Dear Idle Reader:

"Idle reader, you can believe without any oath of mine that I would wish this book . . . to be the most beautiful, the liveliest and the cleverest imaginable."

Miguel de Cervantes

"The book which the reader now holds in his hands, from one end to the other, as a whole and in its details, whatever gaps, exceptions, or weaknesses it may contain, treats of the advance from evil to good, from injustice to justice, from falsity to truth, from darkness to daylight, from blind appetite to conscience, from decay to life, from bestiality to duty, from Hell to Heaven, from limbo to God. Matter itself is the starting-point, and the point of arrival is the soul. Hydra at the beginning, an angel at the end."

Victor Hugo

"My friends, who are about to read this book,
Please rid yourselves of every predilection;
You'll find no scandal, if you do not look,
For it contains no evil or infection."

François Rabelais

"Persons attempting to find a motive in this narrative will be prosecuted; persons attempting to find a moral in it will be banished; persons attempting to find a plot in it will be shot."

Mark Twain

LORD BALTIMORE

John F. Blair, Publisher
Winston-Salem, North Carolina

LORD BALTIMORE

MEMOIRS OF THE ADVENTURES OF

ENSWORTH HARDING

HOW HE WAS ABANDONED ON A HIGHWAY BY HIS FATHER

HIS SUFFERINGS ON A BARRIER ISLAND

HIS JOURNEY THROUGH COASTAL GEORGIA

HIS ACQUAINTANCE WITH LIVERPOOL, TILLY, BRANTLEY,

AND NOTORIOUS ADVENTURERS

WITH ALL THAT HE SUFFERED AT THE

HANDS OF MAN AND FATE

WRITTEN BY HIMSELF, AND NOW SET FORTH BY

S. M. G. DOSTER

Published by John F. Blair, Publisher

*The paper in this book meets the guidelines
for permanence and durability of the
Committee on Production Guidelines for
Book Longevity of the Council on Library Resources*

Library of Congress Cataloging-in-Publication Data

Doster, Stephen, 1959–
Lord Baltimore / by Stephen Doster.
    p.   cm.
ISBN 0-89587-264-1 (alk. paper)
1. Eccentrics and eccentricities—Fiction. 2. Fathers and sons—Fiction. 3. Male
friendship—Fiction. 4. Teenage boys—Fiction. 5. Georgia—Fiction. 6. Islands—
Fiction. 7. Gullahs—Fiction. I. Title
PS3604.O68 L67 2002
813'.6—dc21
2001056499

*Artwork used on title pages and cover—
Sea Island Oaks by S. A. (Shirley) Hunter
Book design by Debra Long Hampton*

CONTENTS

LORD BALTIMORE

CHAPTER 1

I receive an unusual gift
on my eighteenth birthday.
Tsisa a ki ke yu ha . . .

They say a journey of a thousand miles begins with a single step. What they don't tell you is that some journeys begin without your knowing it and without your consent. I offer my summer excursion as a testament to all who feel they've got personal matters just about where they want them. In my case, the journey began with three little words.

"Ensworth. Get in."

Those three words changed everything.

I knew the voice. I knew what the words meant. It's just that hearing my father's baritone at that moment surprised me about as much as if Gandhi had walked up and asked for directions to East Beach, the exclusive gated community where my family resides. My golfing buddies and I stood near the clubhouse entrance recounting the morning's round, just as we had done hundreds of times in the past. My father, by contrast, had spoken about ten words to me in the previous six months, which was about par for him. I rarely saw him outside the house except when we crossed paths in a restaurant or when he raced by on the way to oversee work at one of his construction sites.

So, to hear my father and then turn around and see him startled not only me but my otherwise jaded and unflappable cronies. My first thought was to say, "Dad. What are you doing here?" But as he's the guy who has paid for my golfing lessons since childhood, my equipment, and my club fees, I thought better of it.

"I said," he repeated, "get in."

My friends told me, in unison, "You'd better go," at precisely the same moment I uttered, "I'd better go."

I was barely inside the car when my father hit the gas pedal and sped away. Even so, I recall catching a glimpse of the guard stationed at the foot of the clubhouse driveway. His job was to ensure that only club members and invited guests entered the grounds. The man winked at me as if he knew something I didn't. And he was smiling. Not a happy smile, but a smile that seemed to say, "Hang in there, kid." The only thing I knew about him was that he was a Saltwater Geechee who came from one of the remote barrier islands off the Georgia coast.

Neither my father nor I spoke for a long while as we drove across the causeway from the island of St. Simons to the mainland town of Brunswick, Georgia. For a moment, I thought he might turn into the marina to take us for a ride on our sailboat. But the thought of the two of us alone at sea was too bizarre to contemplate, and I was relieved when he drove past the yacht club.

Other than an occasional coughing fit due to a lingering summer cold, my father made no sound. I assumed something terrible had happened to a family member and that we were going to the hospital. But I also had an inkling that this unexpected visit had something to do with an ongoing feud between us. The root of our differences went something like this:

At the age of fifteen, my grandfather James Norman Harding had hopped a westbound freight train one summer day, leaving behind his family's middle Georgia farm to seek his fortune in the Northwest. There, he learned to cut and sell timber. After many years of hardship, he returned to settle on the Georgia coast and proceeded to cut and sell Georgia pine to a burgeoning resort industry. On the night of his fifteenth birthday, my father, Franklin Parrish Harding, stowed away on a merchant ship docked at the Brunswick port and awoke to find himself steaming toward the Dark Continent. After years of world travel, he, too, returned to settle in the resort community built in great part with pine supplied by my grandfather's mills. So it was only natural that my father, in the name of tradition, having failed with his first two sons, wished to see me follow in his footsteps. However, owing to the fact that my formative years were spent with an English nanny, followed by eight years at prestigious New England boarding schools, the odds of my resembling my father in any fashion seemed remote. I returned to St. Simons to complete my high-school years at a private academy. On my fifteenth birthday, my father offered to send me on a worldwide sailing expedition. Being a timid lad with no inclination to leave the comforts of life in a resort town, I graciously declined. My mother, fearing the worst, defended my refusal to leave. On my sixteenth birthday, my father proposed to put me on a plane to see the world with my oldest brother. Again, I declined. Again, my mother approved of my decision. My seventeenth birthday arrived with my father's appeal to personally escort me on a whirlwind tour of our state. I refused. My mother, bless her, backed me all the way.

So it came to pass that now, on my eighteenth birthday, my father attempted yet again to expand my horizons. I had spent most of that spring and summer on the golf links in preparation for my university days. I intended to pursue a life of diversion and repose at school, to be followed by a life of leisure and procrastination before joining my father's business.

I racked my memory to ascertain the last time he and I had driven somewhere together. My father was not one to spare valuable time from his workday for any of his offspring. As my mother was at the club pool and my brothers and sisters were pursuing various recreational activities, it was just the two of us. A rare occurrence.

We drove across town to the interstate and turned north.

"Your mother and I had a little talk the other day," he said at length.

A war of words would be a better description. "I know. I overheard."

I played back part of their argument in my mind. At one point, he had remarked, "For crying out loud, he doesn't even talk like other kids!" To this, my mother replied, "You were never there! You're more concerned about business than raising your children. You can't send him off to school, pay others to raise him, then expect him to turn out like you."

We crossed several rivers and came to the county line, where he exited.

"You have to understand, Ensworth," he said. "I've done what I could to make things better for you. This is the hardest thing I ever . . ." He broke off and stared straight ahead. "I can't undo what's done."

Soon, we passed through the town of Darien, where we exited on to the old Coastal Highway. After several miles, my father turned off this highway and drove on a winding blacktop road dotted with political campaign signs on either side. It soon became little more than a sandy road barely wide enough in some places to accommodate one vehicle. After a couple more miles, he rolled to a stop and turned off the engine.

"Put those sneakers on," he said, pointing to a brand-new pair of walking shoes.

Oak trees lined the left side of the road as far as the eye could see. Marsh hugged the right. Beyond the marsh, far in the distance, I could see the blue Atlantic.

"I have a gift for you," he informed me at last.

I had visions of a new car, a sailboat, or perhaps a parcel of land. I was sure he would produce a pair of binoculars for me to view the vast landholdings of which I would soon become lord and protector. He got out of the car, and I watched in the rearview mirror as he reached, grimacing, to open the trunk. A rib injury from one of his construction sites? More likely, he had been provoked into a fight.

Rather than field glasses, my father extracted a backpack. He commanded me to exit the car, which I did.

"Son," he said, "I give you a great gift today. See that open road?" He pointed ahead of us. His hand shook.

I nodded and turned to face him once more.

"Your destiny lies down there."

I looked back at the road, scanning far into the distance, trying to catch a glimpse of what on earth he was talking about. Destiny? Could it be the name of a yacht? I saw nothing but trees and marsh.

"You're certain?" I queried.

"Don't let me hear a peep from you until you reach the end of this road. If I do, I will disinherit you. You understand me?"

Again, I nodded. He rarely said anything he couldn't back up and never promised anything he wouldn't deliver. "A promise made is a debt unpaid" was one of his oft-repeated axioms.

"Everything you need is in here," he said, handing me the backpack. "It's not much, but it's more than your grandfather and I started out with."

He then reached around his neck and lifted a slender chain. Attached to it was a weathered Saint Christopher medallion he had worn for as long as I could recall. He placed it around my neck.

"There is a letter inside the pack with a name and address on it. When you deliver the letter in person, then you can come home."

My father grimaced again and held his side. He put his arm around my shoulder and leaned on me for support. It was his first display of affection toward me in years. And had I not known better, I would have sworn he was choking back tears.

He struggled to speak, but nothing came out. "Good-bye, my son" was all he could manage.

He shook my hand, got in the car, wrestled it into a clear space on the tree-lined side of the road, turned it around, and drove off the way we had come.

Before that moment, I had never fully comprehended the meaning of the word *dumbstruck*. When I recovered my senses, I comforted myself in thinking that this was a prank and that the true nature of my birthday gift would soon be revealed. However, that unerring inner voice each of us possesses said very clearly, "Earth to Ensworth. This is not a joke. This is not a rehearsal. This is the real thing. You are standing alone in the middle of nowhere. Do you understand the predicament you are in?"

After a few minutes of deceiving myself into believing I would soon be rescued, my thoughts turned to home. But to what avail? My father was of that breed of Southerners given to understatement. For instance, if he said, "I don't have much use for so-and-so," it meant that person's physical well-being would be in extreme danger were that person to confront him. If you were to ask him about the scar on his hand, he might respond, "I stuck it where I shouldn't have," when in fact he came by the injury during a monsoon in the South China Sea. Aunts and uncles told stories of war medals buried deep in his wardrobe and of acts of heroism he had never revealed to me.

So by this background knowledge of my father, you may well believe me when I say he would strip me of any inheritance. Therefore, I resolved to do his bidding.

I proceeded north on the old Dixie Highway, referred to locally as Geechee Road, once the main route from Charleston to Miami. It now exists only in fragments, mere memories of a bygone era. Few automobiles venture on to it. Instead, the two-lane Coastal Highway and the interstate farther inland are the main routes.

I walked a half-hour or so before fully coming to my senses. Curiosity and hunger fought for my attention as I sat on the roots of an ancient oak and opened the backpack to take an inventory of its contents.

Naturally, I thought to find a cellular telephone, several credit cards, and possibly a note begging forgiveness for this prank gone too far. So you can imagine how disappointed I was upon finding nothing more than a toiletry kit, a box of matches, a pocketknife, a small dictionary, a pocket Bible, a pen, a diary, one hundred dollars in cash, a bottle of Skin-So-Fine, and the sealed envelope I was to deliver. The envelope was addressed to a Mr. Bruce Demere of the law firm Demere, Frederick, and King, located at 326½ Bull Street, Savannah, Georgia. Rummaging further, I found my father's handwriting on the first page of the diary.

"Forgive me," it said. *Aha! The apology begins*, I thought. "A worthy father does not spoil his son. In trying to make your life comfortable, I have neglected to prepare you to survive on your own, which is the greatest sin a father can commit. I know I failed in raising your brothers. I'm determined not to fail you. If I depart tomorrow, you'd be easy prey for the very wolves I try to protect you from. But I worry more about the type of man you are becoming. You seek higher education, but it's one that will be of little service to you if you don't learn some basic facts of life. So I give you travel, a university of sorts, in which experience is the headmaster.

"Your tuition is not free," the letter went on. "The school of hard knocks will demand payment of you by-and-by, but your rewards will far outweigh the costs. First, you'll learn discernment in choosing friends. Second, you'll learn to be careful who you confide in. The kit is for your hygiene. The main difference between a vagrant and you or me is cleanliness. Appearance alone will open doors for you. Study the dictionary not to use big words but to understand a word when you hear or read it. Words are what our world is based on. Those who master the use of words rule in all cultures. Knowing words will open even more doors for you. The diary is for you to document your experiences so that you can recall and learn from them. The Bible is a road map. Follow it and your journey will be a good one."

Coming from a man who hadn't spoken a hundred consecutive

words to me in years, this was an absolute geyser of information. I read on.

"Don't rely on memory alone. Memory has a way of skewing what actually happened into what should have happened. You cannot learn from what should have been, only from what was. This journal will become a textbook written by you, not by a professor. The money is to remind you that a hundred dollars is both peanuts and a fortune, depending on how you use it. For every man with a dollar, there are three men devising ways to take it away. I've told you this a thousand times, but it apparently means nothing to you. Now, you'll learn. Lastly, the envelope. It contains an important item. If the seal is broken, the recipient will know, and he will inform me. If that happens, you know the consequences. Enough said.

"P.S. The Skin-So-Fine keeps mosquitoes away."

You might suspect that I felt very much alone in the world at that point, and you would be right. I became acutely aware of the serenity that surrounded me. This was not the cold, cruel world I had secretly dreaded. In fact, I felt rather comfortable walking beneath the canopy of giant oak trees that soon hugged both sides of the road. A gentle breeze at my back prodded me forward, while a chorus of cardinals, mockingbirds, and cicadas cheered me on. The road narrowed and began to snake its way through a dense forest of oaks and pines. Wild honeysuckle and trumpet vines lined the road.

I was very near a state of total tranquillity when I perceived something or someone approaching on the road behind me. I turned to find an imposing figure quickly gaining on me.

Even from a distance, I could see the fat cigar in his mouth. Great plumes of smoke billowed above him as he puffed away in a manner that gave the effect of a steam locomotive at full throttle. As he neared, I judged the man, by his shoulder-length, graying hair, bushy eyebrows, and long beard, to be in his late fifties or early sixties. His waistline gave clear evidence that the man knew his way to the food trough.

His attire consisted of a white, long-sleeved dress shirt open at the collar and a slightly oversized, dark gray pinstripe coat and matching pants that had seen better days. On his feet were blue sneakers. A gold pocket-watch chain, sans watch, swayed pendulum-like from a vest pocket as he breezed past. He seemed not to notice me standing there. I was admittedly too intimidated to address him. Before long, the only remaining evidence of his existence was an occasional footprint in the sandy road with an indistinct reverse impression of the word *Keds* stamped in the middle of it.

Like a child on his first day at school, I quickened my pace so that I might at least tag along behind someone who seemed to know the territory. But even at a near trot, I could not gain fast enough to glimpse his form in the winding road.

After about twenty minutes, a small cabin came into view. It was a clapboard house with a tin roof. A sign nailed above the front porch read, "Tim's Trading Post." A small boy sat on the front steps slurping a melting popsicle. The Keds tracks stayed on the road. Mine veered sharply into the store, my hope being to find a telephone with which to call the clubhouse to have a certain Mrs. Franklin Harding paged.

Tim turned out to be Timera McIntosh, a plump, middle-aged woman of Creek or Cherokee Indian descent. She made it amply clear, upon my inquiry, that she had no use for phones, faxes, PCs, or "whatever new inventions they dream up to make our lives so-called more comfortable or more efficient." She said this with a mocking smile that revealed two gold incisors.

I bought a candy bar, a bag of potato chips, a tuna fish sandwich, and a Coca-Cola, which cost a mere seven dollars and fifty-seven cents, including tax. I quickly consumed them on her front porch.

Having finished his treat, the boy on the front steps burst into song as I walked off:

Tsisa a ki ke yu ha
Koh wel a khi no hih se
Tsu nah sti ka Tsu tse li
U hli ni ki tih ye hno

I thought I had heard the song before, though I couldn't quite place it. I had just turned a bend in the road when it hit me. I recalled the song from my former days of Sunday school attendance. It was the chorus that gave it away:

Tsis a ki ke yu —Yes Jesus loves me
Tsis a ki ke yu —Yes Jesus loves me
Tsis a ki ke yu —Yes Jesus loves me
A khi no hih se ho —The Bible tells me so

Perhaps Jesus loves you, I thought, regarding the boy, *but where is He now when I need him?* That child had a rude awakening coming to him one day. Oh, to be a child whose biggest care is finishing a popsicle before it melts!

An hour or so later, whether it was the heat of the day or the tuna sandwich or both, I found myself on all fours disgorging the victuals I had recently devoured. I lay supine next to the soupy mixture in a state of weariness until enough flies had gathered that I felt it best to move on.

After several miles, I came upon a spring by the road. It was the source of a brook that flowed about fifty yards through the woods and into the marsh beyond. I stooped beside the pool to drink and to soak my head in its cool waters. Presently, I leaned back on the bare ground, using my backpack as a pillow. The more persistent of the sun's rays penetrated the canopy of trees, dappling my body and the earth about me. I was just about to drift into a welcome nap when I heard a commotion. The events that followed I would not have believed had I not witnessed them with my own eyes.

CHAPTER 2

*In which I stumble
upon a clandestine
meeting in the woods . . .*

A faint humming noise grew louder, and I soon heard what I thought were several trucks approaching on the Dixie Highway from the north. By the time I regained the road, I could only see a cloud of dust indicating their recent passage.

I turned back toward the spring, and a movement caught my eye. At the end of the creek, I spied two boats gliding silently past in a northerly direction. Though they had two large outboard motors each and were built for speed, they were being steered and propelled by men using long poles.

I followed the Keds footprints another hundred yards or so, where I noticed that they suddenly stopped. By this, I mean that the prints came to an abrupt halt and no other prints appeared anywhere around them. That is to say, no other prints of any kind—barefoot, tiptoe, animal, or alien—were to be found, though I searched for ten feet in each direction. An inner voice—perhaps the same one that had spoken to me before—informed me that something was not quite right, as my eyes and ears had observed. This voice furthermore reminded me that I was in unfamiliar surroundings and that it would perhaps be wise to proceed with caution.

The little voice began to say things such as, "Psst. You there, below." In fact, it seemed to increase in intensity, until I believed I could actually hear it with my ears. At that moment, a large bird dropping landed squarely on my head. Or so I thought.

I pulled from my hair a moist piece of resurrection fern. Turning around and looking up, I spotted the elusive gentleman who had passed me earlier on the road. He stood on a large limb about twelve feet above the road and ten feet behind me. A forefinger was pressed to his lips. How his footprints extended well beyond the point where the limb arched over the road was a mystery to me. He passed down a large vine about four inches in diameter and motioned me to climb. Without questioning, I walked back, tossed him my backpack, and then struggled up the vine and onto the limb with his help. He motioned me to follow, and we made our way across the limb to the trunk.

Again, he gestured for silence. He pointed toward a small clearing about thirty yards away. There, through a tangle of limbs and vines, I could see the speedboats nestled in a small inlet. I also saw a pair of sport utility vehicles; these must have been the trucks I heard. One was painted a dark green; the other was black. A number of men were busily unloading small packages from the green truck and transferring them to the boats. The rear of the black vehicle was open. Men were stacking items approximately the size of bread loaves inside it. The windows of the black truck were tinted too darkly for me to see in, but I perceived someone moving. That is to say, I saw what I believed to be a white shirt collar on the other side of the glass. At one point, the window was rolled open, and a hand holding a cigarette rested on the door. On the wrist was a gold watch. A highly starched blue sleeve with a white cuff covered the rest of the arm. Several well-armed men looked on casually. One of them occasionally wandered up to the road.

After several minutes, I heard another vehicle approaching, this one from the opposite direction. Mr. Keds and I moved to a larger limb on the other side of the trunk and hid behind vines as it passed. I could see it was a police car. I was about to make a noise when my tree partner covered my mouth with his hand and slowly shook his head. "Do you believe," he faintly whispered, "that I can secure one of those packages undetected?" I wished he had covered my nose as well, for his breath was a wondrous mixture of tobacco and bourbon. He eyed me with a mischievous grin and winked.

Before I could answer, the patrol car slowed. For a moment, I thought it would pass the concealed clearing. Instead, it turned in and parked. I was certain that gunfire would soon erupt, but that was not to be.

Two officers exited the car. The subordinate man—whom I supposed to be a deputy—was well built, about forty years of age. His face had a pinched, perpetual squint, as if someone had inserted a ratchet in his forehead and wound everything upward and inward. I silently dubbed him Ratchet Face. The taller man was the one in charge. To him, I affixed the nickname Chief. He appeared to be in his fifties, not plump but plumping, balding, and constantly moving, like a coach pacing the sidelines. A dark streak ran from one side of his lower lip almost to the chin; I first thought it was a scar but then realized it was a stain caused by chewing tobacco. His other noticeable habits were constant sniffling and wiping of the nose.

Mr. Keds reached into his coat pocket and extracted a disposable camera. He took photos as the Chief made his way to the black SUV, picked up several packages, and inspected them. Mr. Keds carefully held the camera under his coat while advancing the film, so as to muffle any noise.

The Chief opened one of the SUV's doors and sat on the back seat. Meanwhile, Ratchet Face made his way to the water's edge and met with the man in charge of the boats, a diminutive fellow with a long, white beard and mustache who could have passed for Saint Nick's brother, or at least a distant cousin. Lacking a formal introduction, I nicknamed this person Skipper.

"Any trouble?" asked Ratchet Face.

"Nah. The Coast Guard was too busy rescuing tourists today," the Skipper replied. "Besides, no one's even looking for us in the daytime anymore. Especially boats going out."

From my new vantage point, shielded by vines, I could hear their conversation perfectly. I felt an impending doom and turned to Mr. Keds to discuss a possible departure strategy, but he was nowhere to be seen.

They boasted for several minutes about the superiority of their intelligence over that of the state and federal law-enforcement agencies assigned to apprehend them. While they chatted, the men about them counted packages and loaded them into the boats. I saw a hand reach out of the underbrush at the rear of the black vehicle. I expected cries of "Halt!" or "Stop, thief!" but none came. The fingers gently lifted one of the packages the Chief had handled and then vanished into the bushes. Almost simultaneously, the Chief emerged from the vehicle, and I thought my colleague had been found out. However, the lawman simply stretched and yawned. He was soon joined by his deputy and the Skipper.

"Tim see anyone go by this afternoon?" the Skipper asked, no doubt referring to the Indian princess at Tim's Trading Post.

"Just the Crazy Limey and some hiker," replied the Chief. He stopped to blow his nose and to spit a stream of tobacco-plasm onto an unsuspecting palmetto bush.

"You pass them your way?" the Chief asked the person inside the auto. Though I couldn't hear the reply, I gathered it was negative.

"They must've cut over on the Medway trail. I wouldn't worry about it."

The Chief and the Skipper spoke merrily about selling their goods to support the habits of decadent rich children in my part of the state. By then, the loading and unloading had been completed. The Chief and his deputy returned to their squad car and drove back the way they had come, followed closely by the two SUVs. The Skipper and his crew departed in the same manner in which they had arrived. Soon, the only sounds where those of the forest.

I waited several minutes for Mr. Keds or the Crazy Limey—or whatever other name he might go by—to reappear. But it quickly became apparent that I was on my own once more.

I continued my northward journey with an ear to the rear, for I was anxious that they might return. Soon, I saw to my left what I assumed was the cut-over trail to Medway that the Chief had spoken about.

I was at a crossroads, and my decision could well cost me my life. Should I continue on the road to Savannah and risk being picked up by someone radioed by the Chief? Or should I take the trail to Medway? Even if I were detained and questioned there, I could justify their suspicion that I had not seen anything. The one trail was risky but promised a quick return home. The other was the safer bet, but the detour could cost me a day's time. That little voice was obviously occupied, for I heard nothing from within—or immediately above—to give me direction.

As I had some spare change from the cost of the sumptuous feast at Tim's, I extracted a quarter from my pocket and flipped it into the air. It came down heads. I then realized I had neglected to determine whether that meant to stay on the road or take the trail. I decided that I would proceed on the side trail and hang the consequences.

It didn't take me long to regret that decision, for the Medway trail was so narrow at times that limbs from trees on opposite sides intertwined with one another. I pressed on through the dense under-growth, feeling like a pea passing through a straw. When the path occasionally opened up to small streams and glades, I was struck by a beauty that I was quite certain few but an occasional hunter or fisher-man would ever observe.

At first dark, just as I was becoming concerned about mosquitoes, snakes, bears, saber-toothed tigers, and any of the other monsters that undoubtedly roamed the woods at night, I saw the warm glow of light at the end of the trial. Within ten minutes, the woods disgorged me much as I had done my lunch, and I stumbled out near an aban-doned roadside vegetable stand. I walked the remaining half-mile to the small town of Medway.

CHAPTER 3

I attend a political rally.

The first thing one notices upon entering Medway is the old church. Across the road from the church, you see a cemetery from colonial days. But what most singularly struck this casual observer that evening was the plethora of political signs that battled for space at each street corner and on every light post.

One sign that stood out in the growing darkness was a bright orange poster with the inscription, "Re-Elect Roscoe Pooler, County Sheriff!" Below these words was a drawing of a hand slamming shut a steel jail-cell door. Another sign in the same color read, "Roscoe Pooler Puts Criminals Where They Belong!" This, too, included the afore-mentioned illustration of a jail door being slammed shut, presumably by Roscoe Pooler's hand.

I thought that Roscoe Pooler must be a formidable sheriff, and I even toyed with the notion of reporting to him what I had witnessed in the woods. But a more immediate need beckoned, and that need was my stomach. It sent a steady stream of messages to my brain informing it that sustenance was required to continue in the manner to which I had become accustomed.

My luck seemed to be changing for the better, for on the other side of the church were several tents. Surrounding these tents, a large crowd had gathered to eat barbecue and listen to their favorite candidates speak. To one side, a stage had been set up. Upon closer inspection, I realized that the platform was a flatbed trailer attached to a truck. Black curtains on three sides of the trailer gave it the appearance of a stage.

Half the county's population of mosquitoes was in attendance, held at bay by smoke and citronella candles. I made my way through the crowd to the serving line and filled my plate with what was left of barbecue meat, potato salad, baked beans, corn on the cob, and sweet iced tea. At first, I thought my stomach wouldn't accept heavy food, but I soon consumed the portions on my plate and topped off the meal with a rather indecently large slice of pecan pie. I then settled into a folding chair to rest my feet for a few minutes before taking my leave. A few minutes turned into a half-hour as I got comfortable. Had it not been for an occasional outburst of noise in the crowd, I might have fallen asleep.

Before long, a striking fellow bedecked in a white suit and white hat ran up a short flight of steps onto the stage. He smiled broadly and leaned toward the microphone.

"Hi, y'all," he said in a high-pitched voice. "I'm Glynn Everett. Y'all gather round here. You in the back, come on up. Yeah, you. You, too, Homer. Come on. Come on up," he said, beckoning with his hands.

Though I wanted to leave, I felt compelled to stay on account of having consumed the free food and on account of the onrushing supporters, against whom I would have had to swim upstream.

After several minutes, during which he left no doubt as to who was sponsoring this event—namely, the man at the microphone—or who was backing the candidates about to speak, Mr. Everett relinquished his place to a verbose man half his size named Jimmy Jennings. Mr. Jennings, whose signs I had seen dotting the highway, was running for state representative. He bounded past me and up the stairs to the platform, waving his arms amid the cheers of the onlookers. I immediately noticed that he wore a gold watch beneath a highly starched white cuff attached to a highly starched blue shirt with a white button-down collar. He had jet-black hair graying at the temples and wore after-shave lotion that could have set off a burglar alarm at twenty meters.

He went on about what was wrong with not only Medway but the county and state, and not only the county and state but our great nation and the world in general. Mr. Jennings's argument for change in government centered on what he called the "global economy paradigm," which wove its way from Medway to South America, from South America to Europe, from Europe to Asia, and from Asia to Africa. Somehow, illegal drugs from abroad, the Internet, an influx of immigrants, and a host of other issues I could not follow tied the collective interests of Medwayans to those of international commerce. He spoke with such conviction about keeping Medway's young men and women out of foreign wars that many a patriotic tear welled in the eyes of the assembled. His logic then worked its way back from Africa to Medway, making such common-sense connections on the return journey that one would scarcely believe a Masai tribesman's troubles and a Medway housewife's difficulties were not inextricably linked. And by starting right here in Medway, one could solve each of their problems and change the world for the better.

If his reasoning faltered in Portugal, leaked badly in the Strait of Magellan, and veered completely off the map near Haiti, his supporters seemed not to notice. By the time the future state representative put the final touches on his appeal to save the children, the crowd had risen to its feet. Had someone been present to voice a dissenting opinion, I am quite certain that person would have been tarred and feathered.

He bounced off the stage, seeming to sparkle with the energy generated by his supporters. Not one to miss a photo opportunity, Jennings scooped up an infant from the crowd and cradled it in his arms. The poor child squirmed, gagging on his potent after-shave.

Mr. Everett regained the microphone and droned on some more, not comprehending that a little money and what he considered to be stylish clothing did not impart those qualities that commanded respect and awe in listeners. However, the crowd was well fed, had just been entertained by Mr. Jennings, and was sure to be further inspired by the next candidate. They were not disappointed, for who should trot up onto the stage but Roscoe Pooler, county sheriff—the man I had known up to that moment as the Chief.

The sheriff's speech was similar to that of Mr. Jennings, except whereas Jennings had worked the volume up and down throughout, Sheriff Pooler began his appeal in low tones and gradually increased the decibels. As he spoke, the lawman pointed and nodded at individual people with great effect, until he had touched every section of the crowd. The more he acknowledged people's presence, the more they waved little fans with a picture of Jesus on one side and one of Roscoe Pooler on the other. In short, he worked the crowd admirably. By the time he finished recounting his war years and his service to the citizens of Medway and the surrounding county, there was no doubt that he was the only man for the job. But it was getting more difficult, he pointed out, to maintain the law, what with funding cuts, an increasing population, and the spreading use of drugs.

He paused at one point to wipe his nose with a handkerchief, and I was quite tempted to use the opportunity to stand and confront him about what I had seen just hours earlier. I was close to doing so when he made a humorous remark about "my grandpappy running moonshine in these here parts," with a wink in his eye that didn't bring so much as a blush to the cheek of any woman standing near me. Then my inner voice awakened from its slumber and told me that if someone was bold enough to smuggle drugs in broad daylight, ask his fellow citizens to vote for him, and joke about his grandfather's criminal activities, then that someone obviously had free reign, and a rally at which his supporters were present might not be the most appropriate place to confront him.

As if the good sheriff had not worked his audience into enough of a frenzy, a loud engine started up and a mock jail cell was hoisted onto the stage by a diesel-powered crane.

"Have you had enough of homicidal maniacs walking free?" the sheriff asked the people.

They responded enthusiastically in the affirmative. He marched to a side curtain, where he extracted a lanky inmate, apparently on loan from the county detention facility. The good sheriff escorted him to the cell, pushed the scoundrel inside, and flung the door shut with great force, just as depicted on his campaign posters.

"Are you fed up with perverts running rampant?" the sheriff wanted to know.

The crowd screamed even louder, overlooking the fact that Roscoe had been sheriff for many years and should have cleaned up the mess by now. He marched another evil soul onto the stage and into the mock cell and slammed the door shut. This poor devil appeared to be as sunburned from manual labor as he was malnourished.

The sheriff then raised above his head a package that looked for all the world like those I had seen his men load onto the speedboats.

"Friends," he said, "are you sick and tired of drug dealers corrupting our young and destroying this beloved community?"

The crowd fairly quaked with rage. The poor inmate who was then dragged onstage appeared to be my age. His hair was long and limp, and his sideburns touched his jaw line. He was thrust into the cage trembling with fright, and he had good reason, for many in the crowd would have fought over the honor to execute him right there and then.

"You pull those levers for Roscoe Pooler and Jimmy Jennings, and you won't never have to worry 'bout these type of criminals no more! I guaran-damn-tee it!"

At this point in the proceedings, both Jimmy Jennings and Glynn Everett hurled themselves onstage once more. Mr. Everett grabbed the microphone and bellowed, "Let's hear it for Sheriff Roscoe Pooler and your next state representative, Jimmy Jennings!"

Sheriff Pooler locked hands overhead in triumph with the starched one. They waved, working their way from one end of the platform to the other, totally oblivious to what was transpiring behind them.

I assumed, as probably did most of the crowd, that the convicts were supposed to exit the stage at that point. Which is exactly what they did. Only they departed with such haste through the rear of the jail cell that it was obvious to me that something was amiss.

Mr. Everett, still as clueless as the candidates, took that opportunity to promote his various business ventures. But before he got too far, a voice called from the rear of the crowd, "Hey, sheriff. Where's yo prizners?"

These words had the same effect on the office-seekers that headlights rounding a darkened highway curve have on an unsuspecting doe. Mr. Everett blurted out an expletive worthy of the moment. His remark had the same effect on the audience that a rolling boulder has on a puddle. A wave of panic spread outward from the center in all directions.

Sheriff Pooler wheeled to inspect the empty cell. For a moment, and one moment only, he sagged as though the wind had been knocked out of his lungs. Then, displaying a great ability for extemporaneous balderdash, he took the microphone and calmed the crowd.

"Folks, you don't think we'd be stupid enough to endanger your lives by paradin' real prisoners out here, do you? No! Those were mere actors."

Despite his assurances, squealing tires, excited yelling, crackling gunfire, and police sirens could be heard in the background. But he was up to the task.

"Y'all hear that? Those sounds, my friends, are what they hear every day up there in Atlanta! Listen close. I want you to compare the way things are here to the way they could be if we let our way of life slip any more. We staged all of this for your benefit."

Jimmy Jennings jumped in and reiterated everything he had previously said, only this time starting in Medway and working his way to Atlanta and back. What was apparent to me but not to the Medway faithful was that both their state-representative-to-be and their sitting sheriff now painted Medway as a model of idyllic serenity, as opposed to the hellhole they'd just minutes before claimed it was fast becoming.

As the shouting died down and the sirens became more distant, the sheriff and Jimmy worked their way among the people, shaking hands and kissing babies. After a while, only the sound of an ambulance siren could be heard. Several people remarked that while the loud commands of "Halt or I'll shoot" and the police sirens had delivered the appropriate effect, the ambulances might have been overkill. But since they had eaten freely and been well entertained, everyone left in a good mood, ready to pull the *Pooler* and *Jennings* levers.

After the rally, I drifted toward the center of town, and asked a gas-station attendant where a hotel might be. He directed me to follow the Coastal Highway to the outskirts of town. There, I found the Cherokee Grove Motel, a roadside lodge built in the 1940s. Its white-brick, one-room bungalows formed a semicircle around the motel office. Attached to each bungalow was a small garage. Several were empty, some had cars, and a couple were filled with boxes, appliances, and assorted junk. Two had been enclosed to enlarge the rooms they were attached to.

Because lightning had begun to dance about the sky, I didn't question the thirty-five-dollar room price. The desk clerk, a slim but greasy fellow with long sideburns and slick hair, didn't bother to ask for any identification. As long as I could place cash on the counter, that was identification enough. I later discovered that no hot water was available and that the television received just three stations, none of which was clear or worth watching, though I did so anyway, out of habit.

A few hours later, a storm blew in and the power went out. I lay in the dark room as it became increasingly hot and humid. When the rain stopped, I opened the windows and propped the door open. As the screen door was three-quarters screen and one quarter holes, mosquitoes soon serenaded me with their buzzing.

Peering outside, I noticed a cloud of smoke issuing from the doorway of the cabana next to mine. I jumped into the damp shorts I had just washed and set on the bath curtain rod to dry, then raced next door to rescue the occupants.

"Fire! Fire!" I shouted.

I hurled myself into the room, holding my breath so as not to inhale the smoke. However, my entrance was less than heroic, for someone lying on the floor just inside the door flipped me head over heels into the room.

I lay dazed for several moments while a number of deafening bangs rang out above my head. I saw flashes of light as bullets were discharged and was quite sure one of them had my name on it. It was then that the lights flickered back on and a figure dressed in boxer shorts, a cotton tank-top undershirt, and knee-high black socks emerged through the surreal backdrop of smoke haze and fluctuating lights. A cigar hung out of one side of his mouth. It was him. The Keds Man.

CHAPTER 4

I meet Lord Baltimore.

"You gave me a start," he said in an unmistakably British accent.

I tried to speak but could not and so merely stared at him from an upside-down position as he stood at my head.

He explained that he had stretched out on the cool floor after the power failure and opened his windows and the front door in the hope of catching a breeze, as I had done.

"I always enjoy a good smoke before bed," he said, "and since smoke keeps the mosquitoes away, I was busy fumigating the room when in you barge shouting, 'Fire! Fire!' "

Unfortunately for me, the gentleman interpreted this as meaning, "Fire your weapon." When he reminded me of what we had both witnessed on the Dixie Highway that afternoon, it made sense that he should have viewed my entrance as an assault.

I heard a siren approaching and, thinking quickly, blurted, "We've got to get out of here!"

"Nothing of the sort. If you run, they'll quickly track you down.

Then they will suspect that you fled because of what you saw today. No, my young friend, follow my lead and we shall come to no harm."

He said it with such confidence and calmness that for a moment I believed him. However, it didn't take much for that belief to evaporate.

The officer I knew as Ratchet Face soon arrived. The front-desk clerk peered over his shoulder. The clerk surveyed the damage while the officer questioned us and took possession of the gun, even though my hairy companion produced a license for it.

A large number of scantily clad women also appeared. This puzzled me, though I accepted it as an example of how the other half lived. Then another squad car arrived, and another. Before long, every patrol car in the county, two ambulances, and the fire department were on hand.

Ten minutes later, Sheriff Roscoe Pooler himself walked in with Glynn Everett, who immediately set about assessing the damage. The sheriff leaned against the door sniffling and wiping his nose.

"Damn these allergies!" he complained. "What we got here, Tony?"

Deputy Ratchet explained about the power outage and my failed attempt at heroism, which gave the sheriff and his men a hearty laugh.

The Keds Man stood casually in the center of the room smoking his cigar and looking for all the world like a taller, shaggier Winston Churchill. Another deputy stepped into the bungalow holding my backpack. Sheriff Pooler looked at me in a way I did not care for.

"You boys see anything unusual on the Dixie Highway today?"

The sheriff, crafty devil, was conducting an on-the-spot lie detector test. The suddenness of his question and the burning look he gave me were designed to cause twitches or stammers that might belie my answer.

"I spied a three-legged alligator just this side of the trading post," Mr. Keds responded. "Highly unusual, I would say."

Obeying the instruction to follow his lead, I wove such a verbose story involving the three-legged alligator that I nearly exposed us by way of overexplanation.

"What was you doin' out there today?" the sheriff asked, surveying the Keds Man from head to toe.

Mr. Keds chomped on his cigar, rolled it to the left side of his mouth, and then removed it. "As you know, the Dixie Highway rests upon a sandy ridge created thousands of years ago by the receding Atlantic Ocean." Sheriff Pooler rolled his eyes. "The trail was part of the Creek and Cherokee Nations' network of coastal trade paths that stretched far inland. Later, it became the main route linking Charleston and St. Augustine during colonial times."

"I don't need a history lesson. I wanna know what you was doin' out there today."

Mr. Keds paused to relight his cigar. "It just so happens that on this day two hundred and thirty-seven years ago, a British regiment under General Oglethorpe made a forced march from Savannah to Darien, where it aided the Highlanders garrisoned there in repelling an attack by the Spanish under Manuel Ortega de la—"

"What's that got to do with you bein' out there?" interrupted Sheriff Pooler, to his deputies' amusement.

Mr. Keds puffed several times on his cigar and stared blankly at the floor.

"Crazy man," barked the sheriff, snapping his fingers, "what were you doin' out there?"

"Oh. Well, you see, one of my ancestors was in that regiment. I was retracing his very steps. You can readily imagine the sentiment induced by walking the path of one whose line you are a part of. Add to that the historical significance of the event, and you may begin to appreciate . . ."

The sheriff had heard enough. He motioned me outside and asked me where I was from and where I was going. I answered truthfully. He then put his arm on my shoulder and took me into his confidence.

"You look like a decent boy, and I know you ain't from this county.

But we don't look kindly on trouble from strangers. You know what I'm drivin' at?"

I stated that I knew.

"The best thing for you to do is to pass on through, jes like you was doing. And don't hang out with the Limey. He's teched in the head."

He took me back inside and asked if we had found anything on the road. More specifically, had we seen a package about the size of a bread loaf? We both replied that we hadn't. He then asked our whereabouts that evening. I stated I had been at the rally.

"Hope you enjoyed our little show. And you, Limey?" he asked.

"I was working crosswords, if you must know."

The deputy swiped a crossword-puzzle book off a little table and thumbed through it. "He's lyin'. These ain't even been filled out," he said.

"I do them by memory," replied Mr. Keds, which brought a new round of mocking laughter. "I just completed the one on page seventy-nine."

The sheriff got the book from the deputy and flipped to the page. "Is that a fact? What's a five-letter word for a two-toned whale?"

"That was seven down. *Orcan.*"

The sheriff thumbed to the answer section and paused for a moment.

"Let's see. Thirty-five across . . . ," he began.

"*Quattrocento,*" interrupted Mr. Keds. "Fifteenth-century Italian literature and art."

Deputy Ratchet Face, looking over the sheriff's shoulder at the answer, emitted an expletive. The sheriff drew the book close to his chest on the chance that the Keds Man was somehow reading through the pages.

"Okay, how about a twelve-letter word for wading birds?"

"You've moved back to page seventy-six. The word is *grallatorial.*"

The sheriff slammed shut the paperback and slung it across the room.

"I've heard of people like him," said Deputy Ratchet. "He's one of them idiot saviors."

"Idiot savants," corrected Mr. Keds. "And no, I'm not gifted in that way."

"Enough of this," said Sheriff Pooler. "Frankly, I'm losing interest here."

"I think this might interest you," Mr. Keds announced, pulling a piece of crumpled yellow paper from his pocket. He held it out for the sheriff to read.

"Megiddo Beach? What's this all about?"

"It means nothing to you?" Mr. Keds asked.

The look of consternation on the sheriff's face quickly turned into a mocking grin.

"Fruit Loop, you take the cake, you know that?"

This remark drew far more laughter than would have been the case had someone of a lesser rank made it. With that, the sheriff exited with Mr. Everett. They moved off to visit several of the bungalows, each of which seemed to be occupied by a woman dressed in little more than a thin house robe or undergarments.

After Mr. Keds vowed to make good on the damage to his room, the front-desk clerk departed with Ratchet Face. Soon, the motel grounds were empty of vehicles save the pickup trucks that had arrived after I registered.

I started to leave, but the Keds Man held my arm. "Stay," he commanded. "There are certain things you must know."

He gestured for me to sit at the wobbly table under the whining window air conditioner. As I had nowhere to go and nothing better to do, I obliged.

He sat across from me and extended a hand. "My friends call me Lord Baltimore."

"Ensworth Harding," I said.

"Pleased to meet you, Master Ensworth. You may refer to me as

Your Lordship or Your Grace. Understood?"

He reached behind a curtain beside the air conditioner and pulled out a small flask. "Scotch?"

My stomach felt unsettled, so I declined.

"You're wondering about the women," he said with a wink. "They sell certain wares." He poured a small amount from the flask into a glass. "Until recently, these women worked out of an old farmhouse down the highway. But it burned down under rather suspicious circumstances, and they have relocated here."

He raised the glass. "To the queen!" He then lowered it to his lips and drained the liquid.

"Who is that man dressed in white . . . Glynn Everett?" I asked.

"He is the proprietor of this establishment. The county sheriff, as you have probably guessed, protects Mr. Everett's business investments in return for political support."

In fact, I had not guessed it. He explained that Mr. Everett had set aside several rooms for travelers to make his establishment appear legitimate. I began a moral assault on the community officials, the women in our motel, and the county in general, only to be cut short.

"Don't be too critical of these girls. They've got nothing and will have nothing to show for their work, save a few wrinkles and a degraded spirit. As for the elected officials running this county, well . . . The voter never truly knows who he's put in office, much as a person can learn to his complete surprise that his neighbor is a murderer."

"Did we not see the same thing? That sheriff is trafficking cocaine!"

His Grace held his arms wide. " 'I have seen the wicked in great power, spreading himself like an oak.' " He then added, "Financing a political campaign isn't an inexpensive proposition. Starting with the colonists, rum, slaves, whiskey, and drugs have been smuggled in these coastal waters. It can't be stopped."

"I lost two friends to drugs last year!"

"And I lost many a mate to Jerry in World War II. Life is not fair."

"Jerry who?"

"Jerry who? Jerry the Kraut. Jerry the Hun."

"Well, I hope they caught him."

"Caught whom?"

"This Jerry fellow."

He rolled his eyes and let out a low whistle. "What do they teach in the schools these days?"

I shrugged my shoulders. "The same old things. Math, English, science, history."

"History? Ha! I say."

"What does that have to do with what we saw today? Aren't you the least bit outraged?"

He held up a callused finger. "Fear not, lad. You may have noticed this afternoon that the sheriff departed with one fewer package of money than he anticipated."

"Money? I thought they were smuggling cocaine."

Lord Baltimore shook his head. "No, no. We witnessed different events this afternoon. Each day, cocaine is hauled by road from Florida to points north. And each year, the good sheriff and his men confiscate millions of dollars' worth of illegal drugs on the Coastal Highway. He makes the local headlines with each arrest. Only his official report understates the amount of cocaine seized. While his image is bolstered by the arrests, he sells the unreported part of the seizure back to the drug smugglers, who pay for it in cash."

"You mean to tell me," I said with renewed indignation, "that he is ransoming the drugs back to the dealers?"

"Precisely. Money comes in, the drugs go out. The cash is used to finance real-estate deals and political campaigns for himself and his cronies."

"Like that Jennings who's running for office? I could swear I saw him in the woods today with the others. I saw the starched shirt."

"White collars sometimes hide dirty necks."

I sat back in my chair and reflected on the events of the day.

"So you lifted the sheriff's money?"

"Indeed." He paused to pour and down a second whiskey. "You may be pleased to know that the disappearance of one package is all that is required to bring about his downfall. 'The haft of the arrow has been feathered with one of the eagle's own plumes.' "

"I don't understand," I said.

"He gives the means of his own destruction."

Still, I was puzzled. "Shouldn't we tell someone?"

This remark brought a reproachful stare. "My lad, before assaulting an enemy, you learn the lay of the land. It could very well be that the someone you go to is under the aegis of our esteemed county sheriff."

"Surely, the judge—"

"The judge is his younger brother."

"The commissioners—"

"His first cousin, his brother-in-law, and two of his fishing mates sit on the county commission."

"Well, then, the mayor—"

"No good. The mayor is one of his hand-picked pawns."

"But surely, we have some recourse."

"Where lawmen are above the law, there is no law. Only war. And all is fair in love and war."

"That's not very comforting."

"Ah, but war is nothing more than chess. And I've yet to lose a match."

I again said I was all for marching straight out to inform the world of the wrongdoing I had witnessed. But he assured me that things were already well in hand.

"The seeds of destruction planted today have already taken root. The downfall begins," he said. "Do you believe me?"

Not only did I not believe him, I was wary of this Lord Baltimore fellow.

"How can the removal of one item bring about the sheriff's collapse, if he controls everything?"

"Listen." He reached in a pocket for a pack of matches. "Observe."

He struck a match, held it between us over the ashtray, and instructed me to watch the flame. "What do you see?" he asked.

"I see a match burning."

"Absolute power is a match that, when lit, consumes itself." I looked on as the match slowly extinguished itself. "The match, my young friend, has been lit."

I was unconvinced.

"It's a dreary play repeated daily across the globe. You have seen Act One, the sheriff's entrance. Act Two soon begins in a place called Camelot. You will join me there, won't you?"

I informed him that, darn the luck, pressing duties prevented my accompanying him. What I didn't say was that I had no intention of seeing Act Two.

Dismissing my objection, His Grace instructed me to meet him at the bungalow in six days. "I've prepaid through the week. You may stay here starting tomorrow, if you desire, as I have engagements to attend to elsewhere."

I walked back to my cottage anticipating a deep and well-deserved sleep. Of course, that was not to be. The room had been ransacked. My backpack was disheveled, and all my money was gone save a crumpled twenty-dollar bill I had inadvertently left in my shorts. Whether it was the deputies or the female inhabitants who had robbed me, I could not say.

I flopped onto the mattress too exhausted to care about a trifling amount of money. Soon, I discovered the real reason for my lethargy. The room began to spin, and I was on all fours disgorging the contents of my stomach into the porcelain bowl. It occurred to me that, during my last meal, the meat was not exactly warm and the potato salad not exactly chilled.

I spent the rest of the night swatting mosquitoes and relieving my stomach of bile. After one particularly violent episode, I reflected upon the day's events. I had awakened that morning in a bed made for a king, comparatively speaking. I had eaten a sumptuous breakfast, played an inspired round of golf, and was making preparations for a day of sailing, to be followed by an evening at a local hangout. In less than twenty-four hours, I had been cut off from the life I knew and threatened with disinheritance. I had witnessed a drug deal, eaten two meals I promptly gave up, and seen what I had always thought of as useless phrases take on real meaning, the latest one being "What a difference a day makes."

I resolved to make the next twenty-four hours better than the previous. Naturally, fate, divinity, or perhaps Lord Baltimore had other ideas.

CHAPTER 5

I meet Susan,
learn about the kidnapped child,
and become a business partner.

I awoke well after sunrise, having been drained during the night of vital nutrients and the will to live. Had it not been for the benevolence of several of the motel's residents, I would have perished in that small room. One of them, a red-headed beauty named Susan who was younger than myself, took a particular liking to me.

She did her best to feed me, but by late morning, I could hold down nothing more than a few crackers and water. However, by midafternoon, I was tentatively able to consume a bowl of chicken broth and a small portion of Jell-O. Though she was malnourished and lacking in the social graces, her beauty and charm rivaled those of any debutante I had encountered. A small gap between her two upper front teeth was the only mar on an otherwise striking face.

Susan was usually accompanied by a large woman of about forty-five years named Jewel, who was one of those people who can exhaust any topic of discussion. Even though, in my sickly state, I preferred no conversation at all, Jewel picked random subjects and related her entire database of knowledge of them. For instance, if the subject was barking dogs, Jewel recounted every instance of a dog barking that she had knowledge of, either firsthand or through other sources, and then proceeded to the subject of biting dogs. From there, the talk moved to other animals capable of making loud noises or biting. The result was that every subject touched upon was squeezed so thoroughly dry by Jewel that no one else had the opportunity or the inclination to contribute.

Sometime that afternoon, a large truck, sans trailer, pulled up to Jewel's bungalow, and she made a hasty exit to greet the driver. That gave me the opportunity to ask Susan how she had come about her line of work. She sighed reflectively and said she'd rather not talk about it. I started to apologize for asking but was cut short.

"I got pregnant by my boyfriend just over a year ago," she said. "But he was in a theft ring, got busted, and they sent him to prison. I ran off before Papa knew I was expecting. The shame would have been too much for him to bear. Him being a deacon and all, and Mama dying a couple years ago. So I caught a ride on the highway with the first trucker who came by. He asked where I was going, and I told him my story. He said he knew someone who could help me out. That was Jewel, and that's his truck that just pulled up. Jewel come into the business about the same way I did."

As she spoke, I imagined Susan growing up under different circumstances. Here was a living Cinderella if ever I had met one. It occurred to me that her father might be more saddened by her departure than by an out-of-wedlock child. However, I kept my thoughts to myself on that subject.

"I had no money and never finished high school, so job prospects weren't good. I also didn't want anyone to know where I was, since word might get back to Papa. So I took up the profession, so to speak. After about eight months, I gave birth to a beautiful baby boy in Jewel's room. Soon after, one of the other girls here moved to the trailer park. I took her room, which is where Scotty and I . . ."

Susan began to sob. After several minutes, she regained enough composure to explain that less than a week ago, she had placed Scotty in a shaded crib to nap on the back porch while she entertained a client. A half-hour later, she went to retrieve the lad but found the crib empty. Her worst fears were realized when a policeman informed her that Gypsies from South Carolina were known to be in the area. He further told her that the child would probably be sold on the black market to a couple who could not adopt through conventional means. The officer then said that, though local officials would do everything in their power, the likelihood of finding her baby was slim.

I consoled her as best I could. Presently, Jewel returned and informed Susan that they had best get me to Susan's bungalow. "Now. Pronto!" she said. Apparently, her trucker friend had been listening to his police scanner and was of the impression that the sheriff's office was sending someone by the motel.

Sure enough, not long afterward, a patrol car screeched to a stop in front of the bungalow I had just abandoned. Susan and Jewel ambled outside as they might normally do to investigate a commotion. The day clerk came out of his office. Ratchet Face got out of the car and entered the empty room. Upon emerging, he approached Susan, Jewel, and the clerk, who were standing together. From what I could hear of the conversation, the officer was looking for me. Susan told him she thought she had seen me leave sometime that morning. As the clerk had neither seen me move to Susan's room nor leave the premises, he unwittingly corroborated her story. The deputy told them to call him if I returned, then sped off in a cloud of dust.

I spent the rest of the afternoon napping, listening to Jewel's endless and pointless stories, and trying not to fall in love with Susan.

The night passed pleasantly enough. I awoke the next morning before sunrise to a cool, clear morning. Though fatigued, I firmly believed that listening to Jewel for another day would only worsen my condition. I resolved to quit the premises under cover of darkness, lest the clerk see me and call the sheriff. My rescuers, needy as they were, refused the twenty dollars that remained to me and instead packed me off with a bag of fried chicken, several sticks of beef jerky, and directions to another trail that led back to the Dixie Highway.

You might imagine that I'd choose to hitchhike to Savannah via the Coastal Highway. Or that I'd risk all and return home. However, my new lease on life filled me with determination to complete my journey as my father had instructed. Indeed, recovering from food poisoning and awakening to such a hope-filled day made me feel I'd been given a reprieve from death. It was also quite possible that I wanted to prove to my father and to myself that I could rise above whatever life thrust in my path.

I bade Susan and Jewel farewell and proceeded north on the Coastal Highway, where I'd been assured I would soon reach a dirt road on my right that would take me to the old Dixie Highway. That was the plan. However, on this day, I didn't make it back to the Dixie Highway. Instead, I inadvertently embarked on a new line of work, and it happened this way.

I was not five miles from the motel when a sign appeared on the right side of the road announcing the grand opening of a new driving range. It was the start of the weekend, and every golfer in Georgia was either on his way to a tee time or a driving range. As there was still plenty of daylight ahead for travel, I thought that a few minutes spent sharpening my short game would be a well-earned reward for the last couple of days. It would also keep me in condition for my return home.

Leaving the highway, I discovered the place to be little more than a converted cow pasture. To my surprise, I found a dozen people hitting golf balls. Or to be more accurate, I should say they were vigorously plowing the ground at their feet. The thumping sounds they made were those of hoe-wielding vandals wreaking havoc on a garden.

I entered a small shack next to the pasture and requested a bucket of balls.

"Balls out back in the freezer," a large woman told me. "Two dollar for a small bucket. Three for large."

"Do you rent clubs?"

"Five dollar," she said, pointing at a bag filled with worn woods and rusted irons. When I offered the money, she snatched it from my hand. "Knock yerself out, honey," she said, handing me an empty metal bucket that I guessed might hold ninety balls.

I picked up the bag of clubs and proceeded through the back door to an open meat freezer half filled with golf balls. The range itself was a field of thick grass on which bales of hay sat every fifty yards. A flag stuck out of the top of each one. A small sign marking the yardage leaned against each bale. In addition, two large, empty metal drums were positioned at a forty-five-degree angle about forty yards out.

I was surprised at how well I struck the balls, given the condition of the clubs. My years of play must have shown because I soon attracted a small crowd of people who wanted to know how to hold a club, how to hit this iron or that wood, how to pitch the ball, and so on.

One fellow who had just arrived took a particular interest in me. He was a sandy-looking man—reddish blond hair, pale eyebrows, light, freckled skin, rugged build. His red-and-white-striped shirt was several sizes too large. The rest of his apparel consisted of cut-off jeans and leather sandals. He set up his bag near mine and began to stretch. I didn't notice it at first, but when he took a club from his bag, it was obvious that he had only one arm.

To my astonishment and that of the others gathered nearby, he teed up a ball and stroked it a hundred and fifty yards using a six iron. He repeated this feat several times before advancing to his three wood.

He turned to me and in a thick Scottish accent said, "Betcha a fin ye canno oot drive me seven iron."

"Five dollars? You're on!" I replied.

I teed a ball and laid it up about one sixty-five with my seven iron.

The Scot didn't wait for my ball to settle in the grass before cutting loose a low missile that ended up a hundred and seventy-five yards out.

"Double er nuttin ye canno oot drive me three wood," he taunted.

This time, I let him go first. He pulled out his three wood and ripped a drive almost two hundred and twenty yards. I teed up another ball and laid it out twenty yards beyond his, thus regaining my lost five dollars plus five more.

"Betcha canno reeng yon barrel." He pointed to one of the oil drums. "Betcha twenny dollars ye canno reeng eet in ten goes."

Those who had gathered awaited my reply. I felt it was expected of me to accept the challenge.

"You got it," I said, knowing full well the shot was not hard.

My first attempt was high and wide to the right. The second one missed low but bounced up and struck the underside of the barrel. The next shot nicked the left edge of the oil drum.

"Aye, laddie. Keep yer ee on the ba. Dinno get nervous noo."

I didn't look at him, since I had my stance and range down. I simply nodded. The next shot just missed, but I knew I was close. I eased back in my swing and practically threw the ball toward my target. It clanged around inside the barrel before coming to a rest. My loyal fans clapped loudly and patted me on the back. I thought the stranger would be upset. Instead, he gladly handed over the money. I had regained the cost of the balls and clubs threefold.

"Can ye heet eet past yon bale?" he asked. "Past the three hunnert marker?"

That was the outer limit of my range, given the worn range balls and creaky clubs at my disposal. Even so, I thought it could be done.

"How much?" I asked.

"Thirty dollars," he replied. "In three goes."

I pulled out the aged driver and cleaned its grooves with a tee. I could tell from looking at the treetops on the edge of the field that a wind was blowing out. My first drive was well hit but hooked forty yards left. The next was straight but came up short by about thirty yards. I knew I would have to elevate the ball to clear the three hundred marker.

"Dinna press," he coached.

I teed the last ball slightly higher and closed my stance. The final drive was straight, and I got it high enough to catch the breeze. The ball slammed into the ground about twenty yards short of the last bale but had enough momentum and topspin to bound forward and careen off the marker.

I anticipated he would renege on the bet or continue to "double er nuttin" me until he broke even again. But he had other ideas.

"Ma neme is Bertie," he said. "Bertie McGrady."

"Ensworth," I replied, shaking his outstretched hand.

"Can ah mek a wee proposition, laddie? How do ye feel aboot mekin soom real moony?"

We stepped aside while the other golfers went back to hacking up the ground. The proposition was this: I would accompany Bertie to various golf courses and driving ranges between Savannah and Macon and help him sell devices he manufactured himself. These Golf Enhancers, as he called them, were designed to markedly improve anyone's golf game. I would be a representative of his McGrady line of golfing aids. If they went over big, he told me, several sports-equipment makers were waiting to carry his entire line of products. As his partner, I would be in line for twenty-five percent of the profits. The way he explained it, I would soon be a very rich young man.

I had two reservations, the first being that in order to "sell" these products, I would have to demonstrate their effectiveness. This would require me to pretend ineptitude until I strapped on this or that McGrady Golf Enhancer. Then I was to make shots I knew I was capable of making blindfolded, only I was to feign astonishment in order to impress the onlookers. My second reservation was that Bertie rejected my recommendation to conduct his sales on courses along the coast between Savannah and Jacksonville. I got the uneasy feeling that he had already tried to do so and been asked not to return.

He dismissed my first apprehension with logic I could not easily refute. "Aye, how d'ya think those IBM rascals sol their first machines? They duped people into gettin the proverbial ball a-rollin, now din they?" He further reasoned that if people actually improved their game using his devices, then the end justified the means. "We're sellin hope, laddie!"

My job was to provide that ray of hope. He assured me that all the commercials for golfing aids used experienced golfers who pretended to be inept at first.

He demolished my second uncertainty by insisting that golfers along the coast were far more advanced than their country counterparts, as courses had existed near the coastal resort areas for decades, whereas they were still being built inland.

Bertie suggested I take up residence down the road at the Twin Oaks Apartments. He told me to be at the highway the next morning at daybreak.

"Better go now, lad. The rain'll be a-plumpin doon ere noon," he said, eyeing the clouds.

With a handshake, an entrepreneur was born and an enterprise begun.

An hour later, I came upon the Twin Oaks. I entered the manager's office just as a cloudburst descended. It passed quickly while I waited in what had formerly been a roadside motel lobby and was now a laundromat with the proprietor's apartment in back. The building was one long wing of a dozen apartments paralleling the highway. A parking space fronted each room. Across the highway was a mini-market with two gas pumps out front.

As no one emerged from the proprietor's apartment despite my knocking on the door, I began a search of the grounds. I found a man in back of one apartment working on an air-conditioning unit. The nametag on his blue shirt identified him as Willie. The logo above the name indicated that he also either owned or worked at the mini-market across the road. Willie was a thin, deeply tanned, muscular fellow with well-greased, black-dyed hair, a matching mustache, and long sideburns. His two other salient attributes were pearly teeth and a gold necklace. I assumed the watch to be his statement to all who cared that he had risen several social notches above where he started.

He informed me that he had no apartments available but that he rented a number of mobile homes in the clearing behind the apartments.

I looked up and saw nothing but aging, weather-beaten vacation trailers—the kind a family might have pulled behind a 1963 station wagon on the way to Yosemite.

"Where are they?" I asked.

Willie threw down his screwdriver in disgust and pointed. "Right there! You gotta be blind, boy!"

I glanced again. "Those aren't mobile homes. They're travel trailers."

"It's got wheels. People live in 'em. They're mobile homes!" he said with more than a hint of frustration.

I sensed that he had tried to explain the concept to first-time inquirers on many occasions.

Regardless of what it was called, I surveyed the only available trailer—a small green-and-blue thing—and found it acceptable for my purpose. That is to say, it had running water, lights, a stove, a tiny bathroom, and a bunk bed. Willie also showed off the makeshift shower he had attached to the back of the trailer. It consisted of a mildew-laden curtain attached to a metal ring, a plastic water pipe, and a chain that, when pulled, would deluge the bather with a thick stream of water. It appeared to me that it was intended to drown, rather than rinse, its victims.

"Two hunnert a month," he said. "Fifty up front."

"For that? It's not even air-conditioned."

"Take it or leave it."

I started to leave it.

"Okay. For you, one-fifty a month."

"I'll give you thirty a week."

"Done."

I handed over the money and moved into my new domicile by simply slinging my backpack onto the narrowest bed I had ever seen. At least I had a roof over my head. From this humble beginning, I would help forge a flourishing business that would impress my father and put to rest his concern for my future. Now, I would be able to match stories from his past, stories of survival in strange lands under trying conditions. In my tales, the trailer would be downgraded to an abandoned hut, Willie would become a jealous jungle prince bent on my destruction, and the highway would be an alligator-infested tributary.

I spent the afternoon writing in my diary, napping, and going to the mini-market for a snack. That night, to occupy my time, I began reading a novel left behind by a previous tenant. It centered around an irritating character prone to landing in one unfortunate circumstance after another, each one the result of his own erring judgment. Sleep came upon me during an imagined interview with a leading business publication, in which I revealed the secrets of building a sports-equipment empire from the ground up.

CHAPTER 6

We scheme to make money.
I am deceived.

The next morning at about a quarter past six, the thick fog had not yet ascended, and I could see no sign of headlights approaching. I was close to calling it off when a VW minivan burst through the mist without its headlights on. As it pulled up, I saw Bertie at the wheel.

"Hop in, dude!" he exclaimed. "Got a big day ahead of us."

"What happened to your accent?"

"Aye, the best-laid schemes o mice an men gang aft a-gley. Foggage green o no foggage green, yon birkie an cuif'll bear the gree an dare fer the gowd!"

I asked him to use the English language, if he didn't object. It was then that he laid out the entire scheme to me.

"Look, I'm just an old country boy. But I do know a coupla things about sellin.' The McGrady name and the Scottish accent are all part of the packaging. We're marketing a product, boy. Remember, you're selling hope to hackers. And hope has to be wrapped up nice, or no one'll buy it. Who better to make golf products than a Scot? What does it matter whether the Scot is real or not, as long as someone's game improves?"

Again, his logic was irrefutable. That is to say, I hadn't the skills to refute it.

Neither could I refute the fact that Bertie had grown another arm overnight. For while he changed gears with one hand, another was firmly attached to the steering wheel. And that second hand was firmly attached to a second arm that clearly extended to his body.

"You have two arms?"

"Yeah."

"But why did you hide it yesterday?"

"Hey, with one arm, I can usually get a couple bets going in a pickup match. Not many eighty shooters think a one-armed man can beat 'em. Not until about the fifteenth hole."

The back of the van was filled with an array of golf clubs and gadgets I took to be his line of products. Bertie informed me that we had an hour's drive ahead of us, so I took the opportunity to catch up on sleep. My quarters at Twin Oaks had only two small, screened windows that could be opened. An ancient, rusted Westinghouse fan provided what passed for relief. The choice was being kept awake either by the fan's noise or the stifling heat.

I awoke with a start, thinking the fan was exceptionally shrill, when I realized we were at a railroad crossing watching a locomotive go by. A few minutes later, we entered the parking lot of a public golf course somewhere between Baxley and Hazlehurst.

It wasn't long before we were paired up with two men from Lumber City, Stu and Brian, who expressed an eagerness to complete eighteen holes in less than ninety strokes. Stu was a tall, wiry fellow with long arms, while his partner was just the opposite—short and on the obese side. However, the arc of his belly provided a built-in swing template, if only he'd trace it with his arms in the backswing and downswing. Bertie briefly lifted his eyes to the heavens. I suspected he was silently sending thanks for our good fortune. Apparently, these types were prime targets—or I should say, the prime target audience in the market segment we had chosen to penetrate.

We gave our clients the impression that Bertie and I had arrived separately and had never seen each other before. And though I knew the deception to be wrong, I justified it using Bertie's reasoning that I was doing it for the good of the buyer. "People don't buy what they need, they buy what they want," he had informed me. "These people *need* what we have to offer. That's Marketing 101. Everyone knows that."

The first three holes went without incident. I did my best to mimic the twosome in errant tee shots, muffed second shots, and shanked approach shots. It was on the fourth hole that Bertie strapped on the McGrady Masher, a half-harness, half-ratchet device he claimed would straighten out and lengthen his tee shot while at the same time creating "muscle memory," which would allow the user to duplicate the effect without the device after just a few weeks' use. The improvement in his tee shot was immediate and dramatic. On the next hole, a par five, I asked if I might try the golfing aid. The improvement in my drive was equally profound.

By the seventh hole, our two friends demanded that they try the McGrady Masher as well. As Bertie had only the one device, we all shared it until reaching the clubhouse after the ninth hole. We dashed to Bertie's van, where he produced three more Mashers. I was the first to purchase one, using cash Bertie had given me. Naturally, Stu and Brian each bought a Masher.

We proceeded to the tenth hole. With a little encouragement—as well as greater focus on their parts—our clients were indeed able to hit their drives longer and straighter. It didn't hurt, either, that Bertie instructed each golfer how to position his feet and how to engage in a smooth, unhurried swing, instead of the jerky backswing and doomed downswing each had thus far employed. These tips alone would have improved their driving length and accuracy without the device.

It was on the twelfth green that Bertie suggested I employ the McGrady Pendulum to improve my putting. I had been misdirecting putts on the previous eleven holes and had wondered when he'd get around to producing the next instructional aid. While I sized up a six-foot putt, he pulled from his bag a ridiculous apparatus comprised of a leather strap and a plumb-bob, the kind carpenters use to determine vertical planes. He attached the leather strap to my head so that as I leaned over the ball with my putter, the plumb dangled a foot or so from the ground. If the plumb pointed directly at the ball, it meant that my eyes were not staring straight down onto the ball as they should be. If it pointed two inches beyond the ball, then my eyes were in the correct position. If it moved during the putt, it proved that I had moved my head, thus ruining any chance for an accurate putt.

I easily holed the putt and feigned euphoria. Stu and Brian practically scalped me in pulling the useless contraption from my head in order that they might try it.

Bertie didn't wait around to promote his McGrady Head-Alert. It was on the very next hole as I stood over an easy eight iron to the green that he suggested I try it. The Head-Alert was little more than a noisemaker extracted from a child's toy. It was attached to a baseball cap one wore. If I moved my head during the swing, the Head-Alert would make a noise, thus alerting me to the flaw. However, since I moved my head during the course of a normal swing anyway, this aid actually made it difficult to perform the desired shot. But I somehow managed to place the ball several feet from the hole without causing the alarm to sound. That was enough to sell our two clients on the McGrady Head-Alert.

By the time we completed our eighteen holes, we had sold two McGrady Mashers, two McGrady Pendulums, and two

McGrady Head-Alerts.

"Ye daren't tell a livin soul," Bertie warned our clients, "else yer mates will soon be a-drivin an a-chippin good as ye."

Brian vowed not to reveal the secrets of his improved game. Stu further promised to use the devices only in the privacy of his backyard. Each had broken ninety for the first time and was eager to keep his good fortune to himself. I must confess that I couldn't tell if it was Bertie's personal instruction and encouragement or the McGrady products that improved their games. It was possible he was indeed a genius of sorts.

If I thought our day was done, I was mistaken. At two o'clock, we teed up with another twosome. This time, it was cigar-smoking brothers from Macon who introduced themselves as Fleet—short for Philetus, he was quick to point out—and Chester. They shared a custom-made golf cart painted in the University of Georgia colors of red and black. Attached to the back was another cart, which held their clubs and two other people—in this instance, Bertie and me. By the size of their cigars and the newness of their clubs, the pair seemed to be rolling in money. Bertie cautioned me to play poorly until the sixth hole.

It was, in fact, Bertie's pitch shot to the sixth green using the McGrady Head-Alert that captured our new clients' attention. They snickered at first and held their ground admirably until the twelfth hole. But by then, both Bertie's game and my own had improved to such an extent that Fleet had to have a McGrady Masher and a McGrady Pendulum. He didn't seem to be a big fan of the McGrady Head-Alert. This was "in-field research feedback" that Bertie made note of and told me to remember. In this way, we could weed out the slow-selling products and concentrate on the fast-moving ones.

"Hoots, hoots! Dinna press!" he yelled at our clients, encouraging, coaching, refining their game hole by hole.

Needless to say, we also sold Chester before the end of the round.

Again, each customer was sworn to secrecy. However, Chester was so taken with the aids that he inquired as to Bertie's plans to market them. When Bertie revealed that several large equipment manufacturers with international distribution channels were interested in the devices, Fleet and Chester broached the subject of investing seed money in the product line. Bertie got their business cards and promised to think it over and contact them at a later date.

The McGrady Pendulum sold for forty dollars and the McGrady Masher for fifty. Bertie figured we had profited handsomely. My cut of the day's earnings would be one hundred dollars.

"Just refinin the sales pitch," Bertie said of the two rounds. "Now, for some fun!"

My idea of fun was to find a nice restaurant where decent food might be had. Bertie's was to pull into a driving range a few miles off Interstate 16. There, we found thirty or so people digging up the ground.

"We don't know each other," he said as he got out of the van. "Give me bout five minutes."

After the allotted time, I paid for a bucket of balls and took up a position near Bertie. By then, he had found our target audience—a brute of a woman who gleefully and maniacally hammered at one ball after another. As I practiced my slice, I could see out of the corner of my eye that Bertie had begun to coach her. In a few minutes, with his advice and encouragement, she was stroking the ball quite admirably. A duffer in his forties approached Bertie for advice. Soon, he, too, was stroking fine shots. It was then that Bertie gave a half wink at me and pulled some of his devices out of his golf bag. Then he announced to those within earshot that he was test-marketing golf aids and needed a volunteer.

I emerged from the small crowd of onlookers and presented myself.

First, Bertie asked me to strike a ball as hard as possible. I obliged with a drive that sent the golf ball approximately two hundred yards far to the right.

"Aye, a timid swing ye got there, laddie," he growled. "Try the McGrady Power Train," he said, looping a plastic device around my neck.

The Power Train appeared to be a plastic protective edge from a discarded industrial product. Bertie strapped it to my left arm and informed the onlookers that it would keep the arm perfectly straight at all times.

"Noo, take yer cloob back an heet it lak ye mean it," he said.

Though my swing seemed to match the previous one in every manner, I gripped the club less tightly and reached a little farther on the backswing. Then I swung my hips around slightly faster, increasing my club speed on the downswing. The result was a drive that exceeded the first one by seventy-five yards with only a small slice. This feat was accompanied by utter disbelief on my part and by gasps and applause on the part of our audience.

"Aye, laddie!" Bertie beamed. "Noo, let's do somethin aboot that gad-awful slice."

That said, the Scot attached a grip of some sort around my right wrist, all the while explaining to the crowd what causes a slice and how his gizmo—which I sincerely believe he got from a horse stable—would correct any such flaw. The more you wore it, he said, the longer your muscles would recall how to swing. This item, which he called the McGrady Gripper, was to be worn on the left wrist if you hooked your drives to the left. Left-handers wore it on the right wrist.

I stepped up to the ball and sent it two hundred and ninety yards down the center of the range.

"Give me two," I said emphatically, reaching for my wallet. Unfortunately, Bertie had neglected to hand over my share of the day's take, and I had no money to bring forth. But by then, several on-lookers were vying for his attention.

He hushed the growing crowd long enough to place on various parts of my body numerous McGrady golf wonders that dramatically improved my irons, my chipping, my sand-trap play, and my putting. All I had to do was flub the first attempt, then make a correction to my stance, grip, or swing after the gadget was applied. There was the McGrady Chipmeister, a steel rod that attached to the back of one's right arm. There were the McGrady Sand-Blaster and the McGrady Up-N-Downer, discarded industrial products modified to brace, re-spectively, the knee and hip. In spite of the many encumbrances he attached to my frame, I improved all phases of my game right before our astonished customers-to-be.

Upon leaving the range, we stopped inside the small trailer that served as the office. There, Bertie paid a squat man in a tank-top shirt a percentage of our earnings. "Business expenses," he assured me. It was then apparent to me that our enterprise would thrive on ranges whose owners rented us office space, so to speak.

Over the next four days, Bertie and I peddled our wares at a half-dozen public golf courses and as many driving ranges in a three-county area. And we made several thousand dollars in the bargain. Much of it came from golf enthusiasts who begged McGrady to let them invest start-up capital in his product line. Bertie encouraged this by drop-ping the names of large equipment manufacturers he claimed were interested in buying him out. If that occurred, the investors' returns would be considerable, he assured them.

Our daily routine began when Bertie pulled up to my trailer at six in the morning and ended when he dropped me off about eight each evening. Occasionally, on the driving range, someone in the crowd would be used for the simpler shots, such as chipping, at which point I would play the eager spectator and add to the euphoria surrounding the demonstration.

Though I knew what we were doing was deceptive, my personal convictions were sufficiently fluid to allow me to believe in the higher purpose of improving our clients' golf games. However, each evening, an innate sense of right and wrong surfaced from the depths of my conscience to ruin an otherwise enjoyable sail on the peaceful waters of commerce. It was as though my self-assurance set with the sun and my doubts rose with the moon. But this menace, like morning dew, quickly vanished the next day. That is, until the fifth morning, when the waves of guilt that had swept over me during the night still lapped at my feet in the dawn's light.

On a golf course that morning, while demonstrating the virtues of the McGrady SureSpin aid to two unsuspecting clients, I resolved to bring our partnership to an end.

"I don't think so," Bertie informed me in the parking lot after our round. "You're in this for the duration, hotshot."

"How so?"

Bertie smiled a smile that I hadn't seen before, one that made me none too comfortable. "You know very well what we're doing is illegal. Why do you think I tell these bozos not to tell anyone? If the club pros knew . . . Anyway, we've just about milked this area."

I then informed Bertie in no uncertain terms that I had no intention of continuing in his deception and in fact would be on my way to Savannah that very day.

"Look," Bertie explained, again with that unsettling smile, "I've got a new plan. I know who you are. I know who your old man is. He's not gonna want to see the family name dragged into the newspapers while you're on trial for conning these yokels."

"Why would I be on trial?"

"I'll turn you in to the police in a heartbeat and tell 'em it was all your idea. You're not goin' anywhere until I return from seeing your old man. As a matter of fact, I've got an appointment this afternoon."

"Who do you think the police will believe?" I asked.

"Doesn't matter. I've done time. I'll do it again. It don't bother me none. But you ain't got a record. You're the kind whose family name means something. You gotta weigh whether or not you want to drag that into the papers. Just a few payments from your dad, and you're free to do whatever you want."

We continued our routine the rest of that morning, but my shot-making was not up to snuff. The McGrady encumbrances I was laden with seemed to take on new meaning. To me, they became the yokes of a master. In a very real way, I had become Bertie's slave—or paid servant, at least. My father's oft-repeated admonition to "owe no one and have no one owe you" pounded in my head.

I performed so poorly that by noon we called it a day. Bertie assured me that I could be tracked down and that the law-enforcement community would do it for him, should I decide to leave unannounced.

My first foray into the world of commerce had met with disastrous consequences. I was quite certain nothing could further dampen my spirits until Bertie dropped me off at the Twin Oaks around one o'clock and drove off. It was then that I saw smoke billowing from my trailer.

CHAPTER 7

I witness a poker game.

"Fire! Fire!" I screamed as I circled the trailer and raced for the shower hose. My first thought was to deluge the place with water, but I soon discovered that was unnecessary.

"Master Harding," said a familiar voice, "it seems we've done this once before, have we not?"

To my utter surprise, I gazed upon the countenance of Lord Baltimore. While I had by no means been eager to see him again, his presence was welcome.

His Grace sat in one of the white plastic outdoor chairs Willie had provided for his tenants. A matching round plastic picnic table supported his feet. In his hands rested a newspaper with a crossword puzzle, most likely completed yet unfilled. As usual, he diligently puffed away on a Sancho Panza cigar. As the other residents were dayworkers, mostly construction laborers, and Willie was no doubt minding the mini-mart, it was just Lord Baltimore and me.

"You weren't at my bungalow as I instructed," he said, lowering his feet to the ground and plopping the paper on the table. "Perhaps I didn't make myself clear."

"I suppose not," I replied. "How did you find me?"

"By asking. The same way Sheriff Pooler is going to find you."

"What would he want with me?"

Lord Baltimore chuckled. "Five days ago, he was slightly miffed. Three days ago, he was somewhat agitated. Today, from what I gather, the good sheriff is leaving no stone unturned in order to recover the pilfered money."

"The money you stole!" I reminded him.

"A little louder, please. I don't think the proprietor heard you across the highway."

"I'm tired of getting into trouble because of other people."

"Get used to it, lad. It comes with responsibility, leadership, and having children."

How well I knew his last statement to be true. Because of me, Bertie was at that moment speeding to a rendezvous with my father. I recalled what my father had written in his letter. I was to be careful in choosing friends and in whom I confided. Well, I had chosen and confided in the wrong person in Bertie. I was reluctant to make the same mistake with Lord Baltimore. But he seemed to divine my thoughts anyway.

"Bit of trouble brewing?" he asked. "Work not going so well for you? Got yourself in a bind? Hmm?"

In less than three minutes, I mapped out the entire sequence of events from the time I had parted with him at the Cherokee Grove Motel. He simply stared at me until I finished, then roared with laughter.

"And I thought I could stir up trouble in a short period. My lad, you have got it!"

"You don't seem to understand," I said. "My father . . ."

He held up his hand for silence. "Don't fret about events, boy.

They generally turn out the opposite of what you thought, and then you've wasted a perfectly good day worrying for no reason. What you need is a freshen-up, a little sustenance, and a pack of playing cards."

Maybe I needed someone to tell me what to do next, I conceded. So I followed his advice and took a leisurely shower, wishing to scrub myself clean of anything to do with Bertie McGrady.

Twenty minutes later, I made my way around to the front of the apartments and across the highway to the mini-market. Lord Baltimore had already purchased two submarine sandwiches and warmed them in the store's microwave oven. We went outside to a bench and sat down to what I realized might be my last meal as a carefree youth. Whether it was due to the sandwich being rubbery or the fact that my conscience wouldn't allow me to enjoy a meal, I soon lost interest in food. I determined that, inheritance or no inheritance, I had to warn my father of Bertie's plans. I'd rather he hear it from his son. My logic was that I could circumvent his demand not to "hear a peep" from me by contacting someone else at his Brunswick office.

"I've got to make a call," I said, getting up and approaching the ancient public telephone outside the mini-market. Unfortunately, its keypad had been smashed, rendering it useless.

"Here," His Lordship said, rising from his meal. "Flash the switch hook."

"The what?"

He removed the handset from its cradle and placed it to his ear. "Put in the coins," he instructed.

I did so.

"What's the number?"

I told him, and he dialed it by quickly depressing and releasing what he called the switch hook a corresponding number of times for each digit. He then handed the phone to me. To my astonishment, Valencia, my father's trusted assistant for as long as I could remember, answered. She fairly screamed when she recognized my voice and demanded to know where I was. I told her about the arrangement between my father and myself, knowing full well he had already informed her. Then I quickly explained about Bertie.

"That ol red-headed man?" she asked. "He already come and gone."

Bertie had apparently done some fast driving on the interstate to get there so quickly.

"Ensworth, where are you? You know how sick your mama is from worryin'? And your daddy? Shoot, Ensworth, you listenin' to me?"

No matter how I tried to divert her back to the case of *McGrady v. Harding*, she would not relent on begging me to come home. In a strange way, her insistence that I return emboldened me to continue my journey simply to prove I could do it.

"Ensworth, there's somethin' you don't know," she said just before Lord Baltimore took the phone.

"Hello. Yes, the lad's fine. Yes, I see. Go on. Marvelous. Yes, yes, I'll tell him."

He hung up and smiled.

"What? What?" I said. "What happened?"

"You'll see for yourself before too long" was all he would say.

He reached into an inside coat pocket and pulled out a new deck of blue-backed cards, the kind Willie sold in his store. "You go wait for Mr. McGrady," Lord Baltimore said, handing me the cards. "I've a few calls to make. I'll be there directly. Put this deck in your trailer. And be certain not to open it."

I walked back to the trailer, put the cards inside, and sat at the outdoor table waiting patiently for Bertie's return. I tried to work the daily crossword puzzle His Grace had left behind but soon dozed off.

The sound of a minivan skidding to a halt woke me. I could tell from the sound of the engine that it was running hot—as was its occupant. Bertie slammed the van's door hard and approached me carrying a golf club. Though he wore sunglasses, I could tell that his right eye was swollen and discolored. A bloated and blood-speckled bottom lip was readily evident. And the left arm in a makeshift sling was final proof that his encounter with my father had come out about the way I expected.

"How did it go?" I asked innocently.

He replied by swinging the club at my head. I ducked, fell out of the chair, and narrowly avoided a second swing. I grabbed one of the plastic chairs and used it as a shield until he struck a direct hit that dislodged it from my grasp. It was then just a matter of staying ahead of Bertie as he chased me around the trailer park hurling abusive remarks about my "old man." We finally limited our orbit to circling the minivan.

From what I could gather between club-wielding grunts and epithets, my father and several of his construction workers had assaulted Bertie in an unfair and unprovoked attack. I noticed that the van's back window was shattered but didn't stop to ask how that had come about. Bertie's anger subsided—that is, until he swiped at me and knocked a dent in the side of the van, which only served to renew his rage. All the while, I attempted to persuade him to enter into a truce. However, I soon discovered that he who has the upper hand is not inclined to bargain when he can take what he wants. And what Bertie wanted to take was a large piece of my hide.

"Mm-hmm," came a sound from behind us.

We both stopped to stare at the source. It was Lord Baltimore clearing his throat. He cradled a brown paper sack in one arm. Bertie, still flustered and panting, lowered his weapon and faced His Lordship.

"Tsk, tsk," Lord Baltimore remarked. "Using a six iron on a lad his size? Surely, a pitching wedge would suffice."

"This dinna concern ye, friend," said Bertie, raising the club in a menacing manner. "Eets tween me an me partner, yon laddie."

"Tell me," His Grace said, addressing Bertie, "what manner of commerce might you two be engaged in?"

Bertie briefly explained in his best Scottish accent that he and I were merchandising a line of aids for golfers and that we were simply having a business disagreement. Never one to know when to stop talking, he then began his spiel about equipment manufacturers lining up to make us rich. He even invited His Grace to invest.

Lord Baltimore listened until Bertie completed his pitch. "You know," he said, thumping a great lump of ash from his cigar onto the ground at Bertie's feet, "that is perhaps the most absurd imitation of Scottish dialect I've yet encountered. Possibly second only to a grifter I met in Tangiers some years ago. The blighter was peddling a ghastly brown swill as Scotch whiskey. Now, that, sir, was an insult."

Bertie was stunned. I suppose he had until that moment fooled all whom he encountered. His Grace walked over to the table, sat down, and began to lay out the sack's contents. A pint of whiskey, a matchbox, and a travel-sized chess board soon came into view.

"I believe I have a fair picture of your business activity. What would you say if I told you Master Ensworth and I have an appointment that requires the dissolution of your . . . enterprise?"

Bertie dropped the brogue and all pretense of civil discourse. "You, my friend, need to butt outta our business, if you know what's good for you!" These words were followed by a flurry of threats, none of which vexed His Grace in the least.

"That's all and well," His Lordship interrupted at last, "but as you're a businessman, and as you two have a contract of sorts, perhaps I can interest you in an alternative proposition."

"Yeah?" Bertie said. "What kind of proposition?"

His Grace pulled from his pants pocket and plunked down onto the table an astoundingly large wad of cash. He then withdrew from another pocket a small revolver.

"You are a man not averse to risk. Am I correct?"

Bertie nodded, his eyes fixed on the cash as though it were the Holy Grail.

"That is to say, you are not above a small wager now and again. Correct?"

Bertie nodded again.

"Then what I propose is a wager. If I win, Master Ensworth is freed from his business entanglements with you, and I gain possession of your van and all its contents. If you win, he remains bound to you, and you take the money you see here before you."

"That's it?" asked Bertie in a fit of laughter. He could hardly believe the easy pickings that fortune had laid before him. "You got yourself a bet, my man!" He tossed his van keys on the table and pulled up a chair.

"You can't gamble my life away!" I protested.

"I never gamble," His Grace assured me.

"What do you call this?"

"Gambling implies a degree of risk. I perceive no risk here," he said. "Have you a mind for a game of chess?" he asked Bertie, opening the tiny chess set on the table.

"Chess? I ain't playin' no sissy chess."

"Checkers, perhaps," His Grace said, turning the chess set over to reveal a minute checker board.

"Look," replied Bertie, darting his eyes between His Grace and the wad of cash, "it's cards or nothin'."

There was easily enough money on the table to pay for several months' labor on the links, and probably as much as he had intended to get from my father.

"I don't carry cards," His Grace said.

"There's some in my trailer," I volunteered.

"Well, go get 'em!" Bertie said.

"Fetch two drinking glasses while you're in there," added Lord Baltimore.

I got up, unlocked the trailer door, and grabbed the deck of cards I had placed in the drawer next to a set of plasticware. I fumbled around in one of the cabinets and found two plastic cups that were fairly clean.

"It hasn't been opened," I said, handing the pack to His Grace. His hands swallowed the whole deck as he took it.

"Would you care for a Sancho Panza?" he asked Bertie.

"Don't mind if I do," Bertie replied.

Lord Baltimore reached into an inside coat pocket, extracted a cigar, and passed it across the table along with the matchbox. While Bertie was lighting his cigar, His Grace reached into his coat pocket to get a new cigar for himself. In doing so, he also deposited the cards I'd given him and extracted another deck. This new deck also had a blue backing, only the pattern was slightly different. The switch was made so deftly that I wouldn't have been certain had I not seen the other deck up close.

His Grace tore the wrapping off the deck and lightly shuffled it. "Are you a drinking man, then?" he asked Bertie.

"Aye," Bertie replied, too immersed in the Scottish vernacular to completely turn it off.

Lord Baltimore motioned for me to pour drinks. Bertie gulped his down, then tapped on the table for a second shot. I complied. He leaned back in his chair in a relaxed pose, the kind one attempts to project when playing for high stakes.

Lord Baltimore placed the deck between them.

"I must confess, this isn't my game, but I think you'll find me a worthy adversary nonetheless. You cut the deck. High card deals. Low card chooses the game. Fair enough?"

"Why not let Ensworth deal?" Bertie asked.

"This is between you and me."

"Fair enough," Bertie said, eyeing the money. He picked up a small section of the deck. "Seven," he said, showing us the card.

His Grace chose the very next card in the deck. It was the eight of diamonds. "Seems I'll be dealing. What's your pleasure?"

"You know five-card draw?" Bertie asked.

"I believe I recall that game," His Grace said, expertly shuffling the deck. "Best three out of five hands wins. Does that sound reasonable?"

"Mister," Bertie replied, exhaling a long stream of smoke, "deal the cards."

I held my breath as His Grace dealt. Bertie picked up his cards and studied them. After several moments, he discarded two. His Grace replaced them, then discarded three cards of his own and dealt himself three more.

"All right," said Bertie, "let's see 'em."

His Grace laid down a three, a nine, a seven, and two kings. Bertie laughed and plopped down a four, a pair of sevens, and a pair of aces.

"Two pairs beats your one. Deal 'em again."

The next hand went pretty much the same way, Bertie replacing two cards and His Grace four. This time, Bertie showed three queens, a king, and a four, whereas His Grace could manage no better than a pair of jacks and three odd cards.

"Must be my lucky day after all," said Bertie.

I found Bertie's crowing and my looming misfortune highly unsettling.

His Grace discerned my state of mind and posed a question to me: "Do you believe I can still release you of your obligation to this man?"

I indicated that I wished him to do so, but my tone of voice betrayed my doubt.

The next hand, His Grace replaced only two of his cards, while Bertie requested three.

"As they say, read 'em an' weep," Bertie bragged, slapping down a nine, an eight, a seven, a six, and a five.

"I believe you call that hand a straight," His Grace said.

"Yeah, I think that's what they call it," Bertie mocked, blowing a gust of smoke across the table.

"However," said His Grace, laying down an ace of hearts, a jack of hearts, a nine of hearts, an eight of hearts, and a three of hearts, "I believe this is called a flush. I make the score two games to one in your favor."

Bertie tried not to show his displeasure.

In the penultimate hand, Bertie replaced four cards to His Grace's one.

"Check it out, baby! Full house! Yes!" cried Bertie. "Hand over the dough!"

Bertie's hand was two sevens and three jacks. However, when Lord Baltimore laid his cards on the table, Bertie's eyes widened, his brow furrowed, and he looked upon His Grace with a mixture of suspicion and disgust, for staring back at him were four tens and a king.

"I believe four of a kind beat a full house," His Grace casually remarked. "I make us all square after four hands."

"I make it these cards are marked!" Bertie said.

"Really? Perhaps you wish to call off the bet," said His Grace, carefully lifting the stack of money and beginning to stuff it back into his coat pocket.

"No, no! Let's keep playin'.."

In truth, other than his pride, Bertie didn't have much to lose.

"This reminds me of match play in golf. You do play golf, don't you?" His Lordship asked.

"Just deal the cards. And shuffle 'em real good this time."

Lord Baltimore shuffled and reshuffled the cards to Bertie's satisfaction and dealt the final hand. Bertie requested two. His Grace held firm with the cards he had.

Bertie's hands quivered ever so slightly as he laid down a jack, a ten, a nine, an eight, and a seven—all clubs. He stood and raised his arms in triumph. I felt as if someone had clubbed me.

"If I recall," His Grace began, not yet revealing his hand, "the odds against a straight flush are seventy-two thousand to one. I congratulate you, sir."

"I accept your congratulations and your money," Bertie said, leaning forward to collect the winnings.

His Grace covered the cash with his free hand. "If I further recall, the odds of beating that hand with a royal flush are six hundred and fifty thousand to one."

Bertie's face turned slack. "At least," he said, suspicion returning to his eye.

"Well then, sir . . ." His Grace leaned forward and carefully pressed an ace, a king, a queen, a jack, and a ten, all of hearts, next to Bertie's cards. "You will be so kind as to slide your van keys over to me," he said. As an inducement for Bertie to keep his part of the bet, His Lordship picked up the revolver. He then stuffed the money inside his coat pocket.

Bertie's mouth hung open like a gate on a broken hinge. He eyed the six iron leaning against the chair next to him.

"Leave the club be," warned His Grace.

Bertie then reached with his right hand into the sling that supported his left arm.

"Come on. Out with it," Lord Baltimore said, pointing the gun at Bertie. "On the table, if you please."

Bertie gently withdrew the knife stashed inside the sling. He then removed his arm, which appeared not to be injured in any way.

"Never trust a one-armed charlatan," His Grace cautioned me.

Bertie soon recovered from the shock and launched into a tirade that included a parade of expletives. His face reddened to the extent that he appeared to be one large dynamite stick whose fuse was running out. But instead of exploding into violence, he eventually cooled down and began a series of attempts to talk his way out of the bet.

He threatened to turn me over to the police. He proposed they re-play the game with him dealing the cards this time.

"No, sir," replied Lord Baltimore gruffly. "I've entertained all I care to hear from you."

"He still owes me money," Bertie said.

"Is that true?" Lord Baltimore asked me.

"If you mean the money we made over the last several days, you can have it," I said.

I went inside the trailer, collected my share of our earnings, and gladly handed it over to Bertie. In doing so, an immediate sense of relief overcame me.

"What about the van?" Bertie wanted to know.

"Don't worry. I'll take good care of it," replied His Grace.

"I'm not leaving without it!"

Lord Baltimore pointed the gun at Bertie's arm. "You can step aside, or I will wing you. You may get good use of that sling after all."

It turned out Bertie didn't have to decide, because Willie trotted into the trailer park at that moment. I could tell from the look on his face that something was amiss.

"Just got a call from the sheriff's office. They're looking for you two," he said, pointing at Lord Baltimore and me.

Bertie didn't need to hear another word. Knowing full well Lord Baltimore wouldn't shoot him with Willie standing there and the sheriff's men on the way, he snatched his club and the keys, jumped in the van, and was off.

" 'The wicked man flees, though no one pursues,' " Lord Balti-more said softly.

"I had to tell 'em you were here. But damned if I'll help 'em nab you," Willie said. "You best get while you can."

"Ensworth, gather your belongings. We've an appointment to keep."

I dashed into the trailer, stuffed the essentials in my backpack, and raced back outside. Exiting the trailer, I spied His Grace handing Willie the revolver and thanking him for it.

"You can keep it. I got three more hidden around the store. Never know when you're gonna need one runnin' a convenience mart."

His Grace declined. "Now, it's essential that the deputy find these cigar wrappers," he told Willie, pointing at the discarded Sancho Panza seals lying on the ground.

"No problem."

His Grace then asked if there was a trail nearby leading to the Dixie Highway.

Willie pointed to a slim opening in the trees behind the trailer park. "That path goes south parallel to the road 'bout a mile, then east to the Dixie. Y'all better get goin'."

We thanked him and entered the woods.

Being of a suspicious mind at that point, I asked His Grace why Willie would jeopardize his well-being by aiding us.

"The local law is no friend of Willie's," he said. "Observe the impact one man in authority, namely the sheriff, has on the economic condition of his community. A few prosper at the expense of the rest. The inexorable law of supply and demand necessitates that men of commerce overthrow tyrants. No, the sheriff's time is coming, whether we precipitate it or not."

We marched perhaps a hundred yards along the trail before Lord Baltimore stopped. "Look," he said, pointing at the highway, still visible through the undergrowth.

I stared for several moments and saw nothing unusual. Then a sheriff's car came into view and pulled into the store's parking lot.

"Come," His Grace said. "This way to freedom."

CHAPTER 8

Lord Baltimore and I
travel to Camelot.

"Tell me," His Grace said, turning to face me when we at last made the turn east deeper into the woods, "what would you have done had I not been there to confront this McGrady chap?"

I pondered for a moment. "Gotten beat up?"

"That's not good enough!" he snapped. "Here, block me thus."

He demonstrated how I was to block him, then lunged at me with such force that I was knocked down and rolled backward.

"Not like that. Like this," he scowled, showing me once again the correct movements.

This time, a pine sapling broke my backward tumble. I could tell by his stern countenance that my progress didn't please him.

"We'll do it in slow motion this time," His Grace said.

I started to protest, but he made it clear that the sooner I cooperated, the sooner we'd be on our way again. The manner in which he blocked the path ahead of me clearly indicated I could not flee in that direction. And as I was surely not backtracking to the Coastal Highway, I acquiesced long enough to learn several basic self-defense moves.

When he seemed pleased with what I had learned, we resumed our previous pace along the path. It was then that he set me straight on what really transpired between Bertie and my father.

"According to the person I spoke to—"

"Valencia?"

"Yes. She informed me that Mr. McGrady had no sooner begun his blackmail proposition than your father sprang from his chair and sent him into full retreat with a few well-placed blows. Mr. McGrady immediately fled in his van—not, however, before your father hurled a telephone directory through the rear window. He invited Mr. McGrady to call anyone he wished about your activities, and the more the better. A brilliant move, I might add. For it at once punished the crook and removed any incentive for him to continue the crime. Mr. McGrady then had nothing to gain by telling anyone of your misdeeds and, indeed, risked exposure to prosecution himself."

Valencia's account seemed in keeping with the father I knew. Even so, I couldn't dwell too long on it, having to be on constant alert, as His Grace was prone to lunge at me without warning to ensure that his self-defense lessons stuck.

Something was gnawing at me, and I finally brought it to light. "I intended to give some of that money Bertie just ran off with to Susan," I said.

"Not to worry. I've already provided for her and Jewel. The former has relocated to the county north of here. The latter is on a bus to live with her sister in Oregon."

"Where are you getting all this money?"

"Money begets money," he replied. "Tell me something. Do you feel better for being rid of income made through deceiving your fellow man?"

I revealed Bertie's angle that we were selling hope.

"You weren't selling anything of the sort. Your transgressions far exceeded those of the common thief."

"How so?"

"A robber steals tangible possessions. You stole man's trust in his fellow man. Undermining faith in mankind through trickery is the far greater crime, in my humble opinion. Indeed, a burglar has the decency to state in unequivocal terms, 'I am here to steal.' But a charlatan steals through deception."

"Well, then, what do you call that card game? Did you not gain Bertie's confidence and then deceive him?"

His Grace laughed so hard he nearly walked into a pine. "Nothing so perturbs a flim-flam artist as being the recipient of deception. This morning, he had a going business concern. Now, he has a bruised head, a van with a missing rear window, and a load of merchandise he can't move without the assistance of another. That is a just reward for such a person, in my estimation."

"His mistake was in trusting you," I said.

"His mistake was in allowing me to deal the cards," he corrected.

And with that, he sprang at me again. This time, I was ready and successfully fended him off. By the time we gained the Dixie Highway five or six miles farther, he was satisfied that I had at least learned to ward off an opponent's initial invasion.

His Grace looked cautiously both ways before ushering me on to the road. He told me to be silent, so we might detect any automobiles approaching.

We soon came upon a tiny, wooden church set off the road several hundred feet. We went inside.

"You're to stay here tonight. Understood?"

If I start walking right now, I can be in Savannah by morning, I thought.

His Lordship seemed to divine my intention. "The sheriff has the roads into and out of the county locked down," he said. "This is called the Resurrection Church. You're among saints here. You're perfectly safe, provided you stay inside the entire night. Meet me tomorrow morning at the dock. Just ask for directions up the road. If you're not there by noon, you're on your own."

With that, he said a quick good-bye. I watched him regain the highway and walk out of sight.

A passing shower delayed my leave-taking. When it slackened, I opened the church door and poked my arm out to test the elements. It was then that I heard the distinct sound of car tires splashing through puddles. I closed the door and peeked through a front window. A county patrol car crept by. Though its windows were slightly fogged, I could make out the visage of Deputy Ratchet. I held my breath as he passed.

I decided to take Lord Baltimore's advice and spend the evening. All said, it would represent the most time I had spent in a church in many years, surpassing the sum total at weddings, funerals, christenings, and the like. The advantages quickly became clear. Though the pews were made of simple, rough-hewn wood, there were cushions around the altar on which to lay my head. The church was dry, completely enclosed, and mosquito free. Candles were available if light was required.

To while away the time, I read most of the literature lying about. A pamphlet provided a brief history of the church. It had been built by slaves on the nearby barrier island of Zapala, named by an Indian tribe that once ruled the region. After the War Between the States, many of the newly freed slaves relocated to the mainland, to the very spot where I sat. They brought the church with them one board at a time and rebuilt it where the whipping post once stood on an old plantation. It was a deliberate, symbolic act to reclaim evil ground and make it holy, much the same way the cross represents the triumph of good over evil—hence the name Resurrection Church.

I also came across an ancient Bible. Inscribed inside the cover were the signatures of many founding church members, some having simply made an *X*.

I read for a good while before detecting the scent of cooked food. In fact, a basket with a delicious meal of fried chicken, string beans, mashed potatoes, fried okra, squash, cornbread, chess pie, and sweet iced tea sat inside the front door. I hadn't even heard whoever put it there enter. Looking out the window, I saw that it had become quite dark.

As I ate, a gentle rain once again began to fall. It wasn't much later that I drifted off to enjoy perhaps the most peaceful sleep I ever experienced.

When I awoke, the sun's rays were already overarching the treetops and the basket was gone. I scrawled a thank-you note on the back of an offering envelope, put ten dollars inside, and poked my head out the door. This time, hearing nothing out of the ordinary, I proceeded back to the Dixie Highway. The heat of the day was already apparent.

I passed nothing of significance for a mile or so until I reached an unpainted cinder-block building whose sign proudly proclaimed it to be the Mystery Gospel Church. I next came upon a row of shotgun houses, little more than shacks. None had ever been painted, and each looked just like the next. They rested on small columns of bricks about four feet high. Each one was covered with a tin roof.

The first house had a large "Figs, U Pick Em" sign in the front yard.

An elderly woman raked the front yard of the second house. The yard consisted entirely of sand and doubled as a firebreak. I guessed her age to be in the nineties, judging from her emaciated frame, thin, white hair, and sunken mouth. She slowly worked her way backward, raking the sand into a flat, uniform surface, smoothing over chicken scratchings, marks left by the rain, and children's footprints. I passed without her so much as looking up.

Parked in front of the third house was a shiny, brand-new, red sports car. The chrome of its wheels competed with the glare from the tin roof in an effort to blind me. A deep voice called out to me. I turned and saw that someone was sitting on the front porch, but since it was in shade, I could not make out his face. What I could see were a mass of white hair and two eyes that seemed to float in the darkness.

"Yuh, boy, cum ober yuh," the voice commanded.

I obeyed and approached him.

"Yuh, mista. Yo name Answoit?" he asked.

He spoke the local Gullah or Saltwater Geechee dialect, a mixture of African and English that has survived in coastal areas such as this almost unchanged for several hundred years. Those in the more remote areas of the Georgia coast—especially the elderly—possess thick accents that make it difficult for travelers to comprehend them. His mainland Geechee, however, was diluted enough for me to understand.

Drawing closer, I could see the face. It had been weathered by years of toil beneath the same sun that now beat down upon me. I replied that I indeed was Ensworth and asked how he knew. A small child wearing a Georgia Bulldogs T-shirt burst through the creaky screen door onto the porch. He bore a tall glass of lemonade.

"Yuh, drank dis," the man commanded.

The child leaned beneath one of the railings and handed me the drink, which I emptied with delight.

"Where yuh goin?" the man asked.

"Savannah."

"Yuh b'lieve in ghos?"

I was taken aback by this question and asked that he repeat it.

"Haints, boy. Yuh b'lieve in em?"

"Well, I suppose . . ."

"Yuh b'lieve in de Holy Ghos, doan yuh?" he asked, daring me to say otherwise. "Well, doan yuh?"

"Sure," I replied.

"Den I gots sumpin fuh yuh. Ken Junior, fetch muh glasses," he instructed the child.

The boy disappeared into the house and came out with a box.

At that point, the elderly gentleman told me a remarkable story. I learned that upon passing his fishing business to his son, Kenneth, he had worked for a number of years at a nearby army base. Indeed, a United States Army patch decorated the overalls he wore. I further learned that over the years, he had collected discarded blue-colored shreds of top-secret glass he called "filamenz," which were being developed by the army for night-vision binoculars. He told me he had taken the shreds and made them into lenses for sunglasses, which he sold to passing tourists up on the Coastal Highway. Apparently, those filaments, when ground up and melted with regular glass, allowed the viewer to detect the thermal remnants of people who had been present only minutes before. Furthermore, the old man had discovered one night that a particular batch of discarded filaments, thought to be worthless due to an overexposure of radiation, actually revealed to the viewer the spectral images of "live" ghosts, if one can use that word. In fact, one week prior, he had seen a whole column of ghostly figures march by his house in the middle of the night! I immediately recalled Lord Baltimore's improbable tale of the British regiment walking this very road two hundred and thirty-seven years previous.

After relating his fantastic story, he opened the box that Ken Junior held and pulled out a pair of blue sunglasses housed in red-and-white-striped frames. He assured me this particular pair was the last of his collection.

I disguised my excitement. *Whoever possesses these glasses can have them analyzed, cloned, and mass produced*, I thought. While my mind whirled with computations of production costs and sales volumes and how the discovery could be applied to military and crime-detection uses, I calmly related that I had no personal interest in his glasses. However, I did have a cousin in Savannah who might wish to view the many ghosts that still inhabited that historic town. I then casually inquired as to how much money would induce him to part with the shades.

He did a little computing himself and told me fifty dollars would suffice. As I had only twenty, he acquiesced and said he would consider himself lucky, since he saw no real use for the glasses and since none of his family members seemed interested in them.

Confident that I had made a bold financial coup, I gladly exchanged my last dollar for the glasses and promptly put them on, fully expecting to see a parade of ghosts. I was then informed that they worked only at night, and then only if ghosts were present.

He took the money and promptly spit on it. I had heard that superstitious people did this in the belief that it would cause the money to stick to them and attract more of the same. Then he stuffed the bills into his shirt pocket.

I thanked my host for the drink and the shades and picked up my backpack to leave.

"Doan stay on dat road," he advised. "De sheriff come yuh tuh visit presently. Daze uh paf half a mile tuh de right. Tek it."

"A path. Take the path?" I asked.

"Jus tek tuh de paf," he replied, "lak ah tol yuh."

I didn't comprehend exactly why I should take the trail, but an urgency in his voice and in his eyes caused me to believe I should follow his instructions. I strode quickly for five minutes—and in doing so almost walked right past what looked like an animal trail. I ducked into this trail and wove my way for several hundred yards until I smelled a campfire ahead. Only it wasn't a campfire. As I got nearer, I detected the aroma of a cigar.

The path came to an end at the foot of a rickety, aging dock that extended about ten feet over a tidal river. Nearby, Lord Baltimore stood statue-like in the shade of an ancient oak, his back to me. He seemed not to notice my approach and stared across the marsh at an island on the horizon, puffing on his cigar.

When I stood beside him, he addressed me without bothering to look: "Always take meat from over the burner."

I thought he was having a conversation with an imaginary person until he looked at me and said, "You ate spoiled food at the political rally. When eating catered fare, take the portions directly over the burner. They don't spoil as quickly."

I thanked him for the tip, given about a week too late. I then recounted what had transpired after he and I parted the previous day. My amazing business transaction, I was certain, would make me a millionaire and please my father in one bold stroke.

Lord Baltimore continued to puff on his cigar and stare at the island.

"What's out there?" I inquired.

For a moment, he said nothing. Then he pointed toward the island. "Camelot."

After several more minutes of staring and puffing, he turned to me. "Did you say 'ghost glasses'?" he asked, eyebrows raised.

I confirmed that he had heard correctly.

"From an elderly gentleman?"

I related again the circumstances of my acquisition. He stared at me with more admiration than before. He had obviously misjudged me but now recognized that he was in the presence of an extraordinary young man.

"And you invested your last dollar in those?" he asked, pointing at my sunglasses.

I replied in the affirmative.

"Astounding. Simply astounding. Did you learn nothing from your previous get-rich-quick endeavor?"

I explained that I had learned my lesson but that the dynamics of this business deal were totally different. He shook his head in wonderment.

I was preparing to leave when he spoke again. "Young master, a boat will be here shortly. Would you care to visit Camelot with me?"

"I think I'll just continue up to Savannah by myself."

"The good sheriff is on a rampage, Master Ensworth. I suggest you accompany me if you value your life." The semblance of a smile made itself visible on his face but quickly subsided.

"He doesn't even know where we are," I countered.

Lord Baltimore's smile broadened. "He knows where we were last seen. He knows where we are not. We're not in town. We're not at Willie's. We're not at any of the main docks. And we haven't been seen leaving the county by road. He's already deduced our general vicinity. You've no doubt seen the patrol cars. The net is drawing tight. I'd say he'll have us in another forty-five minutes. And I don't like our chances of even getting to trial. Most likely, he's of another mind altogether concerning our fate." He said these things with such detachment that he might have been referring to two other wretches in a distant land.

I pondered my predicament. Common sense said, "Take your chances with the law. You've done nothing wrong. You're one phone call away from help." However, my instincts told me something quite different. Although I couldn't articulate exactly what it was, I knew that turning myself in or attempting to continue by myself would be a grave mistake.

Five minutes later, a small white trawler pulled up to the dock. The name *Mattie III* was painted in brilliant red upon the bow.

"He's with me," said Lord Baltimore, half shoving me aboard.

The owner and captain of the *Mattie III* was a large man named Kenneth who possessed an iron handshake and a mischievous grin.

"Sheriff been busy, Lawd Balt'mo," he said in a deep, resonant voice as we pulled away from the dock. "Seems someone shorted him on a bidness transaction. Been all up and down Dixie Highway axing questions. Been axing bout you and a backpacker, too," he said, looking at me. "Sheriff hornet-mad."

Lord Baltimore shrugged his shoulders. " 'He whom the gods would destroy, they first make mad.' "

Kenneth steered cautiously down the winding waterway, careful to hug the shoreline. We soon came to a broadening in the river, where he pulled back on the throttle.

"It's all open from here," he told us. "He probably got people watchin."

I sensed that he was giving us the option of backing out if we desired to do so. Lord Baltimore casually gestured for Kenneth to proceed. Within two minutes, we were well into the open sound. Several porpoises raced ahead of the trawler. Kenneth stopped to check a crab trap and emptied a load of the crustaceans into a large storage bin.

"That's Zapala," said Kenneth, pointing to the island Lord Baltimore referred to as Camelot.

I pulled out my new sunglasses and put them on for better viewing in the harsh glare. Kenneth saw them and rolled his eyes. Lord Baltimore attempted to subdue a chuckle.

"How much?" Kenneth asked.

"Twenty dollars," I proudly responded.

"I have *got* to have another talk wit Papa!" he shouted above the engine as we pulled away from the trap.

It was then that I saw my investment evaporate. My father's words, "For every man with a dollar, there are three men devising ways to take it away," took on meaning.

I didn't have long to dwell on my thoughts. Kenneth's grin soon disappeared, and he throttled back to a crawl. Up ahead, I saw an orange object bobbing in the water.

"Not good, Lawd Balt'mo," Kenneth said. "Not good at all."

"Not good" was an understatement, for we soon drew alongside the lifeless body of the drug dealer I had known as the Skipper. He was face down in the water, a life jacket keeping him afloat. It looked as though the back of his head was bashed in.

"Cap'n Sandy," said Kenneth, whose mood had grown decidedly worse. "He was a good un. Jus got into the wrong trade." He shook his head. "Shrimpin got too hard. Chasin dat dollar. An look where it got im."

Lord Baltimore puffed on his cigar and looked down at the corpse with little compassion. I was numbed with horror and fear. Horror over viewing the decaying body of someone I'd seen just a week before. Fear over the realization of what I was involved in.

"This ilan surrounded by big water," Kenneth told me. "Sheriff can't harm you none dere. But a hur'cane blow up, you get off de ilan quick. You hear?"

I affirmed that I had heard. I also noticed that Kenneth's accent had taken a decided Gullah flavor upon nearing Zapala.

Fifteen minutes later, we were creeping along a tidal river that hugged the western shore of the island. We soon came upon an oyster-encrusted dock that looked even less reliable than the one on the mainland.

"I'm makin de Savannah-Lanta run tonight," Kenneth told Lord Baltimore. "See you at de cabin tomorrow evenin."

"Excellent," replied His Lordship, rubbing his hands as if about to make a tidy profit off some scheme or another.

"Y'all be safe here til the storm blows over on de other side," Kenneth said as he shoved a burlap sack into my hands.

"What other side?" I asked.

Kenneth nodded in the direction of the mainland. "That de other side to Zapala folk."

I peered into the sack. Inside were a tiny skillet, a number of smoked mullet, and beef jerky.

Kenneth handed Lord Baltimore a small vial. "Medicine for ol Janey."

His Grace nodded and took the bottle.

"An I got some sturgeon egg for yuh," Kenneth said, tossing me a small peanut-butter jar half filled with what looked like jam.

"What ho! We'll sup well tonight," replied Lord Baltimore as we stepped gingerly onto the dock. "Cheerio, then."

His Grace waved to our escort, then turned for a small trail leading into the island's interior with me close behind. Before the last rumblings of the *Mattie III* 's engine faded away, I knew I had entered a new world. His Grace seemed to bask in the island's ambiance.

After approximately twenty minutes, he stopped on the path. I fully expected him to lunge at me again. Instead, he pointed ahead. There, beyond majestic white sand dunes, lay the grand Atlantic. To our left was an open field where a small herd of wild horses chewed contentedly on grass. To our right stood a dense forest of palmetto bushes and live oaks.

"Welcome," he said, "to Camelot."

CHAPTER 9

In which we meet Brantley
and experience strange and
wonderful events in Camelot . . .

Though Lord Baltimore described our surroundings as Camelot, I thought Eden a more appropriate name, for Zapala was virtually unspoiled by the hand of man. His Lordship sketched a map of the island in the path, using a thin oak branch. He then carefully explained Zapala to me, beginning with the south end.

"This part of the island is uninhabited," he said, pointing to our location. "A mile or so north of here, we cross territory that is home to a small band of Creek Indians. The rest of the population is Gullah. The island is approximately twelve miles in length. Pigge Hammock is here," he said, digging the branch into the dirt, "in the middle near the western marsh. It is strictly a farming community. We will camp near Pigge Hammock tonight. A mile or two northeast of this hamlet is Devil Swamp. That's where Tilly lives."

"Who's Tilly?" I inquired.

"Zapala's resident root doctor."

"What's a root doctor?"

"She uses plant roots and other herbal ingredients to concoct potions to ward off evil spirits. She descends from a long line of witch doctors stretching back to Africa. Among other things, she steers hurricanes away from Zapala."

I laughed. "Surely, you don't believe that."

He did not confirm or deny it. But he did note that no major storm had directly struck the island during Tilly's watch.

"And just how does she accomplish this feat?" I asked.

Lord Baltimore studied our surroundings as if he did not wish to be overheard. The gentle breeze had died down, and it seemed even the birds had stopped singing to eavesdrop. I, too, looked around.

"The islanders believe," he said, "that hurricanes are spun off the western shore of Africa by witch doctors."

"Why would witch doctors go and do a thing like that?"

"It is believed the witch doctors hurl storms at this continent to punish the white man for taking Africans from their homeland. Be that as it may, Tilly has nothing to do with their hitting or missing Zapala. The island happens to be tucked snugly into the crotch of the East Coast. The odds of any storm coming ashore here are very low.

"Now," he continued, "Folktown lies on the northwest edge of Zapala. The residents of that community are primarily fishermen, shrimpers, and crabbers. The rest take a boat each day to the mainland—the 'other side'—to work. By tomorrow evening, we should reach a cabin located here, near Folktown."

He stood up and erased the map with his foot. For a moment, I thought I heard the faint sound of drums in the distance. But the noise abruptly ended, and I thought no more about it.

We followed a trail that paralleled the beach. It branched off to another trail that led back into the island's interior in a northwesterly direction.

A constant stream of cigar smoke flowed over Lord Baltimore's shoulder. From my caboose perspective, he again resembled a train engine surging forward on the sandy path, belching smoke in his wake. The billowing subsided every half-hour or so—just long enough for him to light a new cigar. The curious thing was that he always tossed the butt beside the path, then, a few minutes later, bit off the end of the new cigar and spit it onto the path. A minute or so farther along, he lit the new cigar and similarly dropped the match. Then he littered the path with the paper cigar ring about fifteen minutes after that. He repeated this process numerous times.

Finally, I could no longer stifle my curiosity. I asked him why he littered the path in such an unorthodox, yet methodical, manner.

Lord Baltimore stopped and turned. He held a hundred-dollar bill in front of me. "You tell me why I litter the path, and this is yours," he said.

I watched the money go back into his pocket when I could offer no answer.

Occasionally, he pointed to a plant and called it by its common name and then its scientific name. For instance, the sago palm he named *Cycas revoluta*. The live oak, *Querus virens*. Spanish moss, *Tillandsia usneoides*. He then related the plant's history, medicinal properties, hallucinogenic qualities, and other uses while I dutifully recorded the information in my diary, as he seemed to expect.

"The natives," he said, meaning American Indians, "called moss 'tree hair.' Frenchie," he continued, meaning French explorers, "referred to it as *barbe Espagnole*, or 'Spanish beard,' as an affront to rivals in the New World. Later settlers called it 'graybeard.' "

The lichen that gave the ruins of a small chapel a pinkish hue he identified as *Chiodecton sangueneum*. "This house of worship was built by the Hazzard family. The father of that clan made the unwise decision to kill a Wylly in a heated moment. The Wyllys were connected by blood to every other planter on the island. From then on, the Hazzards were ostracized to the extent that they built their own chapel. Consider that the next time you wish to assail a neighbor."

We passed a small pond, where he pointed to the remains of a cypress stump on the bank. This was where, according to legend, the pirate Blackbeard had buried a treasure of South American gold looted from a Spanish galleon. Blackbeard's men planted the cypress to mark the spot. But they never returned to reclaim the treasure, as Blackbeard was soon captured by the British off the Carolina coast and beheaded. Lord Baltimore related how the Creek Indians had discovered the treasure after a powerful hurricane in the late 1800s caused part of the gold to spill into the pond. To this day, he said, the descendants of those Indians wore pieces of that gold to symbolize their potential for material wealth and their rejection of it.

"You mean Timera's gold teeth—?" I started to ask.

"Blackbeard himself once fondled the gold in her smile," he responded. "Perhaps Cortez as well."

A mile or so farther, we came upon a grove of small, thorny orange trees.

"Seville oranges, brought over by Spanish missionaries in 1500," said His Grace, handing me a dozen to put in my backpack. He pointed to a row of low, vine-covered walls made of tabby, a mixture of oyster shells, lime, and sand combined with salt water. "Were you standing on this spot in 1531, you would have seen a large band of Creek Indians emerge from these woods to massacre the Franciscan missionaries who occupied this site."

Several hundred yards later, we came across a pile of ashes. His Grace stirred them with a stick and studied them. Then he surveyed the area immediately around us.

"Carolina Gypsies lying low from the law, heading north," he muttered.

The path widened considerably as we approached the central portion of the island. Open fields revealed a wide array of seemingly abandoned orchards still bearing fruit. Here and there were small vegetable gardens belonging to people Lord Baltimore referred to as "anchorites."

Perceiving the anchorites to be a cult of some sort and a threat to outsiders, I expressed a keen desire to vacate the area as quickly as possible.

Lord Baltimore patiently explained that the anchorites were nothing more than hermits. He then proceeded to lecture me on the pitfalls of being uneducated. He pointed out that undue mental and physical duress could be caused by the launching of one's imagination upon hearing a mere snippet of news.

I retorted that his inability to communicate was what led to such stress.

His Grace went about collecting a few potatoes and carrots from one of the gardens. He then carefully placed a fresh cigar on a nearby stump. As he did so, a small herd of deer emerged from the woods and sprinted across our path.

"They say the deer can talk to the Creeks and Gullahs of Zapala," he said.

I wished I could speak Gullah so that I might ask a passing deer whether my traveling companion was leading me to my doom.

He certainly didn't elevate my confidence by suddenly turning to me, holding a hundred-dollar bill in my face, and quizzing me with riddles. "Answer this," he began. "He doesn't move yet climbs ten stories."

I could not answer, and we proceeded onward.

Another nonsensical puzzle, posed to me before we had covered two hundred paces, went something like this: "He soars overhead and never leaves his seat."

These were thrown at me indiscriminately for several miles. The more I was unable to answer, the more incensed he became. "Have you not learned to think, boy?" he bellowed. "You could be a wealthy young man by now."

"I am a wealthy young man," I said.

He didn't bother to respond, and I considered it a victory for me. But it soon occurred to me that my wealth, though assured at some point in the future, was not yet legally and actually mine. At that very moment, I had exactly no money to my name—at least none I could readily put my hands upon.

In spite of this revelation, and though I was uncertain of Lord Baltimore and of my prospects, Zapala's charm lifted my spirits. What had happened to me on the mainland during the previous week—indeed, during my entire eighteen years—seemed to belong to a distant time and place.

About midday, we came upon the ruins of what must have been an elegant mansion in its day. As we sat on what remained of the front steps eating the beef jerky Kenneth had supplied, he recounted its history.

"We're on the old Couper estate. This was James Couper's house. All that remains of the mansion are these crumbling tabby walls and two enormous chimneys made of Glasgow brick."

I picked up several small stones that looked out of place.

Lord Baltimore took one in his hand and studied it for a moment. "Tosca stone. Imported from the Costa Blanca region of Spain. Probably placed around a doorway."

Piles of bricks covered in vines dotted the landscape around us. I remarked that they could be reused by the locals.

"After your Civil War, islanders pilfered the bricks to build their houses," he said. "But they have considered it bad luck to do so ever since the hurricane that uprooted that cypress tree I showed you. Everyone who took building material from this site suffered greatly from that storm. Afterward, as you can see by these piles, they returned the bricks."

I asked why they were superstitious.

Lord Baltimore proceeded to tell me that most of the island locals were descendants of James Couper's slaves. A few of those slaves never took up Christianity but continued to practice Islam. Some retained other African religions, including witchcraft. Those religions—or rather an amalgam of beliefs—were passed down to the current inhabitants. However, the little-understood power of the root doctor was passed down to only one person in each generation. That person was Tilly.

I expressed disbelief in her powers.

His Grace reiterated the curious fact that Zapala had gone unscathed since Tilly's birth, while the surrounding islands and the mainland had been wracked with storm devastation.

A sudden weariness descended upon me, whether from the heat of the day or my recent bouts of sickness. It occurred to me that if I could engage my host in conversation—which seemed an easy thing to do—I could slow the pace of our hike. Seeing that he was preparing to forge ahead, I brought up technology, one of the few topics in which I considered myself well versed.

"Your world of computers has no use for me," Lord Baltimore gruffly replied. "I can offer only great truths and personal experience, not virtual truths and virtual understanding. Just the real thing, which might be of little value to many." He said this matter-of-factly.

Undaunted, I expounded on the subject of golf, the only other topic I deemed myself competent to discuss. He seemed impressed with my golfing acumen and plied me with compliments. And so I moved on to subjects of which I had only a passing knowledge and about which I had no new insights. I spoke a good while before he intervened.

"Do not be fooled by adulation, my lad," he said. "Flatterers have ulterior motives. Mine was merely to gain a few more minutes in which to cool my feet. The soil is hot and burns through these sneakers, you know."

You might assume that his words pulled the rug from beneath my burgeoning ego, and you would be right. But I chose to look upon it as a lesson learned at no monetary cost to me. Lord Baltimore consoled me by explaining that since I offered to teach him something about computers, he had reciprocated by teaching me the lesson of being deceived by flattery.

We continued down the trail at the same pace as before and soon came upon a man leaning on the gate of a small cemetery. I assumed the plot belonged to the family that had owned the plantation.

"Get on frum yuh!" the man bellowed at the headstones. I looked around but couldn't detect anyone else present. "You doan b'long yuh. Nah, scat!"

His hair was a mass of matted gray and black. His eyes were blood-shot and fiery. A hole-ridden white shirt and baggy black pants some-how clung to his tall, thin frame. Tattered shoes adorned his feet. He waved a scruffy, black raincoat at his imaginary foes as one would do to scare off a pack of dogs.

"Shoo! Go on, nah!"

We passed silently by. The man appeared not to notice us.

"What was that?" I wanted to know.

My companion smiled. "He's what they call a Shadow Man. Keeps the spirits at bay."

"What?"

"They say he was born with a double caul. That gives him the power to see spirits—or, as the islanders call them, shadows. They say he sees better in the shadow world than in ours."

Fortunately, I didn't have to pursue the matter further because Lord Baltimore then began an unasked-for lecture on heraldry, in which he carefully explained the descension from duke to marquess to earl to viscount to baron. The lecture then turned to the history of heraldry and the basics of escutcheon design. Midway through his description of armorial bearings, just as I was beginning to pine for the subject of shadows and spirits, he stopped and sniffed the air. I, too, detected a faint scent. He tossed the butt of a cigar beside the path, then stooped over what appeared to be a fresh footprint.

"He couldn't have picked a better hiding place than Zapala," said he, nodding with approval. Before I could ask who "he" was, Lord Baltimore pointed at the print. "See how he turned abruptly into this side path? He came upon it unexpectedly. Notice the mud that fell off the side of his shoe." The mud was still moist. "He's been staying off the main trails, walking through marsh. Note, too, that the print is a tennis shoe similar to mine. It is not made for traversing marsh and woods. It appears to be standard prison issue."

He looked up and scanned the trail ahead. The island was a maze of interconnecting paths of various sizes. Some were little more than deer or wild boar trails. A helicopter search team hovering ten feet above the tree line would not see us in many instances.

We took the side path and had not gone two hundred feet before the source of our olfactory teasing was revealed. Just ahead stood a cluster of live oaks. Behind the largest one, we spied a young man sitting near an artesian well.

"You, there," called Lord Baltimore, "may we join you?"

The man jolted upright and appeared ready for flight. But perhaps because he saw he had nowhere to go or because he was too weak to run, he sat back down and simply waved us over. I approached guardedly and sat across from him on the ground. His Grace sat between us. I was quite certain I had seen this person before.

"Y'all might as well get it over with," the man said, wiping his bloodshot eyes.

His clothes seemed a few sizes too large, and he obviously had not recently bathed. Beside him on the ground was a small fire. An opened can of beef soup sat bubbling in the flames.

Lord Baltimore reached into his coat pocket and withdrew a cigar from what I had come to suspect was an endless supply. "Get what over with?" he asked.

"You're bounty hunters, ain'tcha?"

We avowed that we were not, and it was then that I recognized him.

"You're the escaped prisoner," said His Grace, eyeing the young man steadily and tossing his match into the fire.

He was none other than the convict with long sideburns who had escaped from Sheriff Pooler's mock jail cell at the rally.

Lord Baltimore removed his tennis shoes and stuck his bare feet in the cold spring water. He then lay on his back with his eyes closed while the young man devoured the contents of the soup can. Seeing how hungry he was, I offered a smoked mullet, which he greedily consumed.

"I'm Brantley," he said.

Then, without provocation, he revealed how he had come to land in Sheriff Pooler's jail. I was quite prepared for a tale of woe, but to his credit, Brantley admitted he was a thief and that it was through nothing more than laziness and the desire to turn a quick profit that he had slipped into a life of crime.

It had started in his early teens with the theft of a few tires that he foolishly sold to a cousin of the person from whom they were stolen. From there, it progressed to petty theft during summer vacation and larceny with several older acquaintances. This led to his robbing gambling joints and convenience stores—in particular, a convenience store in Sheriff Pooler's jurisdiction.

His recent escape had transpired in the following manner. After slipping out the back of the cage with the other inmates, Brantley had the presence of mind to duck beneath the truck attached to the flatbed trailer that served as the sheriff's stage. While the lawmen chased the fleeing convicts, he waited there until everyone left, then rode away under a tarpaulin on the flatbed. A few miles north on the Coastal Highway, the truck stopped at one of the roadblocks. But a south-bound rig hauling Georgia pine to a paper mill had approached the roadblock too rapidly and jackknifed, causing the logs to spill. In the darkness and confusion, Brantley raced into the woods and made his way to the Dixie Highway. There, he stumbled across a trailer park and made off with someone's shirt and trousers, left on a clothesline to dry. The next morning, he located a dock near the one where the *Mattie* had stopped for us. He stowed away on a boat laden with goods for the people of Pigge Hammock. Upon reaching the main dock on Zapala, he grabbed several cans from the stock and slid off into the water. After that, Brantley had wandered aimlessly for days before making his way to this spot.

He concluded by saying he had fallen in with a bad crowd at an early age and was intrigued by the lifestyle, even though he knew what he was doing was wrong. But as it was the only life he knew, he resolved that it would ever be thus until the day he died.

"It's not with whom you're bred but with whom you're fed that determines the kind of person you are," said Lord Baltimore, rousing from his slumber. "Yours is a tale told a thousand times a day. The end is certain ruin. However, you're young yet and can amend your habits, God willing."

"God!" cried Brantley. "Where's He ever been when I needed Him? I asked God to help me, an' look where I am now."

"What did you ask for?"

"I wanted to get out of jail."

"Well, you're out."

"This ain't out, man. This is bein' on the run."

"Then perhaps you should be more careful of what you request of the Lord."

"Man, I just want a sign. You show me one little sign from God, an' I'm joinin' the first church I come across. The sheriff won't quit 'til I'm caught or dead, 'specially with this election goin' on."

Lord Baltimore waved off Brantley's remark as if it were a gnat. "The good sheriff is in the grip of the demon cocaine. The simple move of a pawn was all that was needed to make his world begin to unravel."

"He's addicted?" I asked with genuine surprise.

"Did you not notice the constant running of his nose?"

"You mean his allergies?"

Brantley snickered.

"Allergies? Not likely," said His Grace.

Brantley informed us that several inmates in the detention center helped smuggle money out of the county while on work detail, in exchange for early release. "They don't call him the 'high sheriff' for nothin'," he allowed.

It appeared that Brantley and I, though from different backgrounds and circumstances, had arrived at the same place and time in roughly the same condition. We agreed that we had little to show for our efforts and little to look forward to if we had to depend on our own knowledge and skills.

"You believe your future prospects are limited, do you?" asked His Lordship.

Brantley sneered. "It's called reality."

"Is it?" His Lordship inquired. The thought seemed to amuse him. He pointed at the sun. "What do you boys see there in the sky?"

"Looks like the sun to me," Brantley said. "A big, ol', hot chunk of rock."

"And you, Master Ensworth. What do you see?"

"I see the sun. A star. A gaseous orb."

"What else do you see?"

"That's it," said Brantley. "Ain't nothin' else up there."

I concurred.

"Aha!" said His Lordship. "It's the only star you see. It blinds you to the fact that there are other stars out there, many of which are much larger. Just as what you perceive to be reality is nothing more than one reality. You can't see the others because you're blinded by the one."

Brantley looked at me for confirmation that we were indeed in the company of a crazy person.

"You mean that maybe we have abilities we don't know about?" I asked.

"You have no idea of the possibilities you possess."

Brantley let his view be known by clearing his throat and expectorating an aquatic missile an impressive distance.

"The potential that lies within both of you is infinite. But potential is nothing without action. Only when you allow your erroneous self-perceptions to fade like the setting sun will you begin to see a new universe of truths."

While I felt something—not quite a revelation but a definite stirring of the soul—Brantley appeared to gain nothing.

"Here," continued His Grace. "Close your eyes. Both of you."

I complied.

"Now, open them. You, Ensworth, describe the object I hold in my hand, using exact details."

Because of the lighting and the angle at which His Lordship held the object, what I saw was a silhouette.

"I see a small, dark circle," I said.

"How big of a circle?"

"Maybe half an inch."

"Now, Brantley, you describe what you see, using exact details."

"I see a brown cigar with a gold wrapper on it."

"What shape do you see? How long?"

"Like a cylinder. 'Bout six inches."

Lord Baltimore appeared deeply satisfied, but only for a moment.

"And the point is?" asked Brantley.

"The point is you both looked upon the same thing, yet your perceptions of it disagreed entirely. That's reality."

"You mean," continued Brantley, "reality is a cigar?"

"Reality is what things look like from your perspective. It's all in your hands. Don't you see?"

"The reality is I'm in deep trouble. I'm a fugitive. I don't know what you're talking about, man."

"Exactly my point. That's your perspective. The reality of your predicament from my point of view is quite different. You'll soon see what I mean." His Grace then rose and announced, "Come. We must be off."

"What for?" I asked.

"If you want to live, do as I say." He turned and made for the path.

"Is he crazy?" Brantley asked me with some alarm.

"I think so. But he seems to know his way around."

Brantley hesitated, then decided to fall in with us.

"He goes by His Grace, His Lordship, or Lord Baltimore," I informed him.

Brantley scoffed. "I ain't callin' no dude 'His Grace,' I guarantee you that."

It was then that His Grace wheeled and attacked Brantley, who fell back momentarily, moved aside, then swung wildly, all the while shouting curses that involved His Lordship's mother.

"Did you see that?" Lord Baltimore asked me with a note of excitement. "Did you notice how the lad held his ground and countered? That's your next lesson. Stand and deliver!"

With that, he turned and was once again off on the trail.

"Man, this dude's nuts," Brantley whispered.

The rest of the day passed peaceably enough. Brantley, too, picked up on Lord Baltimore's habit of littering the path with butts and cigar wrappers. His Lordship made him the same offer he made me—that is to say, if Brantley could guess why Lord Baltimore acted in this manner, one hundred dollars would be his.

By late afternoon, we reached the other side of the island, having crisscrossed its width several times for reasons Lord Baltimore would not explain. Occasionally, we stopped to snack on berries and honeysuckle.

Brantley started singing a bittersweet song, "He Stopped Loving Her Today." Since he knew only the chorus and a smattering of verses, we were treated to an endless, half-told tale of romance gone awry, minus most of the plot and the main characters. It occurred to me that Brantley had forgotten the "reality" of the dire straits he thought himself to be in. It further occurred to me that it was possible to be in the midst of a troubling situation and in a carefree state of mind at the same time.

My thoughts were interrupted when His Lordship came upon a beehive situated in a hollow tree. "I'm going in," he informed us. He removed his overcoat and shirt, so as not to get honey and beeswax on them. Then, puffing furiously on his cigar to "keep the buggers at bay," he reached inside the tree and extracted enough honeycomb to provide Brantley and me a treat. We could not help seeing the scars that covered His Lordship's upper arms and shoulders—long, wide disfigurements that protruded from the edges of his tank-top under-shirt. Neither of us mentioned them. I did my best to eat the honey, though my appetite had waned.

We made camp on the west side of the island on a bluff overlook-ing the marsh. That evening, we dined on the smoked mullet Ken-neth had given His Lordship. The fish were smothered in a Seville orange sauce. They were accompanied by sweet potatoes cooked in hot ashes, carrots boiled in a large tin can, and the raw tips of pal-metto bush stems. Lord Baltimore opened the jar of sturgeon eggs but found no takers in Brantley and me. For dessert, we had wild berries. I thought the meal quite tasty. Brantley expressed his delight by way of forceful belching. I, too, emitted several errant noises. We looked at Lord Baltimore as if it were his turn to complete the trium-virate. He grasped our intent and politely explained that he could not burp, belch, spit, whistle, perspire, or perform any other disagreeable bodily exhalation, due to what he called his "royal gene."

"You see, gentlemen," he said, "as I descend from royal blood, you may easily understand that I have inherited a rare DNA mutation that denies me the pleasure of performing common bodily functions most people take for granted."

Brantley pointed out that the royal family members he was aware of behaved rather shabbily.

"The common man loves to set celebrities upon a pedestal and then knock them off it," said His Grace, "especially the royal family. Great sport for the masses."

It occurred to me that His Grace had set me up with riddles that day and relished knocking me down when I couldn't answer them. I asked if Brantley and I could solve the puzzles and receive the previously offered monetary reward. His Grace readily accepted.

"He doesn't move yet climbs ten stories. Who is it?"

We shook our heads.

"What kind of man doesn't move and yet climbs a ten-story building?"

We conceded defeat.

"A man in an elevator!" he replied. "Any child could tell you that."

"I see," I said, catching on. "So a man who soars overhead without leaving his seat . . . is a man . . . He's a man who . . ."

Brantley nodded his head in unison with mine, the answer on the tip of his tongue.

"He is a p—," His Grace began.

"A p—," Brantley and I repeated.

"A pi—," said His Grace.

"A python!" blurted Brantley.

His Grace put the bills back into his pocket.

"Not a python. A man who soars overhead without leaving his seat is a bloody pilot," he growled.

Being young men and so inclined to the proclivities of our kind, Brantley and I soon shook off this attack on our egos by telling exaggerated tales of our experiences with women. On the subject of unlikely opportunities, I was the clear winner, though Brantley made a valiant attempt. However, on the topic of improbable conquests, Brantley easily exceeded my storytelling.

Lord Baltimore grunted his disapproval. "You two are sculptors," he told us. "Two fine, young sculptors."

"What's that supposed to mean?" asked Brantley.

"A sculptor," began His Lordship, "is one who . . ." He groped for a moment, as if the words would not come. "Ah," he said, "perhaps a poem will explain."

Brantley and I exchanged glances, but before either of us could object, the poem was begun.

They each took their turn sculpting away
Sanding by night, chipping by day
Turning this goddess, this visual feast
First into a mortal, then into a beast

Each was an artist in his own style
A lover of women, at least for a while
By tip-tipping here and tap-tapping there
They fractured the idol beyond all repair

Out went her Faith, then Honor, and more
What once was Belief lay strewn on the floor
Then her Self-Respect and Confidence rose
And left with Affection while she held a pose

His Grace paused to relight his stogie, and I thought for a moment that our torture was over. But the moment the tobacco caught fire, he picked up where he had left off.

Like knights in white armor, each one turned her head
They courted and charmed her but never to wed
While visions of romance danced through her dreams
Each plotted an exit by various means

The hunted soon captured, the trophy now won
Their interest waning, the sculpture undone
And she like a Venus, wounded and hurt
Sought yet another to finish the work

Skilled was each sculptor in the finely tuned art
Of taking and shaping and breaking the heart
Of sanding down Hope to a fine-powdered dust
Scraping off Love, blasting out Trust

Til nothing was left but a fault-riddled stone
Bitter, afraid . . . fragile, alone
They each took their turn sculpting away
Then one by one left her to seek finer prey

"That, my friends," said Lord Baltimore, shoving the cigar back into his mouth, "is a sculptor."

Brantley didn't quite make the connection between the poem and the topic we were discussing. As for me, I found it compelling but saw little relationship between the sculptors and myself. The main reason for this was that my tales of sexual pursuit were entirely untrue but so well recited—having been frequently practiced in the company of my golfing friends—that I had come to believe them. Lord Baltimore's poem brought me to the reality that my sculpting days, if anything, were ahead of me.

Brantley began a related topic that treated of women who "asked for what they got." Lord Baltimore expressed his disenchantment with our conversation by wandering off into the dark stand of pines, palms, and scrub oaks. He should have lingered, for Brantley then told a story with such sincerity that I knew it to be truthful. It was filled with regret and sorrow.

"She was way too young. . . . We went out anyhow. Her papa didn't care for me, but we met on the sly. I was gonna change my ways and ask her to marry me, and then I got busted and was sentenced to a year. When I got out, she was gone. I followed her as far as Brunswick but couldn't find her."

His mood changed as he spoke. I had the sense that his heart felt injury in merely saying the name Susan. He described her from head to toe, and I listened with interest as he mentioned the gap between her two front teeth. At that point, I could not doubt that the Susan he spoke of was the same Susan from whom I had recently departed. But something prevented me from disclosing what I knew. Perhaps it was best that he not learn of her newfound profession, or of the child, or of the child's kidnapping. Perhaps that would have been too much, in light of his current state of affairs.

Brantley continued his story. After failing to locate her, he had searched every town on the coast to Savannah. Broke and broken-hearted, he returned home. Upon reaching Darien, he stopped at a convenience store to buy refreshments, when he noticed that the main street seemed empty. He had learned an old trick from a former jail mate who had been in the business of robbing stores. The trick was to call the police and claim that a bomb had been planted at city hall and was set to go off in thirty minutes. Brantley knew that city hall was a mile on the other side of town, which would give him enough time to make good his heist and escape. He placed a call to the Darien Police Department from the public telephone outside the front door of the store.

His decision to rob the convenience store was strictly spur of the moment and decidedly a bad idea. For upon his request for Jirline, the clerk, to be calm and hand over the money, she instead screamed and fainted dead away. Her sister, Maxine, the other clerk, pushed a button that alerted the police. Brantley's strategy was flawed in that his truck remained parked at the convenience store, where in-store cameras had documented his every move, including his phone call. His strategy was further flawed in that Darien's city hall was quite old and was undergoing repairs at the time. Temporary facilities were located on the second floor above the Darien Planters Bank, located just across the street from the convenience store. He also didn't know that several depositors were queued up inside the bank. One was none other than a county deputy and the sheriff's right-hand man, Tony Adrian, the man I knew as Ratchet Face.

No sooner did Jirline hit the floor than a number of sirens could be heard converging on the convenience store. Deputy Adrian, on foot, beat the patrol cars to the scene. As if that weren't enough, the bank camera across the street had also documented Brantley's moves.

The district attorney thus had his choice of videos to show the jury. He submitted telephone records that detailed the time the call was made, the phone number dialed, and the phone number from which it was dialed. Fingerprints on the telephone proved to belong to Brantley. Most of the jury knew the store clerks and the arresting officer. The only question they had to answer was not whether Brantley had done the deed but how long he should pay for doing it. As he was embarrassingly inept at this line of work, and as he had used no weapon, he was handed a mere five-year sentence. He had still been awaiting transfer to the state penitentiary when Sheriff Pooler hauled him trembling before the political rally.

Brantley finished his tale and asked that I reciprocate by telling how I had arrived at this point. I began my life's story and was half-way through a recitation on the fundamentals of gripping a golf club when I noticed that my audience had fallen into slumber.

I set off on the same trail down which Lord Baltimore had disappeared and would have walked right past him had he not spoken out of the darkness: " 'We blunder and brag, die and are forgot, and some other fool takes our place.' "

I peered into a thicket and found His Lordship nestled in thick vines that hung from a large oak.

"Our friend is asleep?" he asked.

"Yes."

"What do you make of him?"

"I don't know. Seems to be in a fix."

I recounted Brantley's story and told him I believed the Susan at the motel was Brantley's long-lost love.

"Mother dressed me as a girl in my early years, as was the custom in those days," he replied. "It was generally believed that Gypsies would not steal young females. Thus, many a male spent his early childhood in long hair and skirts."

At that, Lord Baltimore sighed deeply and stared transfixed at the moon. He seemed to drift into a deep, reflective mood.

Presently, I heard the distinct sounds of a man deep in the arms of Morpheus. It was apparent that Lord Baltimore's royal gene was defective, for he could be heard snoring from a good distance. In fact, I suspected that Brantley shared the gene, since he could be heard just as easily when I reached a point equidistant from both.

I resolved to stay near the campfire no matter what the cost in sleep. I gently rolled Brantley onto his side and found that sufficient to end his clamorous inhalations. And it wasn't long before visions of my father and mother, cigars, a devilish par four, and Sheriff Pooler filled my dreams.

CHAPTER 10

We visit Pigge Hammock.

The next morning, I awoke to find Lord Baltimore kneeling over a crackling fire. He poured hot water from an aluminum pot into a cracked ceramic mug. Next to him stood a muscular though quite thin man with graying hair.

"Master Ensworth, meet JV."

I got up and shook the stranger's hand. His grip rivaled Kenneth's. However, he did not possess Kenneth's perpetual smile, but rather an intense gaze chiseled in a granite face. Lord Baltimore offered me a sip from his mug, which I accepted hesitantly. I expected a large portion of it to be whiskey but tasted only a pleasant blend of herbal tea.

"Thought you could use a decent breakfast," JV said, nodding to a backpack about the size of mine lying on the ground at his feet. He had brought a pot, several chipped mugs, eating utensils, and food.

"He found the cigar I left when we picked his vegetables," Lord Baltimore informed me.

"You took four taters and four carrots," JV said.

He poured hot water through a strainer laden with tea into a second mug and handed it to me. I declined on the grounds that I was not a breakfast person, but Lord Baltimore insisted I take the brew and also a helping of smoked ham and chopped potatoes, as we had a long stretch ahead of us that morning.

"It's imperative we reach the north end of the island by noon," he said.

He walked over to where Brantley lay sleeping and stirred him awake. While Brantley and I ate, Lord Baltimore and JV spoke in hushed tones near the bluff. JV then loaded his backpack and retreated on the trail going south. His Grace, Brantley, and I made haste in a northerly direction.

It was a good thing Lord Baltimore made us eat, because the pace he maintained that morning was brisk. We stopped for respite only twice, and briefly at that.

"Who was that guy?" Brantley wanted to know during our first stop.

"JV?" said Lord Baltimore, lighting a new cigar. "He's one of the island's hermits. Grew and rolled the tobacco for this particular cigar. Not bad, eh?" He took several puffs stretched out on the ground in the shade of a palm tree. "He's a rather interesting fellow. Apparently a highly sought athlete in his younger days. Served four years in your war on the Indochinese peninsula."

"Which war was that?"

"Your Vietnam War. He's been on Zapala about ten years, I'd say. If things go as I expect, he will play a role that will directly impact your lives in the very near future."

Our rest soon ended. An hour later, we passed through a hamlet that was nothing more than a row of shacks on either side of the trail. Most were painted in shades of blue or green. Behind each home was a small vegetable garden. A large, black pot stood in a common area.

A small fire beneath the pot simmered water. Two women using forked poles boiled clothes and hung them on a line strung between two oak trees. Lord Baltimore took from his pocket the bottle of medicine Kenneth had given him. Then he knocked on the door of a blue clapboard house and went inside. A minute later, he reappeared with a small sack.

We walked another twenty minutes before stopping under a small stand of cedars. His Grace sat beneath the largest tree, rested his back against it, and opened the sack to reveal a half-dozen fried chicken wings.

"That," he said, "was Pigge Hammock. This," he said, offering the bag to us, "is courtesy of Miss Jane."

Brantley grabbed two wings, as did I.

"Why is it called Pigge Hammock?" I asked.

"The residents there descend from a pig farmer of Couper's plantation. They added a *g* and an *e* to make *pig* sound more palatable to the ear."

This bit of trivia was lost on Brantley, who gnawed on the wings until nothing but bones remained. These he broke open and sucked the marrow out. He finished his meal about the time I was done with one wing.

Brantley eyed the bag in Lord Baltimore's hand. For a moment, I thought he had designs on licking the inside of it. "How come you wear a pocket-watch chain but no watch?" he asked.

"This?" His Grace said, fondling the chain. "It's my constant reminder to think outside the scope of conventional wisdom. This was given to me the day of my forced retirement. After decades of service rendered to queen and country, I was called upon to serve in a final capacity as chief scapegoat in a political crisis, though I had warned the appropriate officials of the very problems that developed. They ignored my advice and, upon realizing their mistake, thrust full responsibility on my shoulders, so as to be rid of me and to acquit themselves.

"I won't bore you with details," he continued, "but the watch was given to me as a symbolic token of appreciation. I chose to look at it more as a symbolic monument to ambition-blinded men condemned to a lifetime of conventional wisdom. The moment they placed it in my hands, I snapped the watch from the chain and flung it as far into the Thames as I could. Why, you ask? Because time is a man-made constraint. There is no such thing as time. It's something man invented to keep appointments. What does a tree care for one o'clock? What is eleven thirty-seven to a dolphin?"

I began to respond but was cut short.

"Nothing! Nature's time is nothing more than the rising of the sun, the incoming tide, the changing of the seasons. God made the universe in six days, but it was man who determined what length six days represent."

I wondered why, if time didn't exist, it was so important for us to be at the north end of the island by midday.

Brantley soon discovered his mistake in asking about the watch chain, for Lord Baltimore's ranting spilled over into larger issues. However, I was not overly displeased, because the more His Lordship spoke, the more time we had for rest.

"It is man's imaginary borders that create prejudice," he continued. "All people are either 'one of us' or 'one of them.' Man strives to understand everything in creation and then goes about altering it, often to his detriment. Man wishes to name everything, his first step in claiming ownership. But it is man's constraints on nature that ultimately imprison him."

"How so?" I asked, egging him on.

"Have you never raced the clock or chased the almighty dollar? At the simplest level, there's no difference between men and amoebas. We seek warmth. We seek shade. We seek food. Everything else is based on desire. Desire is the root of avarice. And avarice is the root of all evil. No matter how much we have, we desire more. In all history, man has never had it so good. You two ride in chariots called automobiles that a king one hundred years ago could only dream about." Then, catching himself—and perhaps realizing my ploy to stall for time—he said, "Sometimes, I speak too much. We must be off."

With that, we were on our way again. We soon came upon a fork in the path.

"That way leads to Folktown," said Lord Baltimore, pointing to the path leading north. "This one crosses Devil Swamp. We'll take it."

"Why's it called Devil Swamp?" Brantley wanted to know.

His Grace looked around, then said in a lowered voice, "Some locals maintain that this swamp is a portal through which Satan enters our world. Many islanders claim to have seen him skulking about here. I prefer to believe that the root doctors who came before Tilly named it Devil Swamp so folks wouldn't enter their sanctuary."

"Who's Tilly?" Brantley asked.

"Oh, just a witch doctor," I informed him.

I was all for the swamp passage, as it would take us off the beaten path. I had the sense to know that I was traveling with an escaped prisoner—Brantley—and possibly a wanted criminal—His Grace.

However, Brantley was not equally disposed to crossing the swamp. "You two can go that way. I'm going to Folktown," he said. "Ain't no way I'm goin' into voodoo country."

Lord Baltimore replied in a whisper. "Two of Pooler's men landed on the south end this morning. With two bloodhounds." Brantley turned a shade of pale. "They found your jail clothes and correctly surmised you made for Zapala. As for the two of us," His Grace said to me, "JV informs me that the good sheriff is convinced we're behind the disappearance of his precious money. He further suspects that we, too, are on Zapala."

Lord Baltimore finished these words with a final puff on his cigar. He then tossed the butt onto the path ahead of us.

"Hey, Pooler's men can track us by your cigar butts!" Brantley said in a loud voice a split second before I could do so.

His Grace looked at us with a mischievous grin. "Yes? And . . . ?"

"And you're deliberately leading them to us," I replied.

"That's the idea." His Lordship whipped out two hundred-dollar bills and gave one to each of us. "Did I not say I'd give a hundred dollars to whoever discerned my reason for littering the trail? You two came upon the answer simultaneously."

CHAPTER 11

We cross Devil Swamp
and save a man.

We entered Devil Swamp, a low-lying area in the heart of Zapala. This intimidating sanctuary, whose inhabitants were no doubt the direct descendants of prehistoric monsters, was fed by freshwater ponds and surrounded by bluffs and dunes that allowed little drainage to occur. A narrow path that was submerged in places led us to the center of the swamp. Occasionally, we were forced to cross six-inch-wide plank bridges that bounced under our weight. Water moccasins, which were plentiful, did their best to get out of our way. However, one exceptionally large snake, as if to let us know we were intruding on its ground, took its time slithering away from a warm, sandy patch of ground where it lay.

Not far into the swamp, we reached a fork in the path.

"If you take the right path," His Grace warned, "it soon divides. And either path you take next also divides. And so on and so forth.

The islanders call it the Devil's Maze. A man can get lost in there in broad daylight. I suggest we veer left."

We spent the next hour treading gingerly across logs that spanned sloughs and bogs. I didn't care to dwell upon what creatures might lie just beneath the water, waiting for one of us to plunge into their midst. Fortunately, we traversed the heart of the swamp without managing to become a part of it.

In the middle of this morass, we came upon a dark blue clapboard house that rested high atop columns of tabby. Lord Baltimore motioned for us not to make a sound. "Tilly's domicile," he said. "They say she's a changeling."

"What's that?" Brantley asked in a loud and frightened whisper.

"A changeling is one who can alter shape, like Proteus. She might appear as a bird or a spider and you'd never know it. She could have been that snake back there."

We were almost out of sight of Tilly's dwelling when we heard a creaking door. "Don't look back!" His Grace admonished.

No sooner had these words escaped his lips than His Grace froze. Since he was in the lead and the path was extremely narrow, we could not see what lay ahead. He motioned for us to back up. "See that tree behind you?" he said. A scrub oak stood next to the path a short distance to our rear. "Make for it."

Brantley and I, sensing an urgency in his voice, complied. It was fortunate that we did, for Lord Baltimore would have knocked us down otherwise. Brantley reached the tree ahead of me and flung himself upon the first available limb. I grabbed the next limb higher up. His Grace scrambled over us to secure a smaller limb and wrapped his legs around the tree.

Close on the heels of His Lordship, hissing and thumping its tail, was perhaps the world's largest alligator. We remained suspended between earth and sky for several minutes while the monster thrashed the tree trunk with its tail. Brantley declared that it was the witch in disguise. He seized a rotten limb with one hand and flung it. The limb hit the creature hard on the right hind leg. I, too, snapped off a limb and threw it, only to see it bounce harmlessly off the alligator's back. After ten minutes of impasse, the brute decided to move on, either because we were securely fastened to the tree or because of the wealth of projectiles at our disposal.

After that, Brantley and I watched for the next available tree, should one be required. His Grace resumed his usual brisk pace, seeming more concerned with studying vines and water flora than with looking out for carnivorous reptiles.

An hour later, we emerged from the swamp and entered an oak forest. Coming out on the far side of this wood, we spilled over high sand dunes and on to a beach that was being pounded by the incoming tide. We stayed close to the dunes and plowed our way through soft sand for about a mile, where we exited on to a narrow trail near Zapala's northernmost point. This path led to a grassy clearing shaded by huge oaks.

We had just entered the clearing when a loud bang came from our right. Lord Baltimore suggested we seek cover. The three of us plunged into a thick mesh of palmetto bushes. Brantley shook noticeably, convinced that the law was upon him. Soon, we heard another bang. His Grace raised his head cautiously above the palmetto fronds. I fully expected him to return to cover. Instead, he recklessly plunged in the direction of the noise.

"Stop, I say! Stop that!" he shouted.

Brantley curled up into a ball and closed his eyes. I waited in vain for several moments for something to happen. I then heard Lord Baltimore speaking quietly, though I could not understand what was being said. Curiosity got the better of me, so I slowly stood to witness what I was sure would be several deputies aiming their weapons in our direction. The scene I beheld, though, was quite different.

Perhaps thirty yards away was a small river that separated Zapala from a neighboring island to the north. Between the river and where I stood was a large man in a business suit holding a gun to his head. Lord Baltimore stood just a few paces from him. I stepped forward, which startled the man and caused his gun hand to shake. Keeping his eyes on the man, His Grace motioned for me to stop.

"Can't I end it in peace?" the man asked.

At that point, Brantley popped up from the bushes, whereupon the man dropped the gun by his side and exclaimed, "For the love of Mike! Can't a man kill himself without an audience?"

His Grace removed the gun from the man's limp hand and threw it into the woods. He then took the fellow's arm and helped him back to the clearing, where we all collapsed onto the ground. All, that is, except Lord Baltimore.

We learned that his name was Jeremy. He was a real-estate agent from Savannah who had married a woman with a propensity for spending more than he earned. Furthermore, he had acquired several expensive indulgences, such as the speedboat that had brought him to the island and the luxury auto parked at a Savannah marina with the keys still in the ignition for whoever cared to drive it away, since Jeremy did not intend to return.

"My wife and I came to Savannah fifteen years ago. We joined the right clubs and worked our way up through the social circles. The only problem is that it takes money to stay in those circles. I've got two mortgages on a house with a leaky roof in an exclusive neighborhood. I've got a son in college who is constantly getting into situations I have to bail him out of, and a lazy daughter at home who has no intention of leaving."

Lord Baltimore's demeanor changed gradually from concern to contempt as Jeremy spoke.

"The head of my firm is looking for young, ambitious people to replace what he calls 'extinct volcanoes' like me, just as he used me to replace an older agent when I first came to town. I made a few bad investments, then the market went south, and I've got bill collectors calling me at night. To top it off, my wife's connection to old Savannah money isn't speaking to her, so she's not speaking to me. The final straw was when I went to her brother for a loan. This is the guy I helped get situated seven years ago. Now, he's a big shot with the aerospace firm and can't be bothered to return my calls. My only recourse, as far as I can see, is to kill myself and be done with it."

"For the insurance money?" Brantley asked.

"Ha!" Jeremy said. "That's a joke. Who has money for insurance premiums?"

Upon this revelation, Lord Baltimore headed for the woods.

"Where are you going?" I wanted to know.

"To find that gun. He was doing the right thing!"

"What were those shots we heard?" I asked Jeremy.

"The first shot was my failed attempt with the gun against my temple. The second was when I held it under my chin. Something moved my hand each time."

We could hear His Lordship shuffling in the underbrush. He soon reappeared, still in a foul mood.

"Sir," he began, "I am a fool. That much should be clear to you. I should have let you pull the trigger. Nay, I should have encouraged you to do so! Now that I think of it, in addition to being irresponsible, you are a coward who has not the capacity for doing this world the favor of ridding it of yourself. Each man is the architect of his own rise or fall," he continued. "You, sir, have failed as a person in curtailing your personal excesses. You have failed as a husband in curtailing your wife's. You have failed as a father in disciplining your children. Sir, you are a blight on the business world. You are ambitious but have neither the means nor the skills to fulfill those ambitions. Worse still, you do not know your place. Money alone will not sustain you in the rarefied circles you seek to enter. Go, sir! Go now before I find your pistol and shoot you myself."

I made up my mind that His Lordship was capable of carrying out his threat. Jeremy, equally convinced, bounded away like a deer through the underbrush. We soon heard the rumblings of twin inboard motors, followed by the sound of a boat hull pounding on rough water.

"He's going back," said His Lordship. "Back to chasing a brass ring that will be forever out of his grasp. God help poor souls like him."

"Like him? He ain't got no sheriff trackin' him," said Brantley. "If God gets me outta this mess, I'm changin' my ways for good. That there's a promise."

CHAPTER 12

We meet the Latin speaker
and fish from the forbidden creek.

We wove our way through a long stretch of oaks, then plunged into dense foliage that walled in a narrow, sandy path. This path soon ascended to the first real road I had seen on Zapala. It was composed of sand and crushed shells that fairly blinded me with the sun's reflection. However, it remained mostly in the shadows of the tall pines and oaks that lined either side. We traveled west on this thoroughfare for half an hour before coming upon a series of horseshoe-shaped bluffs overlooking a wide river.

"That is called Raccoon Bluff," His Grace informed us as we walked past the first one.

The second was Big Hawk Bluff. The third was Teach's Bluff. When we came to the next one, Lord Baltimore stopped. He brought to our attention the skull of a wild boar nailed to an oak tree that arched over the path leading to the bluff.

"This is Ibo Landing," he informed us. "Under no circumstances are you to come here. You have been forewarned. Have I made myself perfectly clear?"

Brantley and I confirmed that we understood. I thought no more about it, as I didn't intend to be a guest on Zapala long enough to visit that place.

After passing about a dozen more bluffs, we turned south on a trail overgrown with underbrush. A hundred yards into this trail, we came upon a wide glade surrounded by tall pines and chinaberry trees. To the right was a small vegetable garden of corn, squash, tomatoes, pepper plants, watermelons, and herbs. Next to the garden was a small freshwater pond. A log cabin attached to a small tabby structure sat opposite the pond. I spied a tidal creek and wide-open marsh behind the structure. Large oak trees stood on either side of the cabin. Wild grapevines covered the front porch. Handmade nets were draped from the porch rafters, and two cane fishing poles were suspended from nails above the cabin's entrance. The adjacent tabby hut looked as though it might have once been a horse stall. Next to it were a hand pump and a trough half filled with water and algae. The hut now served as a storage area for numerous hand-woven baskets, which hung from the ceiling.

We entered the shelter to find in one corner stacks of finished and half-finished watercolors. Scattered about were canvases, brushes, a palette, tubes of paint, and an easel. The paintings were mostly landscapes from different parts of Zapala, some of which I had seen. It was then that I understood how Lord Baltimore knew the island so intimately.

"Make yourselves at home, gentlemen," he said, crossing to the far end of the room. "Have a rest. You will go fishing for your dinner shortly."

He opened a cabinet and pulled down a half-filled brandy bottle. He then blew the dust off three jelly jars and poured a drink into each. Passing the glasses, he proposed a toast: "To the queen!"

Brantley and I glanced at each other and responded in unison: "To the queen."

Civility dictated that we abide by house rules. We well knew that Lord Baltimore was our meal ticket and protector—for the time being.

Brantley consumed the brandy with far more ease than I. That is to say, he sipped it cautiously, whereas I threw my glass back and consumed its entire contents in one gulp. It went down easily enough, and I was about to comment on its smooth taste when the first wave of fumes rose to my head. It was this unleashing of vapors that undid me, much to the amusement of Brantley and the disappointment of His Lordship.

"It's not Coca-Cola," His Grace told me in a tone that said he had wasted good brandy on me.

Lining one wall of the cabin were bookshelves that contained volumes on topics of every kind, including government, poetry, architecture, theater, religion, medicine, and law. Lord Baltimore snatched a book, plopped into a well-worn leather chair, and put his feet up on what was left of an ottoman.

I studied the titles and found myself drawn to those that dealt with medicine. There were new books as well as old. I found the following intriguing enough to write down in my journal:

> *Schamberg's Diseases of the Skin and Eruptive Fevers*
> *Braasch's Pyelography*
> *DeSchweinitz's Diseases of the Eye*
> *Bass and John's Alveolodental Pyorrhea*
> *Haab and DeSchweinitz's Ophthalmoscopy*
> *Ogden on the Urine*
> *Pilcher's Practical Cystoscopy*
> *Gleason on Nose, Throat, and Ear*
> *Mracek and Stelwagon's Atlas of the Skin*

A well-worn edition of *Burke's Peerage, Baronetage, and Knightage* rested on a dusty shelf beside *Smith's Guide to Draughtsmanship*. Brantley picked up the book on draftsmanship and was soon standing by the window eagerly turning its pages, entranced by the illustrations and instructions for building foundations, roofs, windows, and doors.

I wandered through an open door that led to a back room. This room was quite dark, and it took several moments for my eyes to adjust. When I cracked a window shutter open to let in more light, I found myself surrounded by hand-woven baskets and brightly painted animal sculptures made of common tools such as pitchforks, shovels, and hammers. An aged worktable was in a corner of the room. The sculptures were covered with a thin layer of dust. I stumbled over something that turned out to be a drum made from a hollowed-out log covered with animal skin, possibly cow or goat.

The discovery of such works of art was unexpected and exhilarating. I was just beginning to admire the detailing on an old plow that was now an exotic bird's beak when a shriek came from the adjoining room. I ran back to find Brantley gasping for air and pointing at the window. Just outside the glass were two dolls about the size of my hand. One was dressed like Brantley, the other like me. Each hung by a miniature noose attached to the roof.

"Voodoo dolls!" Brantley said. "We're dead men!"

Lord Baltimore looked up from his book. "I was wondering when you'd notice those," he said.

Brantley's face was drained of color. "Don't you know what it means?"

His Grace stared at Brantley quizzically.

"He means, do you think we should leave?" I interpreted.

His Lordship sighed heavily, grabbed an old cigar butt that rested on a saucer, and rose. He lit the stub and strolled outside. He reappeared outside the window, cigar in mouth, eyeing the dolls. Then he reached up, pulled them down, and reentered the cabin with both of them in his left hand.

"Voodoo," he said, setting afire with his cigar the straw-filled doll made in my image, "like any religion, works only if you believe." He flung the burning doll through the open doorway. He then did likewise with the doll made in Brantley's likeness. "I do not believe in voodoo. Therefore, I am not affected. And as you can see, neither one of you has caught fire."

His Lordship's indifference toward the dolls comforted me.

Brantley, though, made a startling announcement. "We ain't gettin' off this island alive," he said in a deliberate, measured voice, staring into the distance.

By what means this revelation came to him, I don't know. Nor did I care. His calm acceptance of his fate was far preferable to the high-strung anxiety he seemed prone to display at the slightest provocation.

"See here," Lord Baltimore said, pulling a pair of scissors from a drawer. "Do you lads believe I can cut a hole in this piece of paper large enough to poke your head through?" He held in one hand a scrap of paper about the size of a business card. "If I can do this, will you believe me when I say that no harm will come to you on Zapala?"

Brantley shrugged his shoulders. Apparently, he'd given up all hope. But I encouraged His Grace to make good on the boast.

He proceeded to fold the card in half, making it even smaller. Then he cut narrow strips parallel to each other from both the folded side of the paper and the side where the two ends met. After several minutes of meticulous scissoring, he made one final snip at the fold and opened the dissected scrap, which expanded to an incredible size. He had indeed cut the paper so as to allow one's head to fit inside a continuous loop.

The point, I understood, was that His Grace's word was to be trusted even though what he told us might not seem possible. Brantley remained doubtful.

An hour later, cane poles in hand, Brantley and I made our way up the path to the main road. From there, we cut over to one of the river bluffs.

"I shoulda caught a ride with that guy to Savannah," Brantley said.

"Who, Jeremy?"

"Yeah. I'd rather take my chances with the police there than stick around here with witches and voodoo and all that."

"You really believe in the supernatural?"

"I seen it!" he snapped. "Old witch back home could turn herself into a chicken. One time, a man found a hen snoopin' 'round his house and shot at it. Hit it in the left wing. Next day, the witch come into town with her left arm in a sling. Ever'body knowed what happened."

There was genuine worry in Brantley's eyes, and I knew nothing I could say would dissuade him from his belief. I changed the subject and speculated on what errand of Lord Baltimore's was so important that he couldn't join our fishing.

"Probably gonna go somewhere and get stinkin' drunk" was Brantley's assessment.

I didn't think so, because His Lordship had departed the cabin without his brandy. He had taken a trail that led south, the direction from which we had been traveling for the last day and a half.

It took us perhaps twenty minutes to reach the first bluff. As the semicircle of lagoon beneath it was filled with driftwood and other debris, we decided to try the next one. Whether we were at Two-Mile Bluff, Pelican Bluff, or Two Creek Indian Lovers Rendezvoused Here Three Hundred Years Ago Bluff, we knew not. It looked equally un-inviting. The third bluff appeared more promising. We positioned ourselves at the center of the bluff's curve and dropped our lines into the water. But after an hour of futility, we raised our poles. We tried one and then another location for the better part of the afternoon and had all but given up hope when we came upon a bluff that gave way to a narrow beach, from which we stood and cast our lines. Within a minute, we had a nibble. Before darkness descended upon us, we snatched two redfish and three trout.

The temperature had dipped perceptibly by the time Brantley and I scurried up the steep bank. From there, we made our way to the main road as Venus brightened in the sky. We then found the appropriate trail and arrived at the cabin as the day's final curtain came down.

An oil lamp lit the cabin from within. Lord Baltimore was crouched over a small fire in the middle of the clearing. He sat on a cinder block weaving a small, square mat approximately six inches long by eight inches wide out of stripped palmetto leaves. He had already completed several mats. A pot of boiling water sat on two logs in the fire. The fire itself was set in a three-foot-wide pit about a foot deep.

Brantley and I gutted and scaled the fish and, following His Grace's instructions, wrapped each in a large elephant-ear leaf. We then put each wrapped fish inside a folded mat and placed the mats along the edge of the pit. Using small pine limbs, we piled sand and hot coals next to the palmetto mats, then covered them with dirt.

"In twenty minutes, you will dine on steamed fish. It's a meal you won't soon forget," Lord Baltimore assured us.

Before that moment arrived, we were attacked by a squadron of mosquitoes. My Skin-So-Fine came in handy as a repellent, as did the smoke from the fire.

Lord Baltimore offered Brantley and me a cigar. I declined, but Brantley accepted the offer and was soon choking on a Bolivar.

"Don't inhale the thing," His Grace admonished. "Draw on it lightly."

Rather than calming Brantley, his comment had the opposite effect. I quickly discovered the real cause of his discomfort. He pointed with a quivering finger toward the path, where I fully expected two more voodoo dolls to be hanging from a branch. Instead, I saw two sinister shadows approaching through the woods. They moved first forward, then backward, then sideways as they wound along the twisting path. At last, the smaller shadow emerged from the woods holding a flaming torch. It was followed closely by an enormous, lumbering giant that must have been a creation of the devil himself.

What finally came into view in the firelight was an ancient man, along with an aging ox that voluntarily accompanied him with no rope or harness of any kind. The man was definitely an islander. He appeared to be little more than skin and bone loosely poured into faded overalls and long underwear. His full head of white hair reached out in all directions. His face was a series of craggy cliffs eroded by eons of sweat and tears. A burlap sack held by a mangled right hand was slung over his shoulder. The only items on his person that seemed of any value were the silver chain hanging around his neck and the Saint Christopher medallion at the end of it resting on his chest.

"What do you make of him?" His Lordship inquired of me.

My immediate impression was unflattering. "I see an old man," I quietly responded. "Uneducated. Poor. Not too impressive." And that was being generous, in my opinion.

The living antique set his bag on the ground, raised the maimed hand to his mouth, and extricated a corn pipe with a chicken leg bone for a stem. Opening his parched lips, he revealed three teeth, one that dangled precariously from the top gum and two that stood like miniature gateposts on the bottom.

"*Inflagrante delicto*," he said, sticking the pointed end of the torch into the ground.

Brantley's cigar teetered perilously on his lower lip, his mouth agape. My attention was divided between the diminutive man and the colossal ox that could easily have destroyed the three of us and the cabin at the slightest command from his master.

Lord Baltimore stepped forward and gently embraced the venerable one. "Gentlemen," he announced with solemnity as he turned back toward us, "meet Liverpool."

"Awright, awright," Liverpool responded, making several abbreviated but gentlemanly bows.

I came forward cautiously. Liverpool accepted my right hand with his good one. I felt in that brief grasp a century of labor. It would be safe to say that no skin lotion had ever touched his fingers. I felt by his gaze upon me that Liverpool could read my entire history and future, while, gazing back, I could discern nothing about him.

"Look well on him," His Grace said, "for he represents the very last of his kind."

Liverpool nodded to each of us and smiled slowly, almost shyly. I noticed that the Saint Christopher he wore and the one that protected me were similar in all respects. He held his gaze on my face and gently tapped with a forefinger the medal that hung from my neck.

"Lawd Balt'mo," said Liverpool, "ain uh seen dis boy afo?"

His Grace hesitated a moment, then asserted decisively, "I'm sure you're mistaken."

Liverpool looked at Lord Baltimore as if His Grace's memory were failing. He shook his head, apparently dismissing the matter.

"*Remaneo*, Bucephalus," he said to his pet ox.

It was apparently a command to wander off and not make himself a nuisance. Bucephalus no sooner found a good spot to graze than he discharged a sound that resembled a trumpet. Its reverberations momentarily disrupted the cacophony of insects that had been tuning their instruments for the evening's entertainment.

Liverpool picked up the burlap sack and meandered toward the cabin, where, I suspected, a glass of brandy awaited.

"Unca, as he is known hereabouts," explained Lord Baltimore, "owns this cabin and most of the land you've been walking on this afternoon. He is also the last of the Latin speakers."

Brantley laughed. "What's that?"

"Someone who speaks Latin, of course. I believe he knows a little French as well." Before we could ask how someone from Zapala, especially one so ancient and seemingly poor, learned Latin, His Grace explained: "His father and mother were house servants at the Couper plantation here on the island before and after the war."

"Which war?" Brantley asked. "Ko-rea?"

Lord Baltimore looked at Brantley with what appeared to be either disbelief or pity. "Your War Between the States."

"The Civil War? How old is that dude?"

"You've met living history, lads. Liverpool was born in the year of the hurricane that uprooted the cypress tree on the south end. Mr. Couper was a Scot who, like other Southern planters of the day, was proficient in Latin and interjected phrases into everyday conversation. Eleazar, Liverpool's father, was the best friend of Couper's son. They both learned Latin from a schoolmaster the Coupers employed. Eleazar passed it along to Liverpool. With him go the last vestiges of that bygone era."

"And this is his place?" I asked.

"One of his domiciles."

"And who made all those baskets I saw in there?"

"Your host. He made the nets as well. The old art forms were passed down to him. And now to Kenneth, who, I believe, is nigh upon us."

I heard what I thought was a screech owl. Sure enough, after a minute or so, someone entered the clearing. By then, the moon had risen enough that I could make out Kenneth.

He halloed us and approached the fire holding two paper sacks and eyeing Brantley. "Who's this, Lawd Balt'mo?"

"This is Brantley. A guest."

Kenneth eyed Brantley. It was obvious that Brantley didn't care for the scrutinizing, probably suspecting that Kenneth would turn him in for a reward.

"A guest? Humph. Lots of guests comin to Zapala these days. I drop two mo guests off at the south end this mornin. Sheriff's deputies step off my boat wif two houn dogs."

The effect on Brantley was immediate. His cigar tumbled to the ground, and his mouth trembled momentarily. But to his credit, he otherwise maintained his composure.

Lord Baltimore, on the other hand, seemed pleased.

"You'll be awright. You on Zapala now," said Kenneth, slapping Brantley on the back. "Watch this here."

Kenneth pulled from one sack what I thought was a jellyfish and carefully laid it in a shallow bed of coals on one side of the flames. He bent down and rolled the object side to side until it became long and thin. Then he picked it off the coals and blew into it, forming a perfect little balloon. He tied the end and bounced the balloon in the air.

"Wild boar bladder," he said. "My firs toy was a boar balloon given to me by Unca."

I heard the door of the cabin swing open and saw Liverpool silhouetted there. "*Eheu, horsum venit vir qui fert xiphias!*" he called out.

"What he say, Lawd Balt'mo?" Kenneth asked.

His Grace pulled the cigar from his mouth. " 'Uh-oh, here comes the swordfish man.' "

"Doggone it, Unca," Kenneth said. "You know that swordfish jump in my net by accident. Now, you treat me right. I just been up to Lanta an Charl'ton an sold a whole mess of yo sculptures."

"What about my paintings? What did you get for them?" His Grace asked.

"Now, Lawd Balt'mo," Kenneth said, holding his hand before

him to calm His Grace, "before you go gettin all riled again, remember they ain't buyin ilan scenes in Lanta or Savannah. Now, Charl'ton, they askin for English landscapes. If Charl'ton want em, it won't be long fo Savannah and Lanta want some, too. You give me summa them type paintings, an I bet I sell a truckload, sho nuff."

Liverpool joined us once more at the fire, this time cradling two glasses of brandy. "*Nunc est bibendum*," he announced, handing Lord Baltimore one glass and raising the other.

" 'Now, we can drink,' " His Grace said, raising his glass as well. "*A votre sante!*"

" 'To your health,' " interpreted His Grace.

The two imbibed—or *bibendum*ed—in what I took to be a ritual they had performed many times before.

"You show Unca yo glasses?" Kenneth asked me.

"The sunglasses? No. Why?"

Kenneth burst into laughter. "Show im. Unca, looka dis."

I pulled the worthless spectacles from my shirt pocket. I could tell from his eyes that Liverpool knew where I'd gotten them. His expression was as sour as if he'd swallowed half a lemon. He looked away, spit on the ground, and mumbled, "Dat no-count tink he same lukkuh buckra."

"Let's not bring up old conflicts," His Grace said. "It's a pleasant evening. The snail is on the thorn, the deputies are on the island, and all is right with the world."

"Ain't gonna be awright when you see dis," replied Kenneth.

He produced from the other paper sack a small stack of cash bound by a rubber band. I guessed it amounted to two hundred dollars. He handed this money to His Grace. He then pulled out a large envelope stuffed with cash, which he gave to Liverpool.

The Latin speaker emitted a plain-English "whoo-doggy" while he counted the contents. "Dis yuh put Jenny in Tech," he said.

"She'll end up on de other side, like Papa," warned Kenneth.

"Not li'l Jenny. She gots de book learnin. She come back wit knowin law an keep de lan stealers away."

"This is intolerable!" His Lordship said, no longer able to watch Liverpool count his take. "Why are they paying high prices for Liverpool's sculptures and so little for my watercolors?"

Kenneth tried to console him. "Hey, dat de art society fo you, Lawd Balt'mo. You know dat well as I do. Cain't no man tell what folks gonna want next."

Lord Baltimore puffed irritably on his cigar. "Bah!" he said.

"Dey wants de folk art. Two year ago, I coulda sol yo paintins fo a bundle. But de market done flooded wif em. Now, dey wants de folk art. Dey sellin dem things fo ten times what they pay me. I done double my price. Mebbe next year—"

"*Degustibus non disputandum est,*" Liverpool broke in.

"Now what Unca say?" asked Kenneth.

Lord Baltimore, still fuming, refused to answer and instead crossed him arms, stared into the darkness, and puffed away on his cigar.

"Dey's ain no disputin bout taste," said Liverpool, interpreting for himself.

"They should be ready about now," said Brantley, concerned about our meal. He poked the sand with a stick, uncovered a steaming bundle, and gently opened it to reveal the contents.

"Say, where you boys get them fish?" Kenneth asked.

"Down at the bluff," I proudly answered. "Caught this bunch in less than an hour."

"In a hour? You?"

Kenneth and Liverpool looked at each other. Lord Baltimore turned toward me, too.

"Which bluff?" he asked.

I shrugged my shoulders. "I don't know. One of them."

"You didn't backtrack the way we came this morning, did you?"

Brantley said nothing. Neither did I.

"Did the bluff have a beach?" His Grace asked, burning a hole in me with his stare.

I could not respond.

"Did-it-have-a-beach?" he asked once more, very deliberately.

"Yes," I said.

No one said anything for an eternity. Even the cicadas ceased their background orchestrations. Kenneth emitted a low, slow whistle. Liverpool simply shook his head. He and Kenneth turned as one and walked off, taking the torch with them. I could just make out their forms as they disappeared down the trail into the woods. The huge, lumbering shadow followed them.

Lord Baltimore looked at Brantley and me with a mixture of despair and anger. The tide had turned. Now, we were the crazy ones who couldn't even follow a simple instruction. However, instead of castigating us, he simply shook his head, marched into the cabin, and closed the door behind him.

"What's the big deal about that bluff?" Brantley said in a whisper.

I admitted I didn't know. Whatever it might be, though, was enough to make me lose my appetite. Brantley, on the other hand, enjoyed at least two trout before his conscience reared its ugly head.

CHAPTER 13

In which we encounter
the one-eyed house and Tilly . . .

The plaintive cooing of mourning doves brought me out of slumber the following morning at daybreak. I stepped over Brantley, who slept contentedly on the pine floor, and walked outside. A mist shrouded the woods. Dew dripped from the trees like a slow-motion rainfall. Looking up, I noticed that several dozen neat rows of small holes ran up one side of a pine tree as far as the eye could see. Spanish moss hung limp from the boughs. The pervading morning quiet was in complete contrast to the hypnotizing chorus of crickets, cicadas, and frogs that lulled me to sleep the evening before. I supposed those revelers to be recovering from their late-night serenade much like partygoers recuperating New Year's morning.

"They're part of the web," a voice said from behind me.

I turned to find Lord Baltimore approaching from the woods on the south side of the clearing. The ever-present cigar was wedged in his teeth. He held in one hand a clean, white T-shirt.

"What about the Web?" I asked, thinking, of course, that he referred to the World Wide Web.

"You were struck by the silence and wondered what the noise-makers were doing now." How on earth he knew what was in my mind escaped me. Perhaps I had been thinking aloud. "The birds help keep watch during the day," His Grace continued. "They'll start up shortly. At night, it's the frogs and insects that sound off. Any disturbance in their immediate area causes a change in their rhythm or in their volume or causes them to cease altogether. Liverpool calls it 'night song.' You can track a man's movements simply by listening to it. It weaves a web from one end of the island to the other, from the ground to the tops of the trees. That's how Tilly knows you're here. That's how I know where Sheriff Pooler's men are. That's why you and Brantley must watch the port at Folktown today. I need to know where the sheriff is at all times once he arrives. It's too easy for an intruder to board this island in the light, given all the day noises."

"What about the drums?"

"What drums?" he asked.

"I've heard drums. They're sending messages."

"Oh," said His Grace. "Those drums. Yes, they're part of the web, too."

I indicated the holes I had been studying. "What are those?"

"That's the work of the sapsucker. He pokes holes in the tree, then departs. The holes fill with the tree's sap, which ensnares bugs. Then the sapsucker returns and collects the fruits of his labor, much like we shall do tomorrow."

"How so?"

"Today and tonight, we poke some holes. The holes will attract our pursuers. Tomorrow, we will collect the fruits of our labor."

Because I was hungry, I opted not to pursue Lord Baltimore's cryptic conversation, turning instead to the topic of food. His Grace stirred Brantley to consciousness, and we soon enjoyed a breakfast of hominy grits and bacon courtesy of Liverpool, who had brought our victuals in a burlap sack the previous evening.

Several attempts by Brantley and me to discern what offense we had committed by fishing at the forbidden bluff were rebuffed by His Lordship.

"Your offense is to the people of this island," he informed us gruffly. "Ask Kenneth or Liverpool. I'm simply disappointed that you disobeyed me."

Lord Baltimore then produced the T-shirt I had seen him holding earlier.

"Master Brantley, take off your shirt," he instructed. "Put this one on. Let's have your shoes as well. You'll go barefoot today."

Brantley obliged, knowing that the attire he wore was known to the police, as was his shoe print by now. He put on the new shirt. The motto "Get Right With God" was emblazoned in bold, green letters across the front. His Grace pulled out a pocketknife and quickly sliced Brantley's old clothing in half.

We were then instructed to take the path back to the road and travel west until it divided. We were to take the road on the right and proceed to Zapala's center of commerce, Folktown. Under no circumstances were we to take the road leading left, to the south. His Lordship was explicit in his instructions. He asked us to repeat his commands, which we did.

"Right. When the sun crests the tall pines, Kenneth will be waiting for you at the one-eyed house. I'll see you gentlemen here this evening." With that, he disappeared into the woods on the south trail.

"A one-eyed house?" Brantley said. "This I gotta see."

I cleaned the utensils as best I could using the pump. When I got back to the cabin, Brantley was fast asleep on His Grace's cot. I grabbed a book—*Fanny Kemble: A Passionate Victorian*—and sat down in the leather chair to read.

The sound of a cardinal pecking at his reflection in the window woke me from my stupor. Realizing I had dozed off, I bolted from the chair and ran outside. I gazed upward and saw that the sun had ascended to the upper branches of the pine trees. I raced back inside and fairly tipped Brantley out of the cot in my haste.

"Hey!" he yelled, still half asleep, swinging at an imagined enemy.

"We'll be late!"

"That dude ain't my boss. He sure ain't my daddy."

"The least you can do is cooperate."

"Naw, man. The least I can do is nothing. Which is exactly what I was doin' when you dumped me over."

I explained to Brantley that since our efforts in Folktown would be chiefly for his benefit, his participation was required. He grudgingly acquiesced.

In five minutes, we were walking west on the main road at a quick pace. We soon came to the fork and, mindful of our instructions, veered right. In another few minutes, we rounded a bend.

Kenneth stood in the middle of the road removing the stems from blueberries he had just picked. To our right stood a small house painted dark blue. Two windows adorned the front. One was boarded up— the one-eyed house. An odd-looking chicken scratched in the ground outside a white picket fence that enclosed a well-kept garden.

"Y'all want summa these?" Kenneth asked, holding forth the berries.

We took a good number from his large hand. A chorus of songbirds chattered noisily around us. They were now on duty. Day song had begun.

"Your house?" I asked.

"Naw. Belong to the Po-lites."

"How long has it been one-eyed?" Brantley inquired.

"Many a year. Mr. Polite bust that window to keep the Wavin Man out one night."

"What waving man?" I wanted to know.

"The Wavin Man is a man who . . . He's a ghost. They keep that window boarded up so's the ghost can't enter but through one window or the front door."

Brantley's attention turned to the creature pecking in the dirt. "That's the weirdest doggone chicken I ever seen," he said.

For a fact, I had never seen such a bird. It looked like it had been spun through a washer and dryer.

"That? She a frizzle chicken. Alluz scratchin in the ground. She scratch up any root someone bury in the ground. Mr. Polite don't take no chances."

"A root?" Brantley said.

"You know, a conjure. A hex some ol root doctor makes up fo someone. They take it an plant it under they victim's doorstep. When the intended step over it, they get the affliction. But the frizzle chicken, she dig up the root no matter where it go."

"That's an odd color for a house," I said.

"That's called haint blue. Keeps spirits away."

"How does it do that?"

"That's another story," said Kenneth. "We ain't got time for it right now. C'mon."

I reassessed my thinking about Kenneth's speech. I decided he switched between mainland vernacular and the Gullah dialect without thinking. In the course of his fishing and art dealing, he had no doubt interacted with people from varied backgrounds, which required him to alter his speech to match whatever social setting he found himself in.

He started off at a brisk pace. His long strides soon had Brantley and me in a half trot trying to keep up.

"This here power walkin," he said. I guessed it was the gait Zapalans had honed over centuries of crisscrossing the island. "Learnt it from Jane Fonda workout tapes," he said with a laugh.

His laughter was met by the sound of hooves on the road ahead of us. Just what creature they belonged to registered immediately with Kenneth. "Uh-oh. I know who that is," he murmured.

A donkey carrying a striking figure rounded a small cluster of cabbage palms and came into view. The rider was bedecked in colorful clothing and wore green-tinted sunglasses. Several dozen gold rings adorned her fingers. She rode with an air of aristocracy, as though she owned the very ground we were on and had come to exact a toll. I was both impressed and stricken with terror.

"I knew I'd fine yuh two sooner uh later," she said.

I didn't need to look to see if Brantley was terrified. I could feel him quaking next to me. We both knew we had come face to face with Zapala's resident root doctor.

The gray squirrels that had been chasing each other among the pine trees wisely disappeared. The cicadas' droning ceased altogether, as if to announce that the master had arrived. The creatures of the forest seemed to hold their collective breath to see what would transpire. So did I.

"Already done been fishin in Ibo Landin," she said.

"How you knew bout dat, Tilly?" asked Kenneth.

The voodoo priestess didn't bother to answer. Instead, she pulled off her sunglasses and unleashed a barrage of mostly unintelligible invectives at Brantley and me. I estimated her age to be between fifty and sixty. And I could not help noticing what an attractive woman she was and what a catch she must have been in her prime. Her dark eyes, high cheekbones, and full lips were what many women sought to emulate through surgery. Her thin nose brought to mind the Baluchi poem I had read in one of His Grace's books the previous evening: "Her nose is like a sharp sword/ a blow from which takes her lover's life/ I will be the smith who gives it an edge." Though her eyes blazed with hellfire, though her nose flared like that of an enraged bull, and though reprimands to last a lifetime flowed like a torrent from her lips, I stood in awe and fascination.

"Yuh heah me?" she demanded to know.

I heard. But I was too entranced to comprehend her blistering attack. "Could you repeat the question?" I asked, resolving to be more attentive.

"Look at dis laig!" she yelled, raising her bright orange skirt and pointing at her lower right leg, which was neatly wrapped in bandages. "Yuh did dis to me!" she said, turning an accusing finger to Brantley.

The alligator in the swamp. Brantley had hit its right hind leg with a tree limb. The witch. The changeling. She'd turned herself into an alligator to attack us. It all made perfect sense.

"Look on dis," she said calmly, pulling a small hex doll from her saddlebag.

The doll somewhat resembled me, though it could have been Brantley. As we looked on, she pierced the doll's midsection with a needle.

I heard a thud and felt something graze my leg. It was Brantley, overcome by the revelation that witches and voodoo did indeed exist, regardless of beliefs to the contrary held by His Grace, Lord Baltimore. I stood ready to take my punishment—whatever punishment fit the crime of fishing a perfectly well-stocked hole.

Tilly didn't turn into a vulture and eat my liver, as I half expected. She simply burned her gaze into my eyes and said, "Yuh gonna brang dat hur'cane on Zapala. Yuh done raised de Ibo ghos. Leave dis place fuh yuh drain all my powers."

"Gwan, Tilly," Kenneth admonished. "Yuh scare dese boys nuff. Dey ain fectin none a yo powers."

"Huh!" Tilly snorted, spurring her donkey on. "Yuh tink yuh big stuff. Tink yuh safe wit Mista high-an-mighty Lawd Balt'mo. Yuh keep Mama's name on yo boat an I might make a doll fuh you!"

Kenneth and I knelt to help Brantley. I looked up after a few moments to ensure that we were safe. Our antagonist was nowhere in sight. We soon revived Brantley and got him walking again.

"She's a witch. A real witch!" he kept repeating. "Did you see that? She put the evil eye on me and purt near turned me to stone."

More like she glanced your way and you hit the dusty trail, I thought. My reason began to return in her absence. Brantley was overcome mainly because he believed in her powers. I was afraid but not overcome because I did not believe to the same extent. It seemed to follow that I might completely shield myself from her domination of will simply by refusing to believe in her omnipotence. My fear would be in direct proportion to my belief in voodoo. I strongly felt Lord Baltimore's presence at that moment.

"It's a bunch of hooey," I bravely ventured, secure in the knowledge that Tilly was not around to hear me.

Kenneth sucked air through his teeth before saying anything. "Sometimes, I don't know," he reflected. "Dang if I know how she heard bout you two fishin at Ibo Landing, less she were hidin in the bush, overhearin us last night. Or less she have an agent."

"An agent?" Brantley said.

"An agent is someone who . . . He play-act with Tilly. He sneak around an spy on folks an tell her what they do. Then next day, she see them an pretend lak she know what they up to, when they know she was plumb on the other side of Zapala."

"So someone could have seen that gator chase us, then told her about it," I said.

"Coulda been her that seen you get treed. She know this island good as any man."

"And we didn't actually see a wound on her leg, just the dressing," I said, my suspicion growing that there was a logical explanation for everything.

Brantley, less than sold on the theory, changed the subject.

"How come everyone's so upset over us fishing offa that bluff?" he demanded to know.

Kenneth stopped. The road had wound back near the river that separated the north end of Zapala from the marsh. It was apparent that he didn't want to speak about the subject. He pointed at the river, which was plainly visible above an outcropping of palmetto bushes. "They used to bring slave ships up this creek. Couldn't never catch em, even when the slave trade got abolished. One day, a northern sloop come in with a new tribe called Ibo. They Ibos were some proud Africans. Some say they a little tetched in the head. Soon as the boat put in at the bluff and let them Ibos off, they walked hand in hand into the river, chanting, 'De water brung us yuh, de water will tek us back agin.' Them bones an those chains still lyin there in the mud at the foot of Ibo Landin. Nobody drop a line in that creek for two hundred years. Til yesterday."

A shudder passed through me like a cold wind. Brantley put his hand on his stomach, as though the food he'd eaten didn't sit too well. As a believer in the supernatural, he likely felt that the fish remains passing through him were haunted. I mumbled an apology I knew was pointless.

No one said anything for the next ten minutes as we made our way up the road. Brantley lagged behind, still clutching his gut. I suddenly remembered that Tilly had mentioned something about a hurricane and asked Kenneth about it.

"Oh, that," he said. "They's a hur'cane comin up the coast. Tilly usually steer them away from here. People believe she protek Zapala from evil spirits and from the hur'canes. This one been churnin up the coast steady for two day now. She believe the white men make

Zapala impure an hurt her powers. That's why she put the hex on you. The mo white men, the mo she cain't protek Zapala from the hur'canes the witch doctors send over from Africa. Her work cut out fo her."

"And," I added, "she thinks her powers are weakened because Brantley and I unleashed the Ibo ghosts on Zapala. That's why she's trying to put spells on us."

This was too much for Brantley, who crumpled to the ground in a heap, holding tightly to his midsection. "I think she's pricking me," he loudly complained.

"Come on," Kenneth said, hauling Brantley to his feet. "I got some antidote to Tilly's charms up yonder to the house."

We got Brantley to a clapboard house a hundred yards farther along. It was built well off the ground. A rusted tin roof covered a wide porch that ran around two sides of the house. A beautiful, young girl about my age sat on the front porch in a rocking chair with a baby in her arms. The only thing that looked out of place was the brilliant red hair of the child lying upon the dark brown skin of the girl. The baby turned his head. His skin was milky white. His eyes were blue.

"Jenny, you finally up," Kenneth said. "This young man got a tummy pain. Needs some root-be-gone."

She looked quizzically at Kenneth as he disappeared inside the house with Brantley at his heels.

"You must be Kenneth's granddaughter," I said in an attempt to break the ice.

"I must be. And who must you be?" she wanted to know. Her accent was decidedly not of Zapala. I took her for being educated on the mainland. My guess was that she spent her summers on the island.

"I'm Ensworth." I stroked the child's head and made funny faces in an attempt to entertain him. He looked upon me much the way I looked at Lord Baltimore when I first thought him curious, if not deranged. "Who's this?" I asked.

"This here is Pumpkin. Ain't got a real name right now. What's Kenneth talking about—root-be-gone?"

I didn't know and didn't hazard a guess. Neither did I ask where she got the baby, though she must have read the question in my face.

"Some of them ol Gypsies left him behind. They come by boat from Carolina and sneak across Zapala to steal from people on the mainland. Only in Sheriff Pooler's county. Other sheriffs watch out for their folks. You ever met our sheriff?"

It occurred to me that she already knew the answer to that question. I wondered if she knew I was hiding from Sheriff Pooler and that Brantley and I had fished out of Ibo Landing. But I was saved from answering when Kenneth opened the screen door.

He shook his head. "Man," he said, "that boy thinks Tilly's workin on him."

"What's a root-be-gone?" Jenny asked him.

"I just mixed up some lime juice an some orange juice. Put some paprika in it to make it taste a little bad, so he'd think it was medicine. Told him it would unhex the conjure. He out back restin on the hammock. I don't think that boy'll be much good rest of this mornin."

Kenneth bent to stroke the child's hair. He then told Jenny about our encounter with Tilly. Jenny informed Kenneth of some minor goings-on in Folktown.

"Well, li'l mans, we gonna find yo papa one day," Kenneth said to the child, rising.

With that, we were off. The baby, who had up until then paid Kenneth and me no attention, waved heartily as we departed.

Since we had some distance to go, I took the opportunity to inquire about the people I had met on the island. "Kenneth," I began as soon as we were out of earshot, "what do you know about JV?"

"You mean Lawd Balt'mo ain't tol you bout JV?" Kenneth drew

a deep breath, as though he were sucking a memory database out of thin air. "JV, he grow up on the other side. Roun Riceboro. He was a high-school ath-a-lete star. Had baseball scouts from the Pirate farm team down there in Brunswick watchin him. Had all the college football coaches watchin him, too. Someone even say Bear Bryant come in-cog-nito. That mean he come in disguise. Took JV one year to take the state championship from Valdosta. Never been done by a school that small befo. One night his senior year, his family get swiped by a log truck while they's on the way to the game. They's knocked off the road an hit a big oak. Next day, you cain't see no marks on the road. Barely a nick on that tree. But three pine boxes laid out at the funeral home. JV run off the day they's buried. Next thing folks hear, he in Vietnam. He do two tours, then he disappear. Then he show up a year later. Then he go back an stay for two mo tours. Then no one hear nothin. Bout ten years back, he show up on Zapala an take to Hermit Town. That all I know bout ol JV, cept he help keep the land planners away. Him an Tilly.

"Don't know why they want to plan homes here. We ain't botherin no one. But they want to bring folks here an move us out. Once, Lawd Balt'mo step in tween some fast-talkin lawyers an developers. Them folks want to build a road to the mainland an force us out. After two hundred years. Cain't scape the white man, no offense to them's present. 'Might as well learn to be like him an stick yo neighbor,' that's what Papa always say. That's why he move to the other side an work on the army base. He pick up a lot of the white man's ways. That's how come he sol you that pair no-good sunglasses. He think he buckra sometimes. That how come Unca Liverpool don't care much fo him. He think Papa act like po white trash."

"What's buckra?"

"Buckra the white man. Buckra has the paper an pencil an books. That why Unca take up book learnin an pay for Jenny to go to school. The man dat uses de pencil, de paper, an de books gets de big house.

The man that uses de ax an de shovel an de hoe work for de man with de books."

It reminded me of what my father had written in his note: "Those who master the use of words rule in all cultures."

"But if Liverpool is educated, how can he be fluent in Latin and not speak English well?"

"Unca, he speak Latin perfect, an he speak Gullah perfect. It's you that don't understand either them languages."

Kenneth then enlightened me on several points of interest concerning Liverpool's long life. "Unca born durin one of the big hur'canes," he began. "He always say he came in with a hur'cane, and he'll go out with a hur'cane. He an my papa, that's Kent, growed up in Pigge Hammock an live the goot life on the island. Unca lot older than Papa. One day, they both move to Folktown an work on the shrimp boats. Unca Liverpool don't care much fo the big water. He come back an take up the plow. But they like brothers an stay best friends fo years. Then my mama, Mattie, come up marrying age in Pigge Hammock, an Unca Liverpool an Papa sets they eyes on her. He an Papa fell in love at the same time with Mama, who my boat named fo. Mama chose Papa fo reasons only God an a woman can understan. Maybe cause she the daughter of Relondo."

"Who is Relondo?"

"He was a slave who ride ol man Couper's race hosses against other planters'. One day, he don't come home with Massa. Old island folk say Relondo have knowledge of de unknown tongue an flew back to Africa. But what really happen was on a racetrack in south Alabama, he jump a fence on de backstretch. Rides down into Florida an takes up with other runaways an Seminoles. After de big war, he go out west an cowboy. Become a bull wrangler an famous in Texas an Mexico. He show up back here years later an marry his childhood sweetheart. They daughter is my mama. Some say she got de rebellion in her like him. Anyway, ever since then, Unca Liverpool calls my papa a shiffless no-count, a fig seller, an a mainlander. Papa calls Unca a two-bit lowlife, a junk maker, an Spanish moss, cause he still jus hangin round the island. Unca cain't stand nothin to do with Papa. But Unca love me, an I know it. He start makin them junk sculptures bout nineteen an sixty. Quit makin em nineteen eighty an somethin. Sells em through me to art dealers on de other side for a thousand apiece. Started out sellin em for cheap, almos nothin. Then it turns into what they call primitive folk art, an I props up de price. Unca make enough to fix up de church an send my girl to school in Statesboro."

"Even though he doesn't care for your father?"

"Ha! Neither one has spoke the other's name in goin on sixty years. Wouldn't look at one another at Mama's funeral ten year back. She buried jus up de road."

"But Tilly said her mother's name is on your boat," I noted.

"That bout right. Tilly named after Mama. Mama's name was Matilda. Mattie short for Matilda. Tilly short for de end part of Matilda. Tilly my older sister. She born with a double caul over her head. That gives her de power to see ghosts an sech. She study de conjure an de voodoo from an ol root doctor name of Dr. Buzzard, an took it up to keep Zapala safe. I think Tilly use it fo power over everyone else. Everyone cept Liverpool an Lawd Balt'mo."

More confused than ever, I decided to change the subject. I asked about Liverpool's deformed right hand and learned that, among his many jobs over the years, he once led alligator sportsmen on night hunts in Devil Swamp. Back then, it was called Gator Swamp. One outing ended with his hand finding its way into the eager jaws of a fourteen-foot alligator. Liverpool took that as a sign the island was displeased with his dealings with sportsmen, so he promptly gave up that endeavor.

"Ever since that, he travel at night with de flambeau."

"The what?" I asked.

"Flambeau. A toach."

"Toach?"

"You know, t-o-r-c-h. Toach. Like he carry last night."

"Say, that ox, what's the deal there?"

"Bucephalus? Unca raise that ox an treat him like fambly. Built that stall on de side of de cabin you stayin in. Built it just fo Bucephalus. Could be cause that ox stubborn an do what he wants. Unca like that sometimes. Unca name the ox atter one of Alexander the Great hosses. Unca got powerful book learnin from de Couper library, handed down from his papa."

An old wooden church painted white came into view on our left. "First African Baptist Church of Zapala Island," a sign out front proudly proclaimed.

"What about Lord Baltimore?" I wanted to know. "What do you know about him?"

Kenneth didn't reply. Instead, he put a finger to his lips. At first, I thought I had violated yet another island law. I didn't realize it, but we had come upon a graveyard. I wouldn't have seen it had Kenneth not pointed it out. I could just make out a few headstones behind several live oaks draped in vines and moss.

"Wanna see Mama's grave?" Kenneth asked in a whisper.

"Sure," I replied with equal stealth.

Once we cleared the small tree barrier, I could see that the cemetery was extensive. Some of the graves were obviously very old. Most were simple plots with granite headstones. A few markers appeared to be made of alabaster and showed signs of premature weathering. The intriguing thing to me was the adornments on some of the graves. Broken china cups, bottles, and a doll's head rested upon one concrete slab. A fractured bathroom sink, a chipped piggy bank, and a cracked alarm clock bedecked another.

"What's all that?" I whispered.

"Folks break personal things for puttin on a grave. The dead person's life, it's broken. It's a symbol. Plus, haints won't step on de graves with broken objects. That way, de dead won't be disturbed. Them other things is favorite reminders of de dead folks. Some folks believe if you put de last thing someone was usin on they grave, de spirit won't wander back to they house."

I pointed to the remains of a cowboy doll that sat on a child's grave.

"That my baby brother grave," Kenneth whispered. "Passed away when he was four." Then he pointed to his mother's grave beside the child's. A simple headstone marked Matilda's resting place. On it were a basket of flowers and a miniature shrimp boat. "Tilly been here," he said.

"How do you know?"

"Seen fresh donkey tracks between de church an here. Them flowers new. She bring Mama new flowers every week."

"A witch doctor? I don't get it."

"Tilly more Baptist than conjure doctor when it come to Mama. Plus, she collect dirt from de preacher's grave. See them pennies over yonder on that grave?"

I looked to where he was pointing and spied half a dozen pennies on a headstone.

"That ol man Daddy Grace grave. He were a preacher. She have to leave some pennies behind so's de spirit don't take offense."

"What does she use the dirt for?"

"She take dirt from his grave fo makin roots. It remove hexes put on folks by black witch doctors. Tilly what they call a white witch doctor. Only protek and take curses off of folks. Cept outsiders. Then she try to make em think they got the root on em an leave. That what she tried to do to you."

I felt a churning inside that could have been sorrow or confusion.

Sorrow for the brother who died at four years of age. Sorrow for Kenneth, who lost his mother. Confusion over who was a Christian and who wasn't.

"C'mon," said Kenneth.

In five minutes, we were passing clusters of houses that resembled Kenneth's. Soon after that, we entered Folktown.

CHAPTER 14

I go to Folktown.
Brantley and I meet the Waving Man.

Folktown unfolded before me like a place from another era. The first thing that came into view was a small park surrounded by a dirt road. Spanish moss streamed from tall oak trees that shaded the grounds. In the middle of the square was a pedestal where a statue had once stood. It now held a pot with a magnificent fern sprouting green stems in every direction. A sunbeam shone on the plant like a lone spotlight, diffusing its colors into a green-gold glow. Across the street from the park were two-story homes leaking small children in a steady stream.

We strode through the common and entered Folktown proper. Rows of shops lined the half-dirt, half-shell main street. The wharf area was paved in brick that, I was informed, came as ballast in ships that sailed over from Europe and the Caribbean in colonial times.

"Dat island Li'l Europe," Kenneth told me, his Gullah becoming more pronounced. He pointed to a small, shrub-covered mound in the marsh on the other side of the river. "European ships come fo Zapala oak an pine. Dey dump de ballast on dat side of de river." He stretched his hands out as if blessing the town. "Dis port once rivaled Savannah fo commerce. Now, jus a sleepy li'l town fo shrimpers an farmers."

We walked past the shops to the dock, where men were busy repairing fishing nets. We came upon a large man, Julius, who was working on an inboard motor.

"He de best beat-on-ayun around," Kenneth informed me.

It turned out that "beat-on-ayun"—"beat on iron"—meant he was a mechanic.

Kenneth asked him if anyone had docked that morning. No one had. He and Julius then engaged in what I learned was a common exchange of information among the islanders. Julius told Kenneth every scrap of news that he had heard in the last several days. Kenneth in turn told Julius about Lord Baltimore, Brantley, me, our fishing at Ibo Landing, and our encounter with Tilly that morning. Though I was embarrassed, Julius took in the information as if he were watching the six o'clock news. In fact, he was. By this means, the islanders were able to spread news far and wide in a short time. It also bound each person to every other and to the island's history on a daily basis.

Kenneth assured me I had nothing to fear in his divulging to Julius our presence at the cabin. As long as he accepted us there, the other islanders were honor-bound to accept us as well and would protect us from any outsiders.

We spent an hour milling around the shops of Folktown, keeping an ear out for approaching boats. To my surprise, everyone in Folktown already knew of the arrival of Sheriff Pooler's men on the south end and of our desecration of Ibo Landing. To my equal surprise, no one behaved with animosity.

"Why is no one upset with Brantley and me?" I asked Kenneth as we left the general store and post office with a newly arrived box of cigars for His Lordship.

"Man, dat ilan philosophy," he replied. "Dis ol ilan seen a heap in its time. Seen Creek an Cherokee. Seen Blackbeard de Pirate. Seen French an Spanish. Seen English gentlemens. Seen plantations an War Between de States. Seen hur'canes."

Kenneth stopped to sit on a bench. I sat beside him and helped him scan the marsh for signs of movement.

"Dis ilan," he said, voice lowered, "don't care who on it. Dey come an go. Us ilan folk won't be here fo'ever. Hur'cane come an wipe de slate clean, an start all over. An she don't care. Dat what Unca say. He say, 'I go to de nex world wif a hur'cane. An Zapala don't take no notice.' "

I picked up a newspaper that had been left nearby. As Kenneth passed the time chatting with passersby, I searched the paper. To my complete surprise, I found no mention of Brantley or the fiasco at the fund-raising event.

"I can't believe there's no story about you-know-who in here," I said.

Kenneth shrugged. "Sheriff get dat story in dere when it suits him fine. Not til then. He'll say yo friend broke out on a work detail, not at some barbecue."

Before long, we strolled back to the dock and boarded Kenneth's boat, the *Mattie III*. Kenneth stayed in the pilothouse, where an array of communications devices resided. He left one tuned to weather information and fidgeted with one of the others until he picked up the voices of Sheriff Pooler's men.

"We got 'em now," I heard over the two-way radio. It sounded like Deputy Ratchet. Kenneth confirmed that the Ratchet was one of the men he had deposited on Zapala's south end the day before.

"Come again. Over," a voice replied.

"We got 'em on the run. Cain't be a half-mile ahead. Over," said the deputy excitedly.

Then a new voice replied, "I'm gettin' fed up with this foolishness. Don't call in 'til you got them in cuffs. You hear what I said?"

It was Sheriff Pooler.

There was a brief pause. "I hear," came the response, less enthused than a moment earlier.

Kenneth chuckled. "Man, Lawd Balt'mo an JV gonna run them deputies in circles all day. They already got the sheriff riled."

"And that's good?" I asked.

"That's the plan. Sheriff been hearin them boys talk nonsense. He wants to come to Zapala when you in custody. Then he can take you back to the jail personal, an be a hero."

The radio conversation came to a halt. I went to the back of the boat and made a nest for myself, using netting and floats. I spent the rest of the morning eyeing the marsh for the sheriff's arrival. Occasionally, I heard Kenneth howling as he picked up another conversation between the Ratchet and the police dispatcher. Each bout of laughter was followed by a commentary from Kenneth shouted for my benefit: "Now, they headin back to Hermit Town," he would say, or "They gone full circle on that path twice!"

When Kenneth announced that a deputy and his dog were chasing us in an easterly direction and another deputy and his dog were hot on our trail to the west, I understood why Lord Baltimore had torn Brantley's shirt in two. I also realized why he had taken Brantley's tennis shoes. The deputies would surely recognize the tracks of prison-issue sneakers.

"Lawd Balt'mo an JV makin liars outta them dogs," said Kenneth, shaking his head. "Ain't no one gonna believe them hounds after today."

I began to appreciate His Grace's ability to improvise on the field of battle. And I better understood the remark that he had never lost a game of chess.

Around noon, we went below and ate tuna fish sandwiches that Kenneth had stored in an icebox. The first thing I spotted upon entering the cabin was a T-shirt draped over a chair. It was a duplicate of the one His Grace had given Brantley that morning.

"So you're the one," I said.

"I'm the one what?"

"The T-shirt."

"That? Tilly give me that las Christmas."

I thought no more about it and went back on watch. I stayed on the lookout while Kenneth tinkered with the engine and kept an ear out for more radio transmissions.

When the sun's rays began to cast the first long shadows of the day, Kenneth came on deck. "I think Lawd Balt'mo an JV wore dem boys down," he said.

"No sign of the sheriff," I dutifully reported.

Kenneth popped the lid on a Coke and handed the drink to me.

"He'll be here," he said. "Jus takin care of bidness fo he come."

"How can you be so sure?"

"Lawd Balt'mo say so. He ain't never wrong bout nothin, cept what people want in de art world," he said with a broad grin.

"Do you fear Sheriff Pooler?"

"Fo sho," said Kenneth. "I don't fear much. I respect de ocean. I respect de gator. I don't fear em. But Sheriff, he ain't right in his haid. I got no use fo crazies lak him."

"What about His Grace?"

"Who?"

"Lord Baltimore."

Kenneth laughed. "People think he crazy, cause Lawd Balt'mo don't fear nothin. Not Tilly. Not the sheriff. So folks think he got to be crazy. But if he crazy, I'm crazy, too, cause I respect that man."

"What about Liverpool? Surely, at his age, he doesn't fear anything. Anything but . . ."

As if on cue, Liverpool pulled alongside the *Mattie III* in a flat-bottomed boat powered by the old man himself. Using a long cane pole, he held his boat steady next to ours.

"Hey, Unca. Whatchoo fear?" Kenneth asked.

Liverpool smiled. "*Timeo periculum quod timetis.*"

"In English, Unca."

"Ah feah de danger which you feah."

Kenneth shook his head. "Dat why you an Lawd Balt'mo get along. Only he can understan you, even in English. Him an dat ol ox." Kenneth studied the horizon. "Time fo you to go on back to de cabin," he told me. "You done nuff watchin today."

It didn't take much prodding, for I was indeed tired of squinting in the sunlight. We carefully boarded Liverpool's boat, and the old man steered us out into the river, which led back to the bluffs.

"Dis here boat called a batteau," Kenneth informed me when we had gone a short distance. "Unca built dis one by hand thuddy years back."

"Shouldn't we lend a hand?" I asked, uneasy about making Liverpool do all the work.

"Nah, nah. Dat why Unca live to a old age. He keep movin. De day he stop to rest is de day he stop fo good. Ain't dat so, Unca?"

Liverpool removed the chicken bone pipe from his mouth to speak. "*Mors est somno similis.*"

"Not de Latin, Unca. Talk right, now."

With a grin, Liverpool delivered the translation: "Det is similar tuh sleep." Then, with a wider grin, and nodding at Kenneth, he said to me, "*Metus mortis.* He feah det."

"Well, I sho don't go courtin it," Kenneth replied. "Seem lak death comin at us from de east an de west. Got dat durn hur'cane stalkin us. Got dat durn sheriff stalkin us. Jus a matter of who get heah firs."

I commented on the way Kenneth switched from mainland talk to Gullah when he was around Liverpool.

"Gullah?" he said with a laugh. "You ain't heard Gullah yet."

"Well, just what is it I've been listening to?"

"You heard me an Liverpool tryin to speak so's you can understan. Listen to dis. Tell me what it means. Hey, Unca, do 'De Lawd Me Shepud.' "

Liverpool removed his pipe again and cleared his throat. Then he delivered the following:

> *De Lawd me shepud!*
> *A hab ebrthing wa A need.*
> *E mek me fa res een green fiel*
> *en E lead meta still wata wa fresh en good fa drink.*
> *E tek me soul en pit em back weh e spos ta be.*
> *E da lead me long de right paat,*
> *fa E name sake, same lok E binna promise.*
> *Aaldo A waak tru de valley a de shada a det,*
> *A ent gwine faid no ebul, Lawd,*
> *kase You dey longside me.*
> *Ya rod en Ya staff protek me.*
> *You don papeah nof bittle fa me,*
> *whe all me enyme kin shum.*
> *You gib me haaty wilcom.*
> *You nint me head wid ail en full up me cup tel e run oba.*
> *Fa true, You gwine lob me en tek cyah a me long es A lib.*
> *En A gwine stay ta ya house fareba.*

Liverpool squinted as though trying to focus on something ahead, then began to pole us toward the middle of the river. I saw an object floating our way. It was a jar large enough to hold candy in a grocery store. It appeared to contain eggs.

Kenneth reached over the side of the batteau with a long arm and snagged it. He opened the lid and reached inside to extract a hard-boiled egg. "Lord Baltimore" was written in a red, sticky substance on this egg, as was "John 3:16."

"Look lak Tilly at work again," Kenneth said. "Dis here another voodoo conjure."

I inspected the jar and saw eggs with my name and Brantley's— misspelled *Brantlee*—written on them. The names were accompanied by other Bible verses.

"Tilly tryin to send y'all down the river," he said. "Cept now, de curse is broke, cause we found dese eggs."

I heard a great snorting and looked up to see Bucephalus following us along the shoreline. Presently, Liverpool poled us into a small inlet on the opposite bank. He picked up a six-foot casting net, gripped one end of it with what remained of his teeth, and expertly heaved it into the narrow waterway. When he drew the net into the boat, several pounds of shrimp fell at our feet.

"Dat dere dinner," he remarked. He stooped to pick up several small trout and threw them back into the water. "Grow, nah, li'l uns. Ah be back fo yuh."

He poled us out of the inlet and into a tributary alongside which the ox patiently waited. We came to a dock. As I stepped off the boat, Liverpool reached over the side and lifted a string of trout. He held it up for me to take.

"Dis yuh fo de cabin folk," he said. "Dese fish clean. Ain't got de Ibo ghos in dem."

I mumbled a thanks, too embarrassed even to apologize for the incident.

We took a trail that soon led to the back of Kenneth's home. Liverpool continued onward, his faithful ox lumbering two steps behind. They headed back in the direction of the First African Baptist

Church.

Kenneth and I gutted and cleaned the trout in a sink at the back of the house. I then rolled them in newspaper while he scraped ice from the inside of a large meat freezer that had seen better days. He stuffed the rolled fish into a plastic bag and threw several handfuls of ice and shrimp inside.

"They'll stay cold til supper," he said.

We entered the back door and came out on the front porch. There, we found Jenny on the swing. Brantley occupied the rocking chair that Jenny had sat in that morning. The baby lay in his arms sound asleep. I noticed that a large spot of drool had dampened Brantley's shoulder. He motioned me to be quiet.

Kenneth sat on the swing beside Jenny.

"They're made for each other," she whispered, nodding toward Brantley and the boy. "They've been playing in the yard all day."

Brantley beamed as he held the infant, gently rocking back and forth.

"I'll take him off your hands anytime," he said to Jenny.

"We'd better get going," I reminded him. "It'll be dark before long."

I knew exactly what Brantley was thinking. He didn't enjoy meeting Tilly on the road in broad daylight. He surely wouldn't like to see her at night.

Brantley lifted the child with the greatest care and handed him to Jenny. When we started to leave, Brantley ran back up the steps and kissed the boy on the head.

"I don't know what it is," he told me, "but I want to be that boy's daddy."

I didn't want to jump to conclusions, but it was likely his wish had already come true.

We kept up a brisk pace past the spot where we had met Tilly that morning. It crossed my mind that she could be lying in ambush anywhere along the road, but I repeated over and over that voodoo worked only if one believed in it.

The air temperature had dropped several degrees by the time we reached the one-eyed house. The Polites, two slow-moving, elderly people, were in the front yard when we went by. The frizzle chicken was nowhere to be seen. Mrs. Polite stared at us in a not-too-friendly manner. Mr. Polite waved, though his glasses were so thick I'm not sure he could make out who we were.

We turned right at the fork in the road, as Lord Baltimore had instructed. That is to say, I took the right path and Brantley followed. He kept his eyes focused on the ground, hoping against hope that Tilly was not around.

After five or ten more minutes, he stopped and looked up. "This is a dirt road. We're not on the right road," he said.

First dark was descending on the island, and the creatures were tuning their instruments for night song. I looked down at my feet. Sure enough, this wasn't the shell road we should have been on. In fact, it had narrowed to little more than a wide path. I then realized that we were to turn right at the fork on the way to Folktown and left on the way back.

"Do you have any idea where we are?" Brantley asked.

"Just calm down," I said in as reassuring a voice as possible. "All we have to do is turn around and go back to the fork in the road."

"Let's ask him."

"Ask who?"

"Him," Brantley said, pointing behind me.

Thirty yards away and a little off the road stood an enormous dead oak shrouded in Spanish moss. Beneath it was a man dressed in black. A white scarf was wound tightly around his throat. Though I couldn't see his feet, I got the impression that his head was on backwards. When he beckoned us to come closer, we started toward him. Though his mouth was open and he seemed to be calling aloud to us, we heard nothing. A bad case of laryngitis, I assumed. With an urgency I could not comprehend, he motioned us to follow. Perhaps someone was hurt and he wanted us to help. Perhaps he was mute. Perhaps he, like everyone else on the island, knew who we were and knew a shortcut to the cabin. He blended with the shadowy woods in the growing darkness until he appeared to be little more than an apparition. As we came closer, he retreated farther into the woods, waving ever more frantically. Finally, all I could see was the white of his scarf.

I had reached the roots of the tree when I felt a cold, trembling hand grip my arm hard. It was Brantley.

"He's not human," he said in a hoarse whisper.

Even though I had convinced myself that things were not true unless you believed in them, and even though I knew that Brantley was prone to overreacting to the supernatural, something inside me said that he told the truth.

"Don't go in there," he said, visibly trembling. "He's tryin' to lure us to our death."

That was all I needed to hear.

We didn't stop running until we reached the fork in the road. Perhaps fearing that our mute zombie friend might be hot after us and that splitting up would give one of us a fighting chance, Brantley made for the cabin and I took off in the direction of Kenneth's house. I figured that Lord Baltimore might not be at the cabin, which helped in my decision making. I also knew that we were roughly equidistant from the cabin and Kenneth's house, and I knew that someone would be at the latter. To his credit, Brantley might have thought it better not to lead our pursuer to the doorstep where slept the child he so adored.

I had not gone far before I came upon the Polites' one-eyed house. Out of concern for their safety, and also because I was exhausted from the run, I decided to warn them about what might be behind me.

In a single bound, I jumped the picket fence and landed in their herb garden. The Polites were on their front porch enjoying the evening. I'm sure they heard my footsteps, the thud of my landing, and the heavy breathing in their front yard.

"Who dere?" yelled Mr. Polite, coming to his feet.

Mrs. Polite grabbed a broom and stood ready for battle.

I panted my name and came within the light that shone through the screen door.

"Boy, whatchoo actin lak dat fo?" Mr. Polite asked. "Runnin up on folks."

I pointed back the way I had come, as if that would explain all.

Mrs. Polite loosened her grip on the broom and let her jaw drop a notch. I believe she comprehended my meaning.

"Who chasin attuh yuh? De sheriff?" asked Mr. Polite. "C'mon in yah. We protek yuh."

"Ain't no sheriff on dis ilan yet," his wife broke in. "You ain't hear no drums, is yuh?"

"There was a man," I said.

"What man?" asked Mr. Polite. "What he look lak?"

"I don't know. He kept waving at us."

"Yuh ain't seen no Wavin Man," Mrs. Polite said, shaking her head.

"Were he haid on backward?" Mr. Polite wanted to know.

"Yes! He kept waving at us to follow him," I said, making the waving motion with my left arm.

"Yuh ain't seen dat man!" Mrs. Polite said loudly, this time with trembling and anger in her voice.

I wanted them to believe me. "But I saw him!"

"I said it!" she snapped back. Mrs. Polite muttered Gullah under her breath and went inside the house, slamming the door behind her like an exclamation point.

"Yuh better go on from yuh," Mr. Polite warned me. "Fraid yuh done let loose de Wavin Man. It gonna be a long naht roun yuh."

"The what man?"

Mr. Polite stepped off the porch. In a low voice, he confided the story of the Waving Man. "Troop a Yankees come tru yuh during de war. Dey roun up all de Couper slaves an ax dem, 'Where de silver buried?' De ones dat know don't tell. De ones what don't know cain't tell. Anyhow, dem soldiers string up all de house servants dey can find an two fiel hand. Dey hang em raht from dat big oak. De oak die dat very same yeah from bein curse by de hangin. De Wavin Man one uh de house servants. Nah, he a ghos from de shadduh world. He wave attuh any Yankee or stranger to dis heah ilan dat walk by de tree. He want to show yuh where de silver buried. Whoever follow de Wavin Man in dem woods never come out again. Ain't been seen in many a yeah. But nah . . ."

Mr. Polite, true to his name, was too polite to state the obvious. Now, he meant to say, I had come along and committed another blunder. Given another day on the island, I felt certain I would invoke the ghosts of the slaughtered Spanish missionaries, if they were still around. And perhaps a pirate or two for good measure.

Mrs. Polite burst through the screen door holding a newspaper and a bulging paper bag.

"Yuh better get," Mr. Polite advised.

The two then proceeded to tack sections of the newspaper over the window and door of the house with a synchronization that suggested they had done it many times before. I babbled some sort of apology for ruining their evening and backpedaled through the open gate. Mrs. Polite pulled two Mason jars from the paper bag. She casually tossed them on the porch steps, smashing them into shards with no more hesitation than if she were spreading bird food on the ground.

It was clear to me then that I might expect a similar reception at Kenneth's home. I therefore decided to make for the cabin. Aside from sprinting past the fork in the road, I took my time.

As I anticipated, His Grace had not yet returned. Instead, I found Brantley huddled in the back room with a hammer in his hand, defending his ground against all the spirits, ghosts, zombies, witches, and assorted ghouls that no doubt plagued Zapala at night.

CHAPTER 15

I confront the Waving Man.
We proceed with Operation Sapsucker.

Lord Baltimore stared at Brantley and me in disbelief. "You actually saw the Waving Man?" he asked, snuffing out his cigar in a turtle-shell ashtray.

Brantley and I looked at each other. How did he already know? We slowly nodded our heads in unison.

"Incredible." His Grace closed the cabin door behind him and tossed Brantley's tennis shoes to the floor. He then proceeded directly to the liquor cabinet. "Did I not clearly instruct you to take the right fork in the road?"

"Yes, you did," I said.

"Good God, boys. In less than two days, you've fished from the forbidden bluff and resurrected the ghost of the Hanging Tree. You two . . ." He tried to go on but seemed at a loss for words. His Grace poured a jigger of brandy and nestled into the leather chair, propping his feet on a basket.

"Well, I can tell you we didn't mean to bump into that thing," said Brantley. "I ain't never been that scared in my life. The son of—"

"It's done," His Grace interrupted. "It's simply incredible, is all."

It was at this point that Brantley and I engaged in a short but furious round of finger-pointing, each blaming the other for our blunders. Lord Baltimore got our attention by pulling from a drawer two slender objects that fit into the palm of his hand.

"Here!" he barked. "I hold in my hand the answer to all your problems—indeed, the answer to any ill fortune that befalls you in the future." Brantley and I gazed at the flat objects with more than passing curiosity. "If you really want to know whom to credit for your prosperity, whom to blame for your adversity, and who it is that will extricate you from misfortune, I suggest you look on these."

He held out one for each of us. I picked up the thing expecting to see an illustration of Christ or some other illustrious personage. Instead, I flipped it over and stared at my own reflection in a pocket mirror.

"Oh, man," Brantley said. "I shoulda known it wasn't nothin'."

"What you see in there is the person who holds all the keys to your successes and failures. Now, you can't say you haven't been warned," said His Grace.

These words brought another frustrated moan from my companion. However, for my part, I felt there was some truth to it.

"Beside you on the shelf is a maple humidor lined with Spanish cedar," His Lordship said to me. "Inside are Cohiba cigars. See if you can extract one without breaking the box, spilling the contents, or ushering forth the ghost of this, that, or some other thing."

I obliged.

His Grace lit the cigar and drew on it several times. "I shall tell you how my day went," he began. "James Van Dora—JV, that is— and I spent the morning running several deputies and two hound dogs in circles. The poor fellows actually backtracked to the south end of the island at one point. It took us most of the afternoon to get them into position for tonight's fun."

"What happens tonight?" I asked.

"That remains to be seen. But if the Wheel of Truth does not lie, we can expect a certain party to arrive this evening."

"What Wheel of Truth?" Brantley wanted to know.

"Nothing that concerns either of you, especially after what you did today."

"How did you know about our meeting with the Waving Man?" I asked.

"I passed by the Polites' house on the way in."

"They're pretty strange. When I left them, they were covering the window and doorway with newspaper. Mrs. Polite broke glass on the front porch like it was nothing."

Lord Baltimore sipped his brandy and pulled on the cigar. "They believe in the old ways. According to legend, ghosts must read every word of written material placed at the entrances of a house before they can come in. If the owners put newspapers outside or affix them to the windows, daybreak will come before the ghosts finish reading the entire text. The broken glass is added insurance to keep the blokes—in this case, the Waving Man—from even stepping on the porch."

"That's nuts," said I.

"No, it ain't!" said Brantley with conviction.

"The Polites," His Grace continued, "are the first line of defense for the residents of Folktown. They're the closest to Ibo Landing and the Hanging Tree. Hence the color of their house—haunt blue. That particular color is supposed to have mystical qualities that repel the living dead." He sipped his brandy and let the weight of his words sink in. "By the way, did Kenneth give you something to bring back for supper?"

Brantley looked at me. I looked at him. We had left the fish by the dreaded Hanging Tree.

"Well?" His Grace demanded to know.

As the day's catch had been entrusted to me, I felt compelled to own up. "You can imagine our terror at seeing—"

"Go get our dinner," he commanded.

He might as well have told me to swim across the Atlantic. "There's no way—"

"You've nothing to fear," he calmly informed me.

Brantley tried to intervene on my behalf, but he, too, was cut off.

"Gentlemen, this is not a complex issue. You were given food to sustain us. Liverpool did not spend his afternoon pulling God's creatures from their domicile so you could leave them as useless carrion for ants. There's a flashlight in the drawer behind you, Master Ensworth. Now, get going. Let's have no more of this nonsense."

To my surprise, and I'm sure to Brantley's, I opened the drawer, removed the flashlight, and slowly made my way to the door. A number of ideas took seed in my head. I could take a cane pole back to Ibo Landing and snare a few fish in no time. I could beg at the Polites' door or at Kenneth's. I could . . .

"Brantley will start the fire. You can be back in ten minutes if you hurry. Besides, this is an excellent time for you to test your mettle. I envy you the opportunity."

With that, His Grace buried his head in a dog-eared book titled *The Tigers of Baluchistan*. I went outside, not quite sure what I was going to do. Brantley followed.

"Man, I wouldn't go back there for nothin'," he said. "That dude's crazy if he thinks he can make you go."

"I've got to go," I replied.

"You ain't got to do nothin'! Let's get outta here!"

Lord Baltimore was right. This was an opportunity to test my mettle. Me against the dark. Me against the unknown. Me against the underworld, no less! How many times would I get a chance to see what I was made of? In a way, Brantley helped me. His unwillingness to confront his fears annoyed me, and when he attempted to deny me the chance to confront mine, I felt anger toward him. I resolved to defy the Waving Man to test myself, or at least to prove to Brantley that he was wrong in not challenging his anxieties.

"Just start the fire," I said. The quiver in my voice probably revealed my true feelings.

As if in a dream, I made my way down the path to the road, then to where the road forked, then on to the road that veered left. With each step, I swore I could see the Waving Man coming toward me. Every noise was surely the Waving Man popping out of the underbrush. I would have been glad to meet up with Zapala's witch doctor at that moment. Even Sheriff Pooler would have been a welcome sight.

I moved stealthily, so as not to alert anyone or anything of my approach. The night song of the crickets, frogs, and cicadas reassured me that all was well. It wasn't until I saw the Hanging Tree outlined in the moonlight that I turned on my flashlight. I shone it close to the ground, not wishing to flood the woods with its light, which might bring forth my mute friend once more. I felt a certain exhilaration knowing that my very presence was an open dare. Terror had put up a challenge, and I had returned to accept it.

After a minute of searching, I found the plastic bag. It was still unopened, still cool to the touch. A few ants traversed the outside. Then I saw it. Next to the bag was a hoofprint. And beside the hoofprint was the faint outline of a sneaker. A sneaker with the faint Keds emblem reversed. Lord Baltimore's footprint.

I picked up the bag. Feeling cocky, and fairly certain I could again outrun whatever it was that I had outrun before, I held my flashlight up and surveyed the tree in front of me. The Hanging Tree must have been three hundred years old. It was a magnificent oak, large enough that five grown men with outstretched arms could not encircle its trunk. Though disease had killed it, the oak still stood with a certain dignity, its huge arms spread in all directions, towering over anyone who would come near it.

"Hey!" I said. "Waving Man!"

My words echoed in the woods.

"You're a ghost. Get it? You're dead! Go on, now. Go on to your reward. You don't belong here."

I backpedaled several steps while waving the flashlight from side to side in front of me, scanning the woods.

"Stop bothering folks!" I yelled, growing in confidence with each unanswered word.

I stood there another minute, feeling almost cheated when nothing happened. Then I turned off the flashlight and began to walk back to the cabin—slowly, like the way a matador turns his back on a bull and feigns nonchalance. I got about twenty yards down the path when the hair stood on the back of my neck. I didn't turn around but flew back to the main road.

I required several minutes of recuperation on the cabin path before my pulse returned to normal. I felt like I had passed through some sort of portal upon entering and leaving the area around the Hanging Tree. If it had changed me in some profound way, I could not tell. But I knew that something was definitely not the same.

Feigning apathy, I strolled up to Brantley, who had by then started a fire. I handed him the bag.

"Well?" he asked breathlessly.

"No big deal," I said. "Just me and the crickets."

"Man, I thought he got you. Heard some caterwaulin' going on."

"Wasn't me. Piece of cake," I said.

I then meandered to the cabin, fully intent on flaunting my indifference to the completed task. However, I was denied the opportunity to display my valor, for without even looking up from his book, His Grace spoke.

"Well? What did you learn?"

"I didn't learn anything."

"You learned nothing about yourself? My lad, you have confronted the very demon that has reduced the bravest of men to sniveling cowards." He laid the book in his lap. "I'm talking about fear. Most men never adequately address that fiend. You have learned a great lesson. There has been a change in you. It's not noticeable. Not just now. But later, you will know that you did something extraordinary. Furthermore, you will know for a fact that you can do extraordinary things for the rest of your life."

I found myself beaming in the glow of His Grace's praise until he added a footnote.

"But was it necessary to taunt the poor devil?"

"How do you know that?"

His Grace looked at me with equal curiosity. "Did I not explain?"

"Explain what?"

He drew on his cigar. "I believe we discussed the night song last evening. You know, the web and all that? Do you recall? Besides, the cabin is not terribly far from the Hanging Tree. You walked a horse-shoe route to get there, you know. I could hear the echoes of your braying through the woods. That was followed by the interruption of night song along the same route you took to get back here. The beads of sweat on your brow betray the fear you experienced and the speed with which you departed the tree."

"If there are such simple explanations for all events," I said, "why do the islanders and Brantley believe in all that voodoo and ghost nonsense?"

His Grace seemed amused by this question. "Dear boy, one doesn't erase centuries of superstition with mere logic. And keep in mind, not all of the islanders believe in Tilly's powers."

"Who, for instance?"

"For instance, Liverpool. He's of Arabic descent. His grandfather was Mohammedan and did not believe in the African superstitions. From the Foulah tribe on the Niger River. The district of Temourah in the kingdom of Massina, if I recall."

"What about Kenneth?"

"Kenneth's family descends from the Mende people of Sierra Leone. However, Liverpool has been a great influence in his life. Kenneth walks with equal ease in a number of worlds. Zapala. The mainland. Savannah and Atlanta. It's not an easy trick to pull off."

"I'm still amazed that these people can believe in myths and superstitions."

"These people? Are you not surrounded by myths and superstitions? You invoke the names of Norse gods each week. Wednesday is named for Woden, the chief Norse god. Thursday is Thor's day, the god of thunder. You call on the Roman gods during the year as well. Janus, the god of portals and openings, lends his name to January. Mars, the god of war, gives his name to March. Indeed, have you not plucked a four-leaf clover or carried a rabbit's foot for good luck? Have you not been wary of black cats or avoided walking under a ladder to ward off bad luck? Have you never seen athletes perform superstitious rituals before a competition? Man, if nothing else, is a superstitious being. He'll pray to and believe in just about anyone or anything he can think of."

I decided to get back to a question I wanted answered.

"What is it you fear, Your Grace?" I asked. It had lingered in my mind since Kenneth and I broached the subject earlier in the day.

He exhaled a long stream of smoke and pondered for a moment. "Fear? I fear nothing. But if you must know, I have a healthy respect for gravity."

"Gravity? You've got to be kidding."

"My young friend, the only thing that tugs at you from the moment you draw first breath until the instant you depart this 'isthmus of a middle state' we call life is gravity. The older you get, the harder it pulls. One day, it pulls you down and you break a thighbone. You recover from that. Some years later, it pulls you down again and you don't recover quite as rapidly. The third time . . . Well, after that, you're not as inclined to rise again and do battle with gravity. You just lie there and wait."

Upon that merry revelation, I decided to bring the interview to an end. I opened the door and started outside before I remembered. "Say," I began. His Grace looked up from his book, irritated that his reading had been interrupted. "Why did I find your sneaker imprint next to a horse's hoofprint by the Hanging Tree?"

He went back to reading. "You didn't find my sneaker print next to a horse's hoofprint," he said.

I thought no more about it and went outside to check on Brantley.

We dined that evening on steamed trout and shrimp. Halfway through the meal, I heard the faint sound of drums coming from deep in the woods, like someone was beating out a coded message.

A bright full moon was ascending the upper branches of the pines when I saw a flame approaching through the woods. It was Liverpool carrying a flambeau, followed closely by Bucephalus.

Liverpool stood outside the firelight and studied Brantley and me. He shook his head as he lit his chicken bone pipe. "Ah doan know," he said. "Ah sho doan know bout yuh two."

"What about us?" Brantley asked.

"Got de Wavin Man outta dat tree. I thought sho he lef us by nah."

Lord Baltimore came out of the cabin and joined us.

"What we gonna do wi dese two, Lawd Balt'mo?"

His Grace's undoubtedly witty reply was interrupted by a low, rumbling cannon blast from Bucephalus. Once more, the beast had no sooner found a spot to stand in than he heralded his arrival. Only this time, we happened to be standing downwind. I knew then why the crickets had ceased their playing the evening before. My meal fought valiantly not to come back up. Only the smoke of the fire and the aroma of Lord Baltimore's Cohiba helped nullify Bucephalus's atomic intestinal assault.

"Do you believe in voodoo?" His Grace asked Liverpool, either to divert our attention from the ox's attack or to show me that Liverpool was above superstitious ways.

The ancient one pulled the pipe from his mouth. As he stared up at the moon, I noticed how young his eyes looked—so round and reflective, like two moons themselves.

"Cain say ah do," Liverpool said.

"Of course," said His Grace. Then he reminisced. "I saw two fakirs in Baluchistan once put hot coals in their mouths and chew on them as if they were eating garden vegetables. Never did discover their trick. But voodoo requires only an accomplice or two to make a whole community believe in its powers."

Kenneth showed up at precisely that moment. He entered the clearing using the south path. At seeing Kenneth, a key piece of a puzzle that had been annoying me fell into place. A moment later, all the other pieces came together. The picture that came into view was that of Tilly receiving information about island goings-on from an accomplice, an agent—Lord Baltimore! It was His Grace who had forbidden Brantley and me from taking the very path on which he and Tilly met each morning to concoct their schemes. What possible objection could he have to our using the path by the Hanging Tree, other than to keep us away from his place of rendezvous with Tilly? And didn't I find his footprint next to hoofprints? He hadn't lied. I didn't find his print next to that of a horse. It was next to the imprint of Tilly's donkey. How else could Tilly have found out about our fishing from Ibo Landing? His Grace had informed her just minutes before she met us on the path to Folktown. He also told her about the alligator we encountered. She had time to ride to the Polites' or to Kenneth's to get bandages to wrap around her leg before confronting us on the road. And had he not arrived just this morning with a T-shirt that matched the one Tilly had given Kenneth for Christmas?

The pieces fit together nicely. The only thing missing was why. However, as His Grace obviously wished to keep it a secret, I chose not to confront him at that moment.

"It's all set," Kenneth said, beaming from ear to ear.

"We know. We heard the drums," replied His Grace.

"What drums?" Brantley asked. "What's all set?"

His Grace rubbed his hands together as if preparing for a feast. "Tonight's entertainment, lads. If my interpretation of the drums is correct, the sheriff will very soon set foot on the island."

It was then that I recalled seeing the crude drum in Liverpool's workshop. I now understood its use.

Lord Baltimore took a piece of paper from his jacket and unfolded it. It was a promotional flyer the sheriff had distributed. "There was a stack of these on the check-in desk at the Cherokee Grove," he reminded me.

The flyer read, "Big Parade, downtown Darien. Starting at noon. Bar-B-Que to follow." Below this headline was a list of sponsors, participants, and speakers. Prominent among the names was Sheriff Roscoe Pooler.

"It seems he's to appear in the event later this week," His Grace continued. "What better way to cap off his campaign than to parade the lot of us down Main Street? Me, a wanted cocaine trafficker, Brantley, an escaped prisoner, and you," he said, looking at me, "our accomplice."

"What is it you got in mind for tonight?" asked Brantley.

It was apparent that he wanted nothing to do with it. It occurred to me that as fearful as he was of the root doctor in broad daylight, he would be even more scared to participate in our nocturnal endeavors.

Lord Baltimore studied him for a moment. "You, sir, are excused from tonight's activities. Your white shirt will make an excellent target in the moonlight. The rest of us . . ."

As His Grace spoke, there was a definite lessening of the night song. We stood silently for several moments. The insect noises ebbed and flowed in a distinct pattern that even I could discern. Slowly, deliberately, Lord Baltimore pointed and turned until his finger fixed on the direction from which the wave pattern seemed to originate.

"It's comin from Folktown, all right," Kenneth said. "Cicadas don't tell no lies."

Liverpool nodded in agreement.

"How many?" Lord Baltimore asked.

Kenneth closed his eyes and cocked his ear. "Sounds like just one."

"It him, aw right," said Liverpool. "Ah know dat walk."

"Gentlemen," His Grace said, "I believe our guest of honor has finally arrived."

For a solid minute, His Lordship moved his finger to track the movement of the person disrupting the song of the cicadas, frogs, and crickets. It became apparent that he was on the main road heading our way. However, if His Grace's pointer was accurate, the intruder took the path that led to the Hanging Tree. Five minutes later, after we heard no gunfire, shouting, or other sign that the Waving Man had shown himself, the night song resumed its normal volume.

"Tis well," His Grace informed us. "The good sheriff will rendezvous with his men in less than an hour. We'll let them settle in for the evening. By midnight, Operation Sapsucker will proceed on schedule."

"I say let sleeping dogs lie," said Brantley with growing agitation. "You ain't seen the sheriff mad. That dude is a lunatic, man. I've seen him kill a prisoner! Whipped out a pistol and—"

"Come now, lad," His Grace said. "Pull yourself together."

Brantley was trembling. "He's got two armed deputies and hunting dogs against us. We ain't got nothin! That ain't exactly what I call a fair fight."

No one said anything for a moment. His Grace appeared to be thinking of other matters.

Liverpool lowered his pipe and commented, "*Pericula magna animos nostros non superant.*"

"Here, here," said His Grace in obvious agreement.

"Unca, you speakin Latin again," Kenneth reminded him.

" 'Great dangers do not overcome our courage,' " His Grace translated. "Besides, we have a number of allies on our side."

"Like who?" demanded Brantley. "Name one."

"I'll name you five. The element of surprise is one. The cover of darkness is another. Our greatest ally is that they still underestimate us. The sheer audacity of our plan gives us an upper hand. Fortune favors the bold. Then there is Bucephalus, who, as you are fully aware, is primed for his part in tonight's excursion. In addition, we have JV, who is watching their camp even as we speak."

We gave the sheriff a good head start before departing. Brantley wished us well and then took a defensive position in the darkened cabin, anticipating a siege of hostile—and mostly imagined—forces. We walked single file down the south path, Kenneth in the lead and Liverpool and Bucephalus behind him. I followed the beast, and Lord Baltimore brought up the rear.

"I have a riddle for you," I whispered loudly over my shoulder at His Grace as we entered the woods.

"Oh, and what would that be?"

"He walks with root doctor's donkey."

Lord Baltimore said nothing for a moment but lessened his pace a notch. "I believe," he said at length, "this is a riddle we should discuss later."

Other than the fact that we were walking straight toward a man who would like to suffer us harm, we enjoyed a leisurely stroll. The moon was bright enough to cast tree shadows on the path at our feet.

We soon passed a clearing in which a cluster of people had gathered for a low-country boil. There were two groups: the cooks and the entertainers.

"Liverpool, you keep dat ox from comin in yuh," called out one of the cooks, a woman of no small circumference.

"*Remaneo*," Liverpool said to Bucephalus, who stayed put.

The four of us made a beeline to the steaming kettle of shrimp, oysters, crawfish, corn, potatoes, and other island bounty. Barbecued coon and collard greens cooked with fatback were also on the menu. Despite the globe-like girth of the cook who had spoken to Liverpool, a number of wiry, elderly suitors orbited her as she stirred a large pot.

Kenneth and His Grace broke away from the circle to speak with several men, one of whom wore a black top hat. A large white feather stuck out prominently from its red hat band.

"Come yuh," Liverpool said to me. "Ken gonna put Tursdy on de sticks."

"The what?"

"Ken tellin dat man bout de sheriff. You see."

Liverpool and I observed a group of men competing in a dance called the Buzzard Lope. Five musicians played while the men danced. One had a slide guitar. Another played a harmonica. A third did what they called "blowing the comb," which meant that he breathed in and out through a regular hair comb wrapped in thin paper. A fourth man kept time by beating on a handmade drum with two thick sticks. The fifth shook several dried gourds filled with seeds. Those who were not dancing or playing instruments clapped to the beat of the drum. The dancers moved in a circle. As the song progressed, it sped up, as did the dancers. Before long, they were rapidly moving in a counter-clockwise direction, raising their arms toward the sky.

I asked what the dance was about.

"Dat de Fly-Away Dance. Some African slaves could fly back to dey homelan. One time, a bunch stop de work in de fiel an start movin fast roun an roun. Den dey up an whirl off in de sky an fly away home."

The dance ended with a flurry of motion, everyone yelling words I couldn't understand.

Then a small group of middle-aged men and women formed a circle around a seated elderly man. The man sang a verse while the others shuffled in a circular pattern around him. The dancers called out in response to the first verse. Then he sang another verse, which was followed by another response.

"Dat called De Shout," Liverpool explained.

His Grace sidled up to us and began to clap, though not in time with the dance. It seemed to me that the calls and responses of the participants could hardly be called shouting, and I commented on this to him.

"The Shout refers to the dances and gestures. It originated with the Arabic *saut*, a holy dance."

I started to ask him another question, but His Grace bounded into the circle and joined the dancers.

"Doan yuh wanna jine um?" Liverpool asked.

"I don't know how to dance."

He laughed. "Dat ain never stop Lawd Balt'mo!"

I declined just the same.

When the dance ended, the man in the top hat stepped forward with a guitar and sat on a wooden box in the middle of the group.

"He Tursdy Jones," said Liverpool. "Bes picker on dis ilun."

Thursday Jones was a slender man of about sixty years whose guitar appeared to be made entirely of metal.

"Thursday? How did he get a name like that?"

"He boan on a Tursdy. He brudder boan on a Mundy."

"And his brother's name is Monday Jones?"

"Dat right."

"Does he have a sister?"

"Sho do."

"And her name is Friday Jones?"

"Huh name June. She boan in June."

As Thursday tuned the instrument, the onlookers shouted requests. He seemed not to take notice until someone called out, " 'Pay Me.' " Upon hearing those words, he launched directly into the tune.

Oh, pay me, pay me, Pay me my money down
Pay me or go to jail, Oh, pay me my money down.
Tink I heah my captain say, Pay me my money down
Tomorrow is my sailin day, Oh, pay me my money down.
Oh, pay me, pay me, Pay me my money down
Pay me, Mister Stevedore, Oh, pay me my money down.
One uh dese days, I'm goin away, Pay me my money down
Wohn be back til Judgment Day, Oh, pay me my money down.
Oh, pay me, pay me, Pay me my money down
Pay me or go to jail, Oh, pay me my money down.
Wish I was Mister Couper son, Pay me my money down
Stay in de house and drink good rum, Oh, pay me my money
    down.

Upon finishing, he continued tuning the guitar while the audience clapped and began to call out more suggestions.

I got caught up in the moment and offered my request. " 'Free Bird'!" I yelled.

You would have thought I said an ugly word, for the title had no sooner escaped my lips than Thursday stopped tuning and everyone looked at me.

Liverpool, bless his soul, covered for me as best he could. "Dat de tune uh wanna heah, too."

"Unca, I doan know that tune," Thursday said.

"Uh taht everbuddy know 'Fee Birt.' " It was painfully obvious to me that Liverpool had never heard the song either.

Thursday Jones shook his head and began tuning again. When the requests resumed, I held my tongue. However, I thanked Liverpool for interceding on my behalf.

"Dat quat aright. Dese folk doan heah much song outside Zapala."

Someone called out, "Play some dat 'High John de Conqueror.' "

Thursday nodded and immediately launched into a rousing, bluesy instrumental the likes of which I have never heard. He slid the broken bottle neck he wore over his left forefinger along half the guitar stings while plucking the rest with his thumb and the free fingers of his left hand. His right thumb and fingers strummed and plucked so expertly that had I not been watching with my own eyes, I would have sworn three guitarists were playing. My disbelief must have been evident, for Liverpool quietly reached over and closed the lower part of my jaw, which hung agape.

"De open mout unseemly in young gen'l'mens."

I thanked him but felt my jaw go slack again as Thursday kicked into overdrive. My head involuntarily swung from side to side until he finished playing. Describing such a song would be like explaining plaid to the color-blind.

"You seem astonished," His Grace said as he approached us.

I caught my breath. Thursday Jones was a buried treasure we had stumbled upon. "I don't believe what I just saw."

"You've seen a master practicing his craft."

"Why doesn't he have a record deal?"

Liverpool laughed and moved off to speak with Thursday.

His Grace looked away, then back at me. "He's pure art. You'll find musicians like him in hard-to-reach places. By the time their art makes it to the populace, it has been diluted to drivel."

"Where did he learn to play like that?"

"From his mentor."

"I'd like to meet that man."

"You have."

"Who?"

His Lordship nodded toward Liverpool. The ancient one stood next to Thursday. They seemed to be discussing fingering positions.

"Before the alligator incident, people would come from miles around to see Liverpool. Back then, they beat the drums on the dock to let folks on the other side know a dance was on. By nightfall, two hundred mainlanders would be here. They danced until dawn."

What happened next I found quite remarkable. Thursday Jones was once more alone in the center of things. He began to bang two square pieces of wood together, which immediately got everyone's attention.

"He's going to put Sheriff Pooler on the sticks," His Lordship said.

"What does that mean?"

"Shh. Listen."

Thursday, now the island news anchor, began to sing in a resounding voice.

> *Juba he live on de other side*
> *Juba come over on de risin tide*
> *Say Juba, huh Juba*
> *Juba he come fo to hunt men down*
> *Fo to tek men back to Medway town*
> *Say Juba, huh Juba*

"What's a juba?" I wanted to know.

"Juba means water," His Grace said. "In their songs, slaves substituted common words for those in authority, usually the master of the plantation or the overseer. *Water* is a safe word to use. In this instance, Juba refers to the sheriff. He could walk through this camp right now and not realize they're spreading word of his presence."

Juba look high an Juba look low
Juba find mo than he bargain fo
Say Juba, huh Juba
Juba go into de swamp at night
Juba lose men on de lef an right
Say Juba, huh Juba

Kenneth had told our plan to Thursday, who was now relaying the information to anyone who could hear. By midnight, the entire island would know our mission.

Juba wear badge an Juba wear gun
Juba alone come de risin sun
Say Juba, huh Juba
Juba go down to Megiddo Beach
Juba he learn what de Goot Book teach
Say Juba, huh Juba

The moment he finished, Thursday threw both pieces of wood high into the air. Everyone looked on in breathless anticipation. The sticks landed with a thud parallel to each other. Apparently, this was a good sign, for the entire gathering burst forth with applause.

A young girl came around with a small basket filled with kumquats. Lord Baltimore took one and began to eat. I hesitated to accept the fruit.

"Go on," said His Grace. "It holds medicinal powers that will give you courage for tonight's work."

Inspired by this knowledge, I grabbed a handful of kumquats and eagerly gulped them down. The effect was immediate. A sensation of growing confidence soon began to manifest itself within me. It was a confidence that was quickly put to the test, for a singular figure emerged from the darkness and made straight for me.

"Shadduh Man, leab de boy alone!" someone called out.

But he kept coming. Before I could react, he was upon me. The Shadow Man took my hand and pumped it vigorously.

"I tank you. You give me merit," he said, smiling broadly.

I hadn't noticed the first time I saw him, but a milky film covered his right eye. In the firelight, his eye and his jagged teeth combined to produce a countenance I seemed to recall from nightmares.

Kenneth smiled, too. "He thankin you fo givin him plenty bidness. Plenty folks need de Shadduh Man now all de ilun spirits upset."

"Dey's plenny ways to ward off shadduhs," the Shadow Man said. "Yuh can tie a rag to de fron gate. Yuh can kill a white chicken an throw her out de fron do. Yuh can bury a root under de do'step." He continued with a litany of ghost-prevention techniques that reminded me of His Grace's long-winded speeches on whatever topic was meandering through his head at that moment. "I knows all de ways to keep shadduhs from yuh. Yuh can break glass on de do'step. Yuh hang up newspaper roun all de house entrance. Yuh paint de frames blue."

This continued for some time. But as his jack-o'-lantern visage was one to be reckoned with, I judged it best not to interrupt.

"That's enough," said His Grace. "Don't give away all your secrets."

The Shadow Man slapped a hand over his mouth and said not another word. He breezed past me and walked back into the shadows from which he had come.

We then returned to the path. It was with a sense of sorrow that I left the gathering and reentered the night. However, I had a very real sense of invincibility by then, fueled by the secret power of the kumquat. I made a mental note to look into marketing an extract of kumquat I would call the "Herb of Confidence," targeted toward those lacking aplomb and self-assurance.

As we marched, I became so mesmerized by the buzz of insects and the hypnotic effect of shadows on the sand that I didn't notice those ahead had come to a stop. That being the case, I walked smack into Bucephalus's backside. In so doing, I caused the beast to emit another breathtaking, ghastly blast. His Grace and I beat a hasty retreat until the effects diminished.

The reason Bucephalus had come to a stop was that JV was on the path.

"Got some news," he told us. "Seems the sheriff has other plans besides parading you through Darien."

"Oh?" said Lord Baltimore. "Pray tell. What are his intentions?"

"He intends for you and Brantley to wind up like Captain Sandy. Said, 'Dead men tell no tales.' "

"Yes, I see. The good sheriff would use me as a scapegoat for his drug trafficking. By eliminating Brantley and me, he can show his constituents just how tough he is on crime. Of course, the beauty of it is that he can also maintain his position as the county's biggest criminal. I admire his boldness."

JV led us through a number of side paths until we came to a circle of trees. Liverpool put his hand on the head of the massive ox and bid him to stay—in Latin, of course. We then ventured another hundred yards or so before coming to a bamboo stand. We made our way into it and peeked through the bamboo.

Zapala's main north-south road stretched out thirty feet in front of us. There, in a small meadow on the other side of the road, partially hidden by foliage, I saw Sheriff Pooler, Ratchet Face, and one other deputy. A small fire burned at their feet. From their vantage point, they could easily observe any movement on the road. From our slightly elevated position, we could watch their movements. Two hunting dogs were tied to a log at the rear of their camp. A gentle offshore breeze blew in our faces, which meant that we were downwind of the dogs. The meadow and the surrounding forest formed a natural amphitheater that allowed us to hear their every word.

"No. We ain't goin' nowhere tonight," the sheriff said. "You boys been chasing these two all day and are sittin' right back in the same camp where you started."

Ratchet Face said, "But Blue and Shoat Thang—"

"Them hounds are just about worthless! Tomorrow, at first light, we're gonna track them boys without those mutts. All they're good for is chasing their tails. Can't even track down one old fool English-man and one hick so dumb he can't pull off a convenience store robbery."

"Liverpool, I believe you know what to do," His Lordship whispered.

"You be careful, Unca," whispered Kenneth.

Liverpool did not answer. He simply turned and exited the thicket the way we had come.

It was perhaps ten minutes before the dogs began barking. I saw the sheriff, Ratchet Face, and the other deputy arm themselves. An-other minute passed before the dim image of Liverpool appeared on the road, Bucephalus in tow. The old man moved at a snail's pace, though I knew he could go much faster.

"Who's that?" growled the sheriff.

Liverpool stopped and turned toward the encampment as if un-aware of its presence. He leaned forward, searching for whoever was behind the voice.

Sheriff Pooler shone a bright flashlight at Liverpool. The beam briefly flashed in my eyes.

"Squint," His Grace whispered.

The sheriff and his men came out to the road where Liverpool stood. The sheriff kept his light in Liverpool's eyes while Ratchet Face and the deputy circled Bucephalus as though inspecting a stolen ve-hicle for drugs.

"Good Godamighty," said the sheriff. "Is that you, Livahpool?"

Liverpool remained motionless, puffing on his pipe.

Pooler shook his head in disbelief. "I thought you passed on thirty years ago. Boys, this here is Livahpool."

"Who's that?" asked the younger deputy, a short, broad-shouldered, stocky man.

"This old fella taught my pappy to track just about anything that lives in the woods," said the sheriff. "Ain't that right?" he asked Liverpool.

"*Filius magni viri non semper est magnus vir.*"

Lord Baltimore, stifling a laugh, fairly blew his unlit cigar through the bamboo thicket. " 'The son of a great man is not always a great man,' " he interpreted in a whisper.

"What the . . . ? What was that?" asked the young deputy.

"Liverpool speaks the Latin tongue," the sheriff said. "Learnt it from his pappy. Only thing he knows how to speak."

This revelation amused the two deputies to no end, and they decided to make sport of it.

"Say," said Ratchet Face, "we want to speak with that Lord Baltimore friend of yours. Need to take him back for some questioning. You seen him?"

Liverpool shook his head. "*Amicus noster in numero stultorum non remanebit.*"

They roared with laughter, not understanding a word.

" 'Our friend will not stay in the company of fools,' " relayed His Grace.

"If you ask me, this guy's as big a fruitcake as that English fool," the Ratchet said.

"*Sapientiam magnorum virorum non semper videmus,*" Liverpool shot back.

" 'We do not always understand the wisdom of great men,' " His Grace whispered.

Liverpool's language must have been just about the most humorous thing the young deputy had ever heard, for he laughed so loudly the dogs began to bay.

I peeked at the others in the bamboo stand to observe their reactions.

Lord Baltimore grinned broadly and muttered, "Liverpool, you impetuous scoundrel."

Kenneth was concerned for Liverpool's safety. "He gonna get hisself shot," he said, almost too loudly.

JV was nowhere to be seen.

"Looky hyar," said the sheriff, unfolding a bundle of cash. "All you have to do is take us to where that prisoner and that Lord Baltimore are hidin'. With this kind of money on this island, you'll be rich and famous."

Liverpool looked at the money and then at the sheriff. "*Pecunia est nihil sine moribus bonis. Vita paucis viris faman dat.*"

" 'Money is nothing without good character,' " His Grace said. " 'Life gives fame to few men.' "

Each of Liverpool's statements brought forth a burst of laughter, particularly from the younger deputy, a man I now dubbed Hyena in recognition of his high-pitched, staccato laugh.

His Grace almost lost control as he interpreted Liverpool's remarks.

"What he sayin? What he sayin?" Kenneth wanted to know.

" 'The man you seek, Lord Baltimore, is there in the bushes behind you,' " whispered His Grace. " 'I jest not. He looks upon us even as I speak.' "

Liverpool, seeing the deputies' delight, kept up the show. "*Vitam sine pecunia non amitas,*" he said with a wry grin.

" 'You do not like life without money,' " said His Grace.

"Now, looky hyar," said Sheriff Pooler. "Do you know where them boys are or not? Just lead the way." He waved the money in front of Liverpool.

Perhaps the sight of the paper bills reminded me of old, musty books. Perhaps there was pollen in the air. For whatever reason, I knew I was going to sneeze. I tried my best to stifle it, but the urge was not to be denied. I turned and covered as best I could.

When I turned back around, Lord Baltimore and Kenneth were looking at me. I was also acutely conscious that Sheriff Pooler had his hand on his gun and was peering in our direction.

"Shh!" he commanded the deputies.

They ceased their merrymaking and shone flashlights at us.

"Steady, lads," His Grace said under his breath. Whether he was advising Kenneth and me or the lawmen, I could not discern.

The sheriff held his revolver in the air. His deputies drew their guns and aimed them toward us.

"Who's in there?" Sheriff Pooler called.

His Grace placed one hand on my shoulder and one on Kenneth's. He slowly knelt and pulled us down with him. He kept the pressure on us until we were all three lying on our bellies.

"Best come on outta there," Ratchet Face said.

No one moved.

"All right, I'm givin' you three seconds," said the sheriff.

Before the third second passed, Sheriff Pooler and his men began firing. I'm not sure how many shots there were. One bullet slammed into a bush just above my head. Another sailed past me through the thicket. The firing ceased in a matter of moments, after which the acrid smell of gunpowder enveloped us.

"Better check it out," said the Ratchet, walking toward us.

His Grace pulled several coins from his pants pocket and jiggled them quickly in his cupped hand in two short bursts.

"Rattler!" shouted the Hyena.

Sheriff Pooler was still unconvinced and was about to investigate further. Liverpool must have realized it, for he provided a distraction to divert the sheriff's attention. The old fossil turned as if to go back in the direction from which he had come. In doing so, he neatly positioned Bucephalus between the lawmen and the small opening in the foliage that led to their encampment.

"He don't know where them two are hidin'," Ratchet Face said. "Old fool don't even know where he is. Just wanderin' around under a full moon like a loony with that big ox."

"*Nidor*," Liverpool commanded as he turned Bucephalus.

"Arm yourselves," His Grace said, rising to his feet. He covered his nose and mouth with a handkerchief.

What we were to ready ourselves for became quickly apparent, for Liverpool had no sooner given his command than Bucephalus obliged with a resounding trumpet blast—or rather, an entire brass section of trumpet blasts. The effect on the deputies was dramatic. They bolted down the south part of the trail bent double with laughter and gasping for air at the same time. The sheriff backed several steps toward us, then followed his men for a distance of about twenty yards. Liverpool and Bucephalus remained stationary, blocking the entrance to their encampment.

The two hounds began barking excitedly at that moment, and for good reason. I saw a figure dart out of the bushes and swiftly move about the camp. In less than twenty seconds, JV snatched up most of the sheriff's and the deputies' possessions. Only the tent remained, though devoid of its contents.

Liverpool waited for JV to disappear into the bushes before he started a slow pace back up the road. "*Vale*," he said, waving good-bye.

Sheriff Pooler and his men cautiously made their way back to where Liverpool had been. The deputies were still snickering, but their chief was no longer amused. They watched as Liverpool made his way up the road.

"Anyone who taught Pappy to track is a sly, old fox," said the sheriff. "Give him a two-minute start, then get on his tail. He'll lead us right to the fugitives. An shet them dogs up! They think they're hot on the trail again."

"Blue! Hush up! Shoat Thang!" Ratchet Face shouted.

But the dogs continued their alarm. Deputy Hyena walked through the camp to where they were tied before he realized the site had been invaded.

"It's gone!" he yelled. "Someone's stole all our equipment!"

Sheriff Pooler and Ratchet Face ran to the camp, shone their flashlights here and there, stomped around in the brush, and then trotted back to the road. Realizing what had transpired, the sheriff let forth a plethora of expletives that amused Lord Baltimore in the same manner that Liverpool had entertained the deputies.

"Go run him down," the sheriff told the Hyena.

The young deputy took off at a gallop.

"Well done, sheriff," whispered Lord Baltimore. "You just reduced your forces by a third."

"I'll get the dogs," said Ratchet Face.

"Leave 'em here!" barked Sheriff Pooler. "If they cain't track worth a durn in broad daylight, ain't no way they're gonna lead us around at night."

"Good," His Lordship whispered. "Separate yourselves from the dogs as well."

The sheriff took his firearm from its holster and reloaded it. "Come on," he growled. "We got some killin' to tend to."

The sheriff and Ratchet Face were soon in pursuit of the ancient Liverpool and his lumbering ox.

With a triumphant air, His Grace announced, "Now, to phase two of Operation Sapsucker."

CHAPTER 16

I get lost in the Devil's Maze.

"Underestimating Liverpool was his first blunder," His Grace informed me as we hiked the main road close on the heels of the sheriff. "Sending that young deputy off was his second. We're three moves away from checkmate."

How a man easily over one hundred years old and an ox the size of a four-passenger vehicle could entrap a pursuer eluded me. I guessed that the sheriff, in his wrath, figured the deputy would catch up to Liverpool and did not think to follow Bucephalus's tracks with his flashlight. Lord Baltimore's plan was apparently working flawlessly.

Kenneth moved swiftly ahead of us on paths that paralleled the road. I could hear Ratchet Face, not far ahead of us, whistle for Deputy Hyena and await a responding whistle.

We had not gone a hundred yards before JV appeared in front of us.

"Well?" His Grace inquired.

"Bucephalus is carrying their equipment back to the cabin," he replied. "They're taking the Cherokee Trail."

"Cherokee Trail? That rascal Liverpool never showed me that one."

"It's not much more than a deer run now," said JV. "Don't tell me they left the dogs behind."

"Can you believe it?" His Grace asked. "We made such liars out of the hounds today that the sheriff will have nothing to do with them."

Juba look high an Juba look low
Juba find mo than he bargain fo
Say Juba, huh Juba

"Speaking of the sheriff, he's going to be back here any minute," I said, worried about our remaining on the road. "He knows by now we have his deputy."

"Where is the poor devil?" asked His Grace.

For the first time, I saw JV smile. I witnessed in him at that moment the ghost of a great athlete and a fearless warrior, someone who relished danger. I believe Lord Baltimore wanted me along that evening to develop a taste for it as well. Why else should I accompany him when I had so little to contribute?

"The kid's all right," JV said. "He won't be making any noise, though."

The buzz of the crickets and cicadas was interrupted by a disturbance ahead of us. It was a faint voice in the distance—an excited, beckoning cry.

"That would be Kenneth," said His Grace. "He's quite good at impersonations. With any luck, our lawmen will think the young deputy is calling out for them."

It then became apparent to me that the plan was to draw the sheriff into Devil Swamp.

"I'll take care of the dogs," said JV, "just in case this boy's right about the sheriff coming back."

He then trotted back down the road toward the still-barking dogs.

I wondered how JV could get near the dogs without being attacked by them. But as Lord Baltimore seemed unconcerned, I decided it was not my business to doubt JV's abilities.

"The thing we have to do," His Grace said quietly as we hurried along the road, sticking to the shadows, "is get those two to completely use up their ammunition. Then we shall have the fair fight that Master Brantley wanted."

I felt a sudden discomfort, for it dawned on me why I had been asked to accompany His Grace. A decoy would be needed in order for our prey to dispose of their bullets.

Every five paces or so, His Grace shone a small, pocket-sized flashlight at the road to study the tracks. At one point, he found nothing. Backing up carefully, he located the spot where the sheriff and his deputy had left the main road for a trail to our right. His Grace stood perfectly still and closed his eyes. For the life of me, it appeared he was sniffing the air.

I now understood how I had overshot Lord Baltimore's tracks the day we first met, when we witnessed the sheriff's drug operation. I had walked about five yards beyond His Grace's position on the limb that extended across the road. By walking backward in his tracks, he had given the impression that he had simply vanished. How he had pulled himself onto the limb was a matter I would have to ponder another time.

"I did not expect them to leave the road this soon," His Grace said. Then he opened his eyes and looked at me. "Something is not quite right with the sheriff. He's acting very irrationally. Blunder after blunder. Not his way at all."

"Perhaps the cocaine . . ."

His Grace held up a hand for silence. Again, I heard faint sounds in the night.

We followed the tracks on to the trail. By now, it was obvious that Kenneth was successfully leading our guests to Devil Swamp. When the insects' chirping and the frogs' croaking reached a deafening pitch, I knew we were nearing Tilly's turf.

After fifteen minutes of brisk walking down narrow, winding, criss-crossing paths, His Grace held my arm. "They've reached the swamp," he said. "And they're about to enter the Devil's Maze. Once we get them in there, the game is over. From here on, stay far enough behind that you can see me. One flash from me means get off the path double-quick. Understood?"

> *Juba go into de swamp at night*
> *Juba lose men on de lef an right*
> *Say Juba, huh Juba*

I understood fine. His Grace didn't want me to be caught with him in the event we unexpectedly came upon the two lawmen. However, I had convinced myself that I would rather take my chances meeting the sheriff face to face than jumping off the swamp trail and into the arms or mouth of a smelly, hairy, or scaly beast.

For the next half-hour, we slowly made our way into the swamp. His Lordship studied what prints he could make out at each bend in the path, while I stayed just far enough behind to see his outline in the moonlight.

It was at one of the numerous forks that an unfortunate thing happened. I saw His Grace bend to study the ground with his flashlight and to feel for footprints with his hand. I clearly saw him stand up. But I didn't see which trail he took. I noticed his graying hair moving in the moonlight on the path to my right. I advanced along that path until I noticed that his hair was not moving forward but side to side. Then I observed that the hair appeared to be levitating. I hurried to the spot and to my astonishment discovered that the moonlit hair was nothing more than a clump of Spanish moss gently swaying in the breeze.

His Grace must have taken the left path. I beat it back to where I had last seen him and scampered along the trail I should have taken to begin with. Just as I feared, this trail also split. I had to make a choice. I could go back to the road, or I could proceed onward. In other words, I could abandon His Grace and Kenneth when they might be in need of my help, or I could be there for them. I determined to go forward. But on which path? One led to Lord Baltimore, the other to what I was sure would be a quick and untimely end to a promising young life.

I wondered what Lord Baltimore would recommend. And the answer to that was that I should remain right where I was. Surely, he would notice my absence and backtrack. I was equally certain that JV would be along. So I sat down and waited.

Sitting on one's backside in the middle of a cursed swamp on a full-moon night tends to put certain thoughts into one's head. Those included one in which two male alligators, intent on impressing a female of their species, fought feverishly over my carcass so the victor could share his spoils with the fair maiden. Another was that of Tilly swooping down in the form of a vulture, tearing various organs from my body, and showing up the next day in Folktown with a necklace made of my teeth dangling around her neck.

Finally, I determined that His Grace would do more than sit on his duff waiting for someone to rescue him. I had seen him close his eyes and listen. So I did the same. Then I used my nose to pick up scents. My ears heard faint sounds that could have come from either path in front of me. My nose picked up swamp smells whose meaning I could not interpret. However, as I sat there yoga-style, my fingers were instinctively drawn to the cool, moist sand. It was by sifting the granules through my fingers that I recalled how His Grace felt the ground for footprints. It then occurred to me that all I had to do was feel for footprints on the paths. Whichever had footprints was the one I wanted.

I spent several minutes moving stealthily along the left path before I gave up. I then came back and proceeded on my hands and knees along the right path. It was not long before my fingers discerned several impressions in the soft sand. I was therefore certain that I had found the right course.

I repeated the procedure of feeling for footprints at each of the next three forks before I realized that something was wrong. What was wrong was that I could no longer discern any tracks. What was wrong was that I was fairly certain I had entered the Devil's Maze.

Soon, I heard footsteps approaching. The sound of any fellow traveler in that place at that hour of the night gladdened my heart. But what might have been a happy reunion turned out to be misfortune on my part. I was in their grasp before I realized that the footsteps didn't belong to His Grace and Kenneth, as I hoped. Indeed, Sheriff Pooler and Ratchet Face were equally surprised to see me dash down the footpath straight into their arms.

"Well, now," the sheriff said. "Looks like we're on the right track after all."

I sensed a certain relief on their part at having run into me. Any feeling of panic they might have experienced up to that moment gave way to a misguided confidence that things always worked in their favor. Perhaps things had gone their way for so many years that they assumed it would always be so. Perhaps they were right.

"He'll do for bait," said the deputy.

After five minutes of interrogation and intimidation, it finally dawned on them that I was as lost as they were and could no more lead them to Lord Baltimore and Brantley than I could lasso the moon.

The deputy was all for doing me in right there and then. Sheriff Pooler, however, was determined to put me to work on their behalf. What that work entailed was not clear to me until we found a dugout canoe that rested on the shore at the edge of the woods. A small island rose from the wetland twenty yards away.

Doing as they instructed, under the duress of having two flashlights and two pistols pointed at me the entire time, I entered the canoe with the deputy. The Ratchet used the oar—or, I should say, half an oar—to row us to the island. Before I got out of the boat, he reached over and snatched the Saint Christopher off my neck. "You won't be needing this," he said with a grin.

I'm sure he thought it was a coin, but upon inspecting it more closely, his expression changed. In anger, he turned and threw the medal far enough that it landed somewhere on the shore. For the first time in my life, I wished my father were present. Though the officer was a fairly large man, I was confident my father could easily handle him.

The deputy left me on the island and rowed back to the shore, where he and the sheriff proceeded to build a small fire of pine straw, cones, and branches.

I didn't understand their plot until perhaps a half-hour later, when I saw two bubbles appear in the firelight's reflection on the surface of the water. I had seen such bubbles before—the kind that never drift apart or burst, the kind that are not bubbles at all but are, in fact, the eyes of an alligator whose body rests just below the water's surface.

"Whoop it up, boy!" Ratchet Face yelled cheerfully. "Whoo, he's a long un!"

By then, the sheriff's plan was obvious. Instead of being Lord Baltimore's rescuer, I was being used to lure him to his death.

Another set of bubbles appeared behind the first, and I heard a rather large splash near the shore of the island to my rear. The island was no more than ten yards wide by about thirty yards long. There was little vegetation on it. The distance from the island to the shore-line behind me, away from the sheriff, was not large at all, maybe ten feet. But it was ten feet I could not jump. To me, it was an abyss of danger and might as well have been a thousand feet.

"Your friends cain't find you if you don't holler, boy!" Ratchet Face yelled.

Yet I refused to make a sound. In fact, other than two owls exchanging calls from either side of us—one of them being a rather sickly sounding bird—there was no noise at all that might attract His Lordship.

My continued silence infuriated Deputy Ratchet. The more he instructed me, the louder he got, as if trying to lure His Grace with his own nasal taunts.

The sheriff, also annoyed that I refused to stick to the script, took matters into his own hands. "Enough of this foolishness," he said, pulling his pistol from the holster. He fired several shots at my feet, which caused me to jump. But he did not achieve the desired effect of causing me to plead for mercy in loud, pitiful, rescue-inducing tones.

That the two of them were making enough noise to attract anyone's attention within a half-mile did not seem to matter. The fact that I would not utter a sound displeased them to no end. The upshot of this was that I was shot—grazed, actually—by the sheriff's third bullet. He wasn't aiming to hit me, but nevertheless, the bullet ricocheted off the ground and grooved a small streak across the inside of my calf. At first, I didn't feel a thing. But the injury quickly began to burn as though on fire. Any thought I had of dousing it with cool water evaporated when I noticed the two bubbles on the water in front of me slowly advance.

To his credit, Ratchet Face had not exaggerated in stating that the alligator was a "long un," for the head alone seemed the length of my torso. As the prehistoric creature emerged from the drink and set foot on my island, I raised my hands and made as large an appearance as possible. This had the temporary effect of causing the reptile to stop. However, he or she soon discerned my bluff and proceeded forward steadily, hissing, eyeing me as though I were a T-bone steak. I in turn proceeded backward, hyperventilating. My firepower consisted of the few pine cones strewn about the island, which I hurled at the predator, who seemed not to notice. The first one missed by an inch. The next two bounced harmlessly off its thick hide.

Any courage imparted to me by the kumquats was quickly evaporating. I was on the verge of saying that I would be happy to lead my tormentors directly to His Lordship when a most unexpected but welcome thing occurred.

The gator's hissing and my hyperventilating were interrupted by a terrific noise and a blinding white light that lit up the entire area. I looked up to see a pyrotechnic device tumbling downward from limb to limb in a pine tree behind the sheriff and his deputy. This was followed by another equally bright comet that plunged into the top of a tree closer to the lawmen. It also tumbled slowly down the tree, fragmenting and emitting blinding phosphorescent sparks as it did so.

The abrupt change in our surroundings proved too much for the alligator, which quickly splashed back into the protection of the murky water. It also startled Sheriff Pooler and Deputy Ratchet. As a third comet hit the top of the tree that sheltered them, they began firing indiscriminately into the woods. Their shooting only prompted another object to appear in the treetop above them, causing them to step back, almost into the alligator-infested water.

I stood in absolute wonderment, observing the luminous spectacle before me. The tree was transformed into a bright cathedral that showered ethereal sparks and scattered pulses of light in all directions. I then became aware of a new noise. This one was close behind me. I dreaded turning around to look. Perhaps it would be less painful if I did not see what was about to attack me.

CHAPTER 17

I am rescued.

I fully expected to be knocked down and devoured where I stood. And I made a quick decision not to look upon what it was that I heard thumping on the ground behind me. But the same curious fascination that has tempted men throughout the ages to see what lies beyond the horizon or inside this or that cave tempted me to turn and confront my new threat. The twenty-foot alligator that my mind had painted in great detail, right down to the bones of its last meal still hanging from its long teeth, was not there. What was there was a splendid and imposing horse. Riding the horse, approaching me and holding his hand out, was His Grace, Duke of Zapala, Lord Baltimore.

"Up with you then, lad," he said with a wink, puffing on yet another cigar.

I didn't need another invitation. Grabbing his arm, I swung upon the back of the magnificent steed.

"Hold on," he told me as we trotted to one end of the small island.

By then, Sheriff Pooler and Ratchet Face had caught sight of us. In all likelihood, they were still partially blinded by the fireworks and could not make out exactly who or what had come to my rescue. Indeed, if it weren't for the glow of His Grace's cigar, I might not have so easily recognized him.

"All right, Pegasus," said His Grace to the stallion, "let's see you live up to your name."

He bumped his heels into the charger's sides, snapped the reins smartly, and commanded Pegasus onward. I felt his powerful haunches churning beneath me as he responded, and we were instantly two passengers on a bolt of lightning. A shot rang out. And another. And a third. But we had already reached the end of the island and were airborne. A large, overzealous alligator leapt out of the water and snapped its powerful jaws at us, but to no avail. Pegasus easily soared to the opposite shore. I clung to Lord Baltimore's waist with my eyes closed and, not knowing when we would touch down, had the wind partially knocked out of me when we landed. We soon disappeared safely into the woods. Several more shots rang out. One bullet bounced off a tree and whizzed by my head.

We glided as if on a magic carpet through the circuitous paths of the Devil's Maze. I could not tell if Pegasus knew his way home or if he was guided by the expert hand of His Lordship.

"They were trying to lure you," I said after my breath returned.

"I know," said His Grace. "We've been following you from the moment you ran into them. I must say you've behaved admirably."

"Did you see that gator?"

"Indeed."

"You saw the whole thing?"

"It was a foolish move by a desperate man. A move easily countered when my knight took his pawn. You might have observed the sounds of two owls corresponding just before the pyrotechnics began."

I replied that I had.

"What you in fact heard was my feeble attempt at imitating a great horned owl, followed by Kenneth's expert impersonation."

We soon slowed to a trot. My eyes had just again grown accustomed to the moonlit darkness when I spied a light shining through the trees ahead of us. We came to a stop at the rear of a house that seemed familiar. His Grace commanded me to climb the back steps and enter. I reached out to pet Pegasus's neck as a gesture of gratitude for saving me. He responded by snorting a snout full of small, granular particles on the front of my shirt. This I took as a sign of affection. His Grace chuckled and led Pegasus to a small structure made of tree limbs and palmetto leaves that served as a horse stall. A donkey's head poked out from one of the openings to see what was going on.

"Are you coming in?" I asked.

"It's a cigar-hostile zone," he replied. "I'll finish it out here."

I turned to go inside.

"And don't bring up the subject of me and Tilly," he said as I climbed the steps.

I reached for the screen-door handle and felt the throbbing pain of the bullet that had nicked me. The blood had begun to clot. Feeling faint from the sight of it, I lurched inside and half fell into the kitchen, where I landed in a chair. A swirl of color moved in front of me, and I looked up into the cold stare of Zapala's resident witch doctor. His Grace had rescued me from the clutches of one enemy and delivered me into the hands of another.

"You boys disturbin my creatures," Tilly said, shaking her head. "I ain't got time fo men's foolishness." She knelt to clean my wound. "Hold still," she instructed.

I watched in dazed disbelief while she tended the injury. The effect of having one's set-in-stone perception of another person so profoundly altered was tantamount to learning God exists when all the logical evidence has indicated otherwise. I would have been no more startled had Sheriff Pooler extended a helping hand upon finding me in the swamp.

I expected her to pull out a patch of moss and weeds or some exotic herbal remedy. Instead, she quickly cleaned and bound the affected area using the same sterilizing agents and bandages available at any pharmacy. From the efficiency with which she tended my abrasion, it was apparent that she had treated many wounds in her day. The fact that I felt no pain and seemed to regain strength just by her presence I attributed to her healing powers.

In the short period it took Tilly to do her business, I had the opportunity to look around the place. Electricity had been strung to her house, just as it had to the homes in Folktown. The room was filled with stuffed animals, live birds, potions, medicine bottles, oils, and powders. The powders, which lined several cabinets, were labeled "Betting," "Love," "Money," "Luck," "Health," and so on. The stenciled letters on several shipping boxes indicated that they were from Egypt and the Far East. A pile of flannel lay on one counter. Beside the cloth was an assortment of roots, sands, bones, rocks, and herbs. These were most likely the ingredients the black-magic priestess used to ply her trade. On another counter were toothpaste-sized tubes of different colors, plastic containers of granulated substances, and more bottles. "Trinitrotoluene," "Silver Oxide," "Sodium Chlorate," and "Potassium Chlorate" were printed on the labels. These I took to be the ingredients that made up the pyrotechnic devices used to distract Sheriff Pooler and his deputy. Undoubtedly, such devices could also produce fabulous displays of her supernatural wizardry. Any traveler moving through this part of the island at night would be amazed and terrified at the sight of a sudden, blinding explosion, followed by the spectacle of a voodoo priestess in full regalia standing in the very spot where the blast had occurred. No doubt, the traveler would share word of his encounter with eager listeners the next day, thus affirming Tilly's supremacy over nature and islanders alike.

"Stay here," she told me. "I have to check on something fo li'l bit."

In a short time, I heard a familiar, high-pitched squeal coming from the next room. I peeked inside and to my astonishment saw Her Mystic Highness sitting next to a computer, the modem of which was squawking like a crow. This part of her house looked no different from any domicile one might wander into on the mainland. A cellular telephone lay beside the computer.

I entered the room. So engrossed in her work was she that she didn't notice me reading over her shoulder. E-mail after e-mail addressed to Dr. Owl appeared on the screen. Letters beseeched the doctor for advice, roots, and amulets to remove spells that had been cast on victims by this or that black root doctor. The messages came from across the United States, South America, the Orient, and even Africa. Several expressed thanks to Dr. Owl for saving marriages or even lives.

"Who is Dr. Owl?" I asked.

"You shouldn't be lookin over folks' shoulders," she replied. Then, after a bit, she admitted, "I'm Dr. Owl. Most of my bidness comes over the Net. Got a lawyer man in Chicago needin a love conjuh. Got a dentist in Zaire need to be rid of the red root some ol witch doctor buried in his yard. Well, I cain't get to everyone at once. Got me some plenty of spells to break right here in this island."

I watched as Tilly pulled up an Internet home page that was tracking the approaching storm. I suddenly understood how she received news about events that occurred far away, then presented that information to islanders, who attributed it to her supernatural powers.

"Looks like it will miss us," I said.

"Huh! He ain't gone by yet. He gonna turn on us tonight cause of you and that fool sheriff and that no-count convict y'all lef back at Unca's cabin."

She rose as she said this and in so doing revealed her lower leg, the same one that she claimed had been hurt by Brantley. The leg was no longer bandaged. Nor did it appear to be injured or scarred in any way.

"Can I send an e-mail?" I asked.

"Sho. Go ahead."

I dashed off a message to my father's office: "I'm okay. With a man named Lord Baltimore on Zapala. Hello to Mama. Love, Ensworth."

I sent the message before I realized I had ended it, "Love, Ensworth." I had never actually said those words to my father, at least not that I could remember, and I was not sure how he might take them. I also realized that he had instructed me not to contact him or anyone else back home until I reached the mysterious address in Savannah. However, I was sure I could evade that demand on the technicalities that (A) his instructions had stated that he was not to "hear" from me, and my e-mail was to be read and not heard and (B) the e-mail would come from Tilly's mail account, not mine.

"Wipe yo feet," she said to Lord Baltimore, who had just entered the back door.

I left the PC and entered the kitchen, where I thanked both of them profusely, His Grace for saving me and Tilly for the use of her horse and for bandaging my injury.

His Grace relayed the events of the evening to Tilly, who said nothing. It was only when he related Liverpool's command of "*Nidor*" to Bucephalus that she responded, nearly falling over backward in her chair. Indeed, she could not refrain from chuckling every so often thereafter. When he got to the part where the alligator crept on to the island with me, Tilly did a most astonishing thing. She walked to my side and briefly hugged me.

"Chile, you po thing," she said. "That was Mo'dred eyein you. He the one got hold a Unca Liverpool's hand. You stay heah with Tilly tonight an stop roughhousing with foolish men."

"I'm afraid we've got more work tomorrow morning," said His Grace.

"You gonna have that hur'cane to work with tomorrow morning."

"The weather reports say otherwise," he retorted.

"Dese boys done broke the spell. Fishin outta Ibo Landin, wakin up the Wavin Man. You kiddin me? Gonna take all my powers to fend off that storm."

Though Tilly had modern communications at her disposal, it was clear that she deeply believed in preternatural powers and the consequences of violating them. His Grace, a man of some intellect and reason—or so I thought—did not argue with her on that point.

"You're quite sure about that?" he asked, to my utter amazement.

For my part, I chose to put my faith in the National Weather Service, which relied on satellites, storm tracking, thousands of observations, and complex computer models to project when, where, and how fast a hurricane might move. I chose not to put my faith in a witch doctor, especially when I saw on a computer monitor a satellite image of a hurricane that was well out to sea and heading in a path that did not threaten Zapala. I also found it ridiculous that the actions two young men had taken a day or two prior could have any influence on the storm's course. Yet His Grace was perfectly willing to accept the word of Tilly over that of the most reliable weather-tracking technology mankind had yet to produce.

I knew it would be futile to pursue the argument. Tomorrow morning would be proof enough of her error. I did, however, take that opportunity to defend technology, going so far as to describe the Internet as the great equalizer.

"Today," I informed them, "everyone has access to all the

information known to man."

This bit of news amused His Grace immensely. "Oh, really. Then that makes you and me equal, I suppose."

I agreed that it did, which amused him even more.

"Tell me," said he, "what is the atomic number of hydrogen?"

My response was that, while I did not know, I could easily and quickly determine the answer by accessing the Internet.

"Well, then," he said, "in that case, an encyclopedia and your local library are also great equalizers. In this world, you move ahead of your fellow man by what you know, not what you might investigate if you have a computer, a telephone line, and a connection to the precious Internet."

Adamant in my belief, I decided to give His Lordship the opportunity to prove one of us right. With Tilly's consent, I challenged Lord Baltimore to a duel with the Internet. He readily accepted, as long as we did not include the topic of popular culture. I sat at Tilly's computer and accessed a search engine.

"Okay," I said, "what is the atomic number of hydrogen?"

"One," said His Grace.

I had not even had the opportunity to enter a string of identifiers into the search engine by the time he answered. But I recalled from chemistry class that hydrogen was the first element on the Periodic Table. Therefore, it followed that its atomic number was indeed one.

"All right," said I, bristling with new confidence, since more of my high-school chemistry was coming back to me, "what does the molecular weight of a compound refer to?"

"It is the sum of the weights of the compound's component atoms," he said irritably. "Must we dabble with basics?"

"Okay, then," I said, moving on to another subject, "which countries border India?"

I hoped that would stump His Lordship long enough for me to

access the answer. As I waited for the data to download, I saw His Grace glance at Tilly and shake his head.

"Is that really the best you can do?"

It was apparent that he was stalling for time. The Web was on the verge of supplying me with a list of sites where I might obtain the information when he rattled off the names of Afghanistan, Bhutan, Burma, Bangladesh, China, Nepal, and Pakistan, being careful to break it down further into the provinces of Punjab and Sind. He even threw in the island of Sri Lanka for good measure.

Undaunted, I pressed on with a series of ridiculously obscure questions, all of which he easily answered. On the topics of law and medicine, he seemed amused by my queries. When I broached the subject of American history, he scoffed at the notion that the United States was old enough to have a history worthy of study.

"I have a cottage in Kent that's twice as old as your country," he told me with a wink.

His Grace had previously said he had never lost a chess match, and I recognized that he was trying to ruffle my feathers. I had experienced such gamesmanship on the golf course many times, and I now resolved to maintain my composure.

"This is tiresome. What's in the bread bin?" asked His Grace, rising from his chair.

"Help yourself. You know where everything is," Tilly replied.

His Lordship proceeded to the kitchen, where he rummaged through cabinets and the refrigerator.

I remained at the computer and took the opportunity to access new databases while he was occupied. Tilly said nothing, simply shaking her head with amusement at my deceit.

"What is the mean distance to Saturn?" I called out.

I heard a glass being filled with ice cubes.

"From the sun?" he called back.

"Yes. Of course, from the sun."

I heard a bottle top pop open and a metal lid fall on the counter.

"In kilometers or miles?"

"Miles."

There was a brief pause.

"Eight hundred ninety-five million, give or take a few."

He was right.

"Where does the word *algebra* come from?"

The sound of a knife slicing something came from the kitchen.

"I believe it's Arabic, is it not? Derives from *al-jebr*, if I recall. It's the first part of a phrase that refers to transferring and removing. I believe it was the title of a book by a ninth-century Arabian mathematician."

Undaunted, I pressed on.

"Who was Giacomo Leopardi?"

The sound of lettuce being torn emanated from the kitchen.

"Leopardi was an Italian author of moral essays and odes. I was always partial to his—"

"Who was Charles the Simple?"

I heard the sound of a knife scraping a jar—mustard or mayonnaise, I assumed.

"That would have been Charles the Third of France, son of Louis the Stammerer, who ruled from about 893 to 923."

It seemed his knowledge was inexhaustible. His answers amused Tilly increasingly, to the point that she could not help laughing at my untenable situation. I began to suspect Tilly and His Grace were communicating, though I saw no evidence of their trick. I soon gave up any pretense of competing with His Grace for the answers, which I'm sure he recognized.

I heard him slice a sandwich on a cutting board.

"Who said, 'Astronomy compels the soul to look upwards— ' "

" ' —and leads us from this world to another.' Plato," he shot back.

I heard a chair slide. He sat down at the kitchen table with his back to me and took a big bite out of the sandwich.

Thinking to trick him, I quoted, " 'The people have always some champion whom they set over them and nurse into greatness. This and no other is the root from which a tyrant springs; when he first appears, he is a protector.' "

His Grace did not answer, and I thought for a moment that I had finally stumped him. But it quickly became apparent he was still chewing. Presently, he took a swallow from his glass and said, "That quote could well apply to our friend the sheriff." Then, taking another sip, he added, "If you're through with Plato . . ."

"Very well," said I, having struck upon a new idea. I decided to test his biblical knowledge. "Who were the Sadducees?" I confidently inquired.

"Ah, the Sadducees."

I perceived immediately that he not only knew about them but was about to impart a short history.

"They were a Jewish sect during the time of Christ. Smaller in number than the Pharisees, but politically influential. Very conservative in many ways, yet open to the teachings of other cultures. Another sect known as the Essenes—"

"Who was Amos?"

"The prophet Amos. He was a shepherd from the region of Tekoa, near Jerusalem. Raised sheep and tended sycamore trees, as I recall. He had three dreams that—"

What astounded me was not just that Lord Baltimore's answers were correct but that he seemed to know a wealth of information beyond what I was looking for.

"Where in the Bible does this come from? 'Glory be to Him who carried His servant by night from the sacred temple of Mecca to the temple of Jerusalem.' "

"I believe you now quote from the Koran."

Of course, he was right once again. I expressed surprise that his knowledge extended to religion.

"Tis nothing any Knight Templar would not know," he replied.

I would have thought nothing of his statement had it not been followed by utter silence. Tilly, too, was suddenly still. It was as though a forbidden topic had been broached. It was as if a dam valve had been opened and they were waiting to see if any water would spill through.

His Grace continued eating his sandwich while I accessed "Knight Templar." A list of links quickly appeared on the screen, one of which was "Knights of the Temple of Solomon." I clicked on it and received a database that I began to read aloud.

" 'Knights of the Temple of Solomon, also known as the Knights Templar. Founded in 1118 to recapture Jerusalem from the Saracens. The Knights Templar were hired by kings to protect pilgrims journeying to the Holy City. Though sworn to chastity and poverty, they accumulated vast wealth, and eventually the Order claimed supremacy over kings, making enemies of monarchs and the Church. In 1307, the Templars were tried for heresy, blasphemy, and unsanctioned behavior. They disbanded in 1314.' "

As His Grace and Tilly did not seem upset by this bit of news, I thought my judgment a minute prior had been in error. That is, until I saw another link, which I read to them.

"Aha! 'Modern Knights Templar Theory.' "

This brought about a coughing fit by His Grace, who had apparently been swallowing at that moment. He sputtered and spewed while Tilly whacked him mercilessly on the back. His coughing continued until she reached around his waist from behind and pulled hard on his diaphragm. Seeing that she had things well under control, I devoted those precious moments to reading more about the Knights Templar. Fortunately, Tilly had a high-speed modem and a good connection to the Web. The link came up quickly.

This new home page informed me that while the old Order of Knights Templar had been defunct for centuries, it was speculated that there still remained a small nucleus of men descended from the order whose mission it was to roam the earth and serve as guides for and protectors of their fellow men, just as their forerunners had protected pilgrims on their journey to the Holy Land. The knights still maintained a vow of poverty. Their main purpose was to act as mentors to those in need and to impart the wisdom of the ages to a chosen few, who would carry the tradition forward after them.

There were many other links, one of which I was on the verge of accessing when a hand reached over me and shut off the monitor.

"If you're done with this inquisition, we must be going," His Grace said. The expression on his face informed me that I was through with the PC for the evening.

"You boys wait while I make somethin fo yo shaky friend," said Tilly.

I watched as the root doctor plied her trade. She laid a piece of blue flannel on the counter and placed on it a root, a handful of dirt from a tin marked "Preacher's Grave," crushed bone, and a lodestone. She then sprinkled various powders and oils onto the arrangement, all the while speaking in what His Grace told me was "the unknown tongue." She wound the cloth around the items and quickly sewed it all together so that it resembled a carrot with the root sticking out one end.

"Give this to that other boy," she said, handing it to me. "Tell him it's a root that will protek him from evil forces an will help in matters of love. Tell him Dr. Owl give it to you, an that he will now be safe from all harm."

I concluded that she was attempting to make amends for the scare she had given Brantley on our first meeting.

I was on the verge of broaching the subject of the alliance between Lord Baltimore and Tilly when Kenneth bounded up the back steps.

"Wipe yo feet," Tilly called out.

Kenneth was out of breath and laughing. "Whoo! Them two lawmen shootin up the swamp out there!"

His Grace absent-mindedly reached for a cigar but was cut short.

"Not in my house," Tilly said.

His Lordship refrained from his favorite habit or addiction—I wasn't sure which.

Kenneth informed us that between Tilly's fireworks—which he and JV had launched with slings into the treetops—and my escape, our guests had used up most of their precious ammunition. By Kenneth's estimation, a few more hours of harassment would cause them to expend the remainder.

"You're not using this boy," said Tilly in my defense. "An you're not using my animals."

"C'mon, Tilly," said Kenneth. "Jus the snake."

"Plenny other snakes in dis swamp," she snapped back.

She did relent, however, by allowing Kenneth to take apart a set of wind chimes made of dried sand dollars that had been dipped in glue and strung together with fishing line. These palm-sized discs made excellent projectiles, according to Kenneth.

"One a these whisk by yo head in the night, you tink it's a bat or a spirit," he said.

"Well," said His Grace, rising, "if you and JV have things in hand here, I'll get this young man back to the cabin. We've a big day ahead of us tomorrow."

As I rose to leave, I mentioned that my Saint Christopher was missing.

"We're jolly well not going back to search for it tonight," said Lord Baltimore.

Tilly offered Pegasus to carry us, but His Grace declined. "He's not partial to one of us," he said to Tilly. They looked at me.

"What? The horse? He adores me. How could he not? Saving me and all."

"Did Peg snort on you?" Kenneth wanted to know.

I admitted that he had. Though I had thought at the time it was a sign of affection, it was becoming evident that my interpretations of many things were incorrect.

In departing, I again thanked Tilly but held my tongue from asking the very thing I wanted to know—namely, why the charade of acrimony toward His Grace and Kenneth in broad daylight, when she was chums with them at night?

We were no farther than a few hundred yards from her house when I raised the question to Lord Baltimore. His Grace had already lit a stogie. My question broke whatever train of thought he was riding.

"It didn't occur to me that you'd find my footprint next to her donkey's hoofprints, much less put two and two together. You have a great gift, Ensworth, my boy. That gift is that people will tend to underestimate your abilities. You can achieve a great deal in this world on that knowledge alone. It can work against you, or you can make it work for you."

I pointed out that he might be underestimating me again if he thought that by skirting the subject and heaping praise on me, I would forget the question I had posed to him.

"I will gladly tell you what you wish to know if you'll answer me this," he said. "What have you learned today?"

He tossed the cigar band behind us onto the path, no doubt for the sheriff's benefit. His question required some thought. The morning seemed like it had happened a week previous. The afternoon was a vague memory as well. But at length, I pieced the parts of the day together sufficiently to get a clear picture of the whole.

"I suppose I've learned that you can't trust your fellow man."

His Grace walked in silence. I could tell that he wasn't pleased with my answer.

"And how did you come to such a conclusion?"

"Simple. Today, you and JV sent those deputies on a wild-goose chase. Then I overheard the sheriff's intention to do us in. Next, we lured him and his deputy into that swamp. Finally, I discovered that you and the resident witch doctor, seemingly enemies, are in fact the closest of allies. Everyone is out to get everyone else. What other conclusion could I draw?"

It was several minutes before he spoke. "You bother me," he said.

"Me?"

"Of course you. You don't see any other blighters out here, do you?"

"But how do I bother you?"

He stopped and held me by the shoulder so as to ensure that my attention would not wander. "In one day, life placed before you a series of lessons, each with its own important message, and the best you can do is come away with a single, pessimistic observation? That is not a pattern of thought that will serve you well over the years. It is certainly not a pattern that leads to happiness. I would suggest that if you wish to avoid becoming embittered by degrees, you should look for the positive lesson in all instances."

"For example?"

"For example, from what you've learned of Tilly and me, you might gather that apparent enemies often turn out to be allies behind closed doors. Remember that the next time you see two rival powers. Things are seldom what they seem. You might also consider that what JV and I did today was a necessary act to save several lives, including yours and my own."

"What about Sheriff Pooler and Deputy Ratchet?"

"That, my friend, is cut and dried. The lesson there is that sometimes you cannot trust your fellow man."

"But that's what I just said!"

"Shh! Do you want to wake the entire island?"

We came upon some oyster-strewn Indian mounds. At that point, the path veered toward the beach. The moonlight began to lose its glimmer as thin clouds passed overhead. I thought about His Grace's comment. Indeed, much of what I had witnessed in the past seven days was not what it seemed. Had I not seen it with my own eyes, I would not have guessed that Sheriff Pooler, while campaigning against crime and drugs, trafficked cocaine and engaged in other criminal activities. Likewise, I would not have guessed Susan's career had I met her under different circumstances. I would not have guessed that Kent and Kenneth were father and son. Indeed, Tilly and Lord Baltimore's alliance seemed merely one of countless intrigues I did not know about.

I pressed him for an explanation of his dealings with Dr. Owl.

"See here!" His Grace said impatiently. "Tilly's power over these islanders depends on their belief in her. In turn, it is she who heals their afflictions, provides spiritual advice, and often defends the island from interlopers who would buy the land and displace its inhabitants with shops and flats. If I can assist her cause with an occasional tidbit of information that makes her appear to be omniscient, then so be it. It is certainly not my intent to generate distrust or ill will among the islanders. The young are lured away to the mainland, where they flee given the first opportunity. That leaves the aging farmers and shrimpers. They have no voice, no leader, no authority save Tilly. That is why she and I pretend to be at odds. Now, you know." He paused to relight his cigar. "I trust you'll keep this between us."

Neither one of us spoke for a while. We left the maritime forest and crossed some low marsh, then entered a tunnel-like path that led through scrub forest. We soon spilled out onto tall sand dunes blanketed with sea oats. His Grace and I climbed to the crest of the highest dune and surveyed the beach. The tide was high, and the wind was strong at our backs. Waves kissed the foot of the dune we stood on. He gazed skyward and out to sea, then spoke: " 'The wind was a torrent of darkness among the gusty trees./ The moon was a ghostly galleon tossed upon cloudy seas.' "

He waited for my comment. I chose not to encourage him and said nothing. I was concerned with the storm that I knew was wreaking havoc not two hundred miles out in the Atlantic. Standing there on the beach, and not sitting in a comfortable home viewing a computer image of the hurricane on the Internet, I began to doubt the forecasters and to favor Tilly's prediction.

"I'm sorry I doubted Tilly's judgment," I said. "But I was surprised that you would take her side. I thought you didn't believe in voodoo."

"Oh, I don't believe in voodoo," he replied, still studying the horizon. "The thing of it is, some people have the gift of understanding nature's ways. Tilly is such a person."

"And you brought me here to show me that it's possible the hurricane might come our way?"

"No. The wind is blowing offshore, which is a promising sign. If it were in our faces right now, that would be a different matter altogether." He slowly spread his arm out, as if smoothing a rumpled blanket. "This is Megiddo Beach," he said, pointing to an area covered by seawater in front of us. "We will part ways here tomorrow morning." He shifted the cigar in his mouth and sighed heavily. "Do you believe me when I tell you that this is the very spot where Sheriff Pooler and I will have our final confrontation?"

"There, in the water?"

His Grace laughed. "No. That part of the beach will be quite dry by morning. The tide has already turned."

His Grace pulled out a pocketknife. He cut several stalks of sea oats and bunched them together in one hand. He then instructed me to walk along the top of the dune to our left and proceed in a northerly direction. Following me, he erased our tracks with the leafy end of the stalks for a distance of about fifty feet. I assumed he did this so our tracks would appear to end at the crest of the dune. We kept to the dunes for several hundred yards before coming across another trail, which we followed back into the woods. It wasn't long before we turned on to the main path that led back to the cabin.

I asked His Grace what else Tilly used the Internet for.

He lowered his voice. "She uses it for the same reason that oracles of ancient times used carrier pigeons to obtain news of battles long before word reached the rest of the population. It's all about knowledge and power. Knowledge is power."

"But what if a power line goes down?"

"She still has her cell phone and her agents," His Grace replied, meaning Kenneth and himself.

Weariness from the long day had reduced my ambitions to thoughts of a warm, dry place to lie down. But His Grace had several more instructions for me, on which he seemed to place a great deal of importance.

"You must leave here tomorrow on Kenneth's boat," he informed me. "I want you to remain with Brantley on the mainland until I find you. Is that clear?"

"Sure, but why should I stay with him? I have to go to Savannah."

"Master Brantley, as do many young men, has a proclivity for attaching himself to mischief makers. He fears taking the trail into Devil Swamp, yet he thinks nothing of following ruffians down more treacherous paths that will put him either in jail or into an early grave. He will soon find himself in the company of those who not only keep themselves down, but who keep their companions from advancing by accusing them of being swell-headed or by challenging their manhood. Indeed, they seek to enslave those around them to their own lowly standards. There's a great deal of good in Brantley that has yet to manifest itself. There are those who depend on him or who will depend on him, and I want you to be there to keep him out of harm's way. Are you up to it?"

At that moment, I had no inclination to keep company with Brantley but every desire to complete the journey my father had assigned me. That way, I could return to a life of leisure far from escaped convicts, cocaine-addicted sheriffs, hurricane-battling witch doctors, and chain-cigar-smoking Englishmen. But as I was tired and wanted no more conversation, I found myself voicing agreement.

"I believe you will be a good influence on him. Do I have your word on it?"

"You have my word."

The words no sooner left my mouth than I realized I was honor-bound to uphold them. Why I was honor-bound escaped me, but at that precise moment, my word and my family name were the most prized possessions—indeed, the only real possessions—that I had. But I felt sure the morning would bring a perspective more favorable to me—one that would allow me to rationalize why the promise I had just given could be broken.

Before I could dwell further on this matter, we entered the clearing of Liverpool's cabin. We went inside and found the place unoccupied. Naturally, my first thought was that Brantley, spooked by the sheriff's arrival, had fled for safety, and that the problem of keeping him out of trouble had thus solved itself. But that problem quickly resurfaced when Brantley entered the cabin door looking tired but happy.

"Been over to see the kid," he explained.

"At this hour?" said His Grace. "He should be asleep."

"He's been sleeping. I just watched him," he said with a heavy sigh. "I want him."

"What you want is a good night's sleep. We've plenty ahead of us tomorrow, and the last thing you should be thinking about—you, a fugitive from the law with a hurricane bearing down on you—is the burden of adopting a boy abandoned by Gypsies. Now, if you two would be so kind as to cease talking and go to bed . . ."

It wasn't long before I was buffeted between the gale-like snores of His Grace and the high-wind wheezes of Brantley. It was no wonder that I dreamed of hurricanes and tornadoes that night. The last dream I remember was that of Liverpool walking along the beach with Bucephalus close behind. A hurricane was approaching the island, and he tried in vain to light his pipe in the high wind. At last, giving up, he looked at me, smiled, winked, and said, "*Pax vobiscum.*" Though I didn't know what he meant, a peaceful calm came over me, and I understood that all would turn out right. In my dream, I turned to leave and then looked back. Liverpool and the ox were gone.

CHAPTER 18

His Grace and the high sheriff duel.

The next morning came far too quickly. I awoke with a start and lumbered outside to check on the weather. Except for a few clouds and a steady breeze off the ocean, it seemed a pleasant day. The only sounds I could hear were an occasional gull's cry and Brantley's snores from inside the cabin. The morning's silence seemed strange and unsettling, though I couldn't put my finger on why.

Someone's whistling roused me from my stupor, and I turned to see His Grace emerging from the footpath.

"Time to move on," he said, marching into the cabin. "Get your things together."

He soon had Brantley up and moving. Before five minutes had passed, we were assembled outside the cabin with most of our possessions. That is to say, I had my backpack, Brantley had a discarded flour sack half filled with his meager belongings, and His Grace wore his coat. Cigars protruded from his vest pocket, as usual.

While fumbling through my pockets, I came upon the root Tilly had prepared for Brantley. "I almost forgot! Dr. Owl, a root doctor, told me to give this to you." Brantley's eyes opened wide. "It will protect you from evil forces and aid you in matters of love. Dr. Owl said you will be safe from all harm as long as you are in possession of this root."

"Aw, man, I can use this!" Brantley said, as though he were a flightless bird that had just stumbled upon a pair of wings.

"You'll need a great deal more than that amulet," said His Grace. "The situation is this, lads. We have a full-blown typhoon bearing down on the island and a distraught and intractable sheriff hunting us. However, a boat waits on the dock, ready to take us away from here. Now, who is for leaving, and who is for confronting the storm and the sheriff?"

It was a rhetorical question. The prudent choice would be to get ourselves down to the dock, but I knew that His Grace had other plans for me. He instructed Brantley to stop by Kenneth's house, collect Jenny and the child, and wait for us at the boat. I feared my task would be to follow him and confront our adversaries. That fear was not unfounded.

We made our way toward the beach. Just as His Lordship had predicted, the tide was out and a wide strand lay before us. The other major difference from the previous night was the strong breeze that blew grains of sand, stinging my legs. The wind now came off the ocean toward the shore, pushing before it an armada of dark, gray clouds. It seemed that fish and fowl alike had vacated the area.

We were near our destination when we saw a cluster of people gathered on a tall dune to our right. In front of this group, standing statue-like at the pinnacle of the dune, was a formidable figure wearing purple-lensed sunglasses. Even though her eyes were covered, I could tell from the slight tilt of her head that she was staring at me. Brilliantly colored raiment fluttered in the stiff breeze behind her. As we marched past the dune, she stretched out her hands toward the sea and began to speak loudly in the unknown tongue.

"Is she addressing us?" I whispered.

"Hardly. Tilly's using her powers to turn back the storm, or at least to deflect it from Zapala's shore."

I looked back every so often in an attempt to catch her eye. I suddenly felt in need of confidence.

"You wouldn't have any kumquats left from last night, would you?" I asked.

"Of course not. Why on earth would I have kumquats?"

"You know."

"If I knew, I wouldn't ask you."

"Courage. Nerve. Remember? Medicinal powers?"

"Ha! Do you really think I was serious about that?"

"You mean . . ."

"Yes, I'm afraid I do mean. Courage comes from within, not from kumquats. You can attribute your valiant actions last night to yourself. Have you already forgotten the lessons of the Waving Man?"

The vast fortune to be made from extract of kumquat evaporated before my eyes. At the same time, I was pleased to know I was capable of heroics—if standing on an island about to be devoured by a scaly brute can be called that. And I was equally pleased to know that for the rest of my life, I would not be dependent on a small, bitter fruit for bravery.

"Position yourself just there," said Lord Baltimore when we reached the exact portion of beach we had visited not eight hours earlier. He pointed at the base of a dune that the tides had shorn into a fourteen-foot vertical cliff. "I will return shortly. I must give the sheriff fresh tracks to follow."

I stood under the dune, close to where the footpath emptied on to the beach. His Grace climbed the face of another dune well away from the path and disappeared over the top. As I waited, I surveyed the strip of sand named Megiddo Beach. It was no more than a half-moon stretch of seashore secluded from the rest of Zapala's shoreline. I imagined Blackbeard landing in a longboat at this very site with a dozen of his most trusted pirates. His ship would have been anchored beyond the wind-driven whitecaps that pummeled the sand bar paralleling the shore. I was musing over this when I became aware of a figure standing above me. What with his long beard, his billowing cigar, and his hair flowing wildly in the breeze, His Grace looked more than a little like the ghost of Blackbeard.

He looked over his shoulder for a good while. At length, something caught his attention. He threw his cigar butt behind him, turned, and hustled down to the beach.

"I'm expecting a certain visitor to arrive shortly," he said. "Crouch here at the base of the cliff. Remain perfectly still, and he shan't see you."

Positioning himself fifty feet away by the water's edge, he removed his coat, laid it over his left arm, and turned to face the ocean. He had no sooner done this than I heard from above me a loud voice.

"Don't move a muscle!"

A moment later, Sheriff Pooler, disheveled and sweating profusely, eased his way down the steep slope of the dune and spilled on to the beach toward His Lordship.

> *Juba wear badge an Juba wear gun*
> *Juba alone come de risin sun*
> *Say Juba, huh Juba*

His beard stubble appeared to have been several days in the making. He looked relieved to have found someone—anyone—at the end of his journey. His Grace pivoted and came face to face with his adversary. Since the wind was blowing in my direction, I could hear every word.

"I said don't move," repeated the lawman, out of breath.

No doubt, the sheriff had once been in good physical condition and could have found his way around in the woods. But what stood before us was a man softened by too many years of sitting at a desk and ordering others to their labor. His clothes revealed scratch marks front and back, as if he had crawled through a forest of briars. He wiped his brow.

"Fruitcake," he said, half threatening, half gloating, "I'm a reasonable man. You took something from me that don't belong to you, and I want it back."

Lord Baltimore didn't stir. He simply stared at the sheriff.

Sheriff Pooler took his gun from its holster and aimed it at His Lordship. "I mean it. I'm gonna do you rhat hyar if you don't tell me where you hid the dough."

"Hid?" asked His Grace. He pulled a small bundle of cash from his hip pocket and threw it over his head. The wind seized the bills and scattered them across and over the dunes.

Sheriff Pooler started toward the money but instantly realized the futility of chasing it. His mouth dropped open in disbelief. "You *are* crazy!"

"Was it not ill-gotten gain you exchanged for cocaine? The cocaine you seized but failed to report? It has been a burden to your conscience. I have freed you of that encumbrance."

"Well, well," said the sheriff, rubbing his chin. "Maybe you ain't as dumb as you make out. Maybe you're a fed."

"Your drug running is no secret. Nor is the fact that you and your cronies are building an empire. Between city hall and the developers, you've been fooling the citizens into thinking you're on their side. In fact, you're responsible for the drug market here and the crime it produces. Meanwhile, the money you make from it funds your political aspirations. But as long as you deliver the votes for statewide elections, no one at the capitol is going to bother you. Then, with your cabal entrenched, the developers can do as they please with the land. Very soon, they will encroach on Zapala."

"Yeah," nodded the sheriff, "that's pretty much the plan."

Lord Baltimore slowly shook his head. "No, sir," he said. "That *was* the plan. It ended the moment you set foot on my island."

A stony silence ensued. The two stared each other down. A dozen pelicans glided by, inches from the surface of the water. I envied them, knowing they'd be sailing past my home on St. Simons in less than an hour.

Then the sheriff said with a smile, "I've been on your trail since you left Twin Oaks Apartments—whose proprietor, by the way, is laid up in a hospital down in Brunswick."

Lord Baltimore made no sign.

"Yeah," continued the sheriff, "I know all about him letting you escape. We caught Bertie McGrady at the county line. Seemed to be in a hurry."

"And Mr. McGrady was no doubt more than willing to provide the information you desired, in exchange for his release."

"I can't have informants turning on me. I suspected you'd get back on the Dixie Highway and possibly head for the island. You left a trail of money and cigar stubs a mile wide over here. Like some dang Robin Hood, stealing from the sheriff and giving to the poor. I bet half these Gullahs got my money. I cain't have that. That money'll fund my campaign and a few others besides. Cain't have someone pulling a stunt like this and getting off clean. Some of my deputies are laughing behind my back. You leave me no choice."

"No choice?" asked Lord Baltimore.

The sheriff looked down and smoothed the sand in front of him with his right foot, apparently in thought. "You're right. I don't have to kill you," he said, still smiling. "You tell me where the rest of my money is and maybe I just take you in and you do a little time. Don't that sound like a better deal?"

"Sheriff, did it not occur to you at some point that this was all too easy?"

The corners of the sheriff's mouth dropped. "What was too easy?"

"You suspected I took your money, because wherever I went, people came into large sums of cash. Certain ladies of the Cherokee Grove Motel suddenly had enough to move away and begin a new life free of your prostitution racket. Then that old rascal Kent walked into your brother's dealership and purchased a red sports car. You made haste to Kent's house, where you learned that his improbable windfall came from my purchasing, in cash, the patent rights to his equally improbable ghost-glasses scam. That little sting was tailor-made for your ego—an ego sufficiently large to let you believe only a fool such as I would make an irrational investment such as that. Kent informed you that his son, Kenneth, had transported me and my young companion, standing over there, to Zapala."

The sheriff turned. After a moment, his eyes fell upon me. I felt my legs begin to liquefy, for I saw in the sheriff's eyes a malevolence that put a deep-seated fear in me.

"That, sir," continued Lord Baltimore, "was done to lure you here, away from your dominion to mine. You easily followed my wanderings by finding cigar stubs and bands haphazardly tossed along the island trails. Actually, they were strategically placed to draw you into my trap. To be more exact, to the very spot where you now stand."

The sheriff was momentarily stunned. But he soon regained his senses and shook his head as if recovering from a blow to the chin. "You mean to tell me," he said with a chuckle, "that you, the biggest durn fool that ever rambled through this county, lured me here?" He thumped himself on the chest as if to confirm who *me* referred to. "Me? The best tracker in these parts?"

"Fourth best, behind Liverpool, JV, and myself."

The sheriff did not respond. He looked hard at Lord Baltimore. They were soon engaged in a stare down. It was the sheriff who finally blinked.

"Aw, enough of this," he said, pointing his revolver at Lord Baltimore's head. He pulled the trigger.

But there was no blinding flash or deafening sound. He pulled the trigger again, then again and again until he had tried all the chambers.

His Grace did not blink. He removed the coat from his left arm to reveal a gun of his own pointed directly at the sheriff. It was the very weapon I had seen him toss into the woods in his effort to thwart Jeremy's suicide. It was now clear that His Lordship had indeed found the weapon, only he hadn't bothered to tell us. He reached into his pants pocket and pulled out a handful of bullets.

"You bluff," said His Grace. "I believe these belong to you."

They were part of what JV had taken from the camp the previous evening. Sheriff Pooler looked at the bullets in disbelief. Lord Baltimore put them back into his pocket, then seized the sheriff's firearm. I could see Sheriff Pooler's neck reddening. I fully expected steam to issue from his ears. Instead, he let loose a barrage of expletives of such force that he had to spit out his wad of tobacco to make way for them. Even then, he couldn't get the words out fast enough, and what came to my ear were hybrid curses such as "tack-schmuther-bun-ova-sitch." His threats upon His Lordship's life were equally distorted.

After exhausting his stockpile of verbal grenades, the sheriff settled down and tried another tactic. "You ain't gonna shoot me," he said, pulling a small, round can of tobacco from his shirt pocket. He shook the tin and realized it was empty, which agitated him even more. Cursing anew, he flung the can into the air. As the wind caught it and the tiny vessel curved in a graceful arc toward the dunes, His Grace aimed, squeezed the trigger, and expertly cleft it in half just above my head.

The sheriff wiped his brow again, staring at the can's remains by my feet. Then he looked at Lord Baltimore with grudging admiration. "That's some fancy shootin', but I still say you ain't fool enough to kill a man in cold blood."

"Of course not," said His Grace. "We'll settle once and for all with a good, old-fashioned duel."

This knocked the wind out of Sheriff Pooler. I could have sworn I heard Brantley say, "That dude *is* crazy!" But I quickly realized it was my own thought.

"I would have preferred to do this beneath the pines," His Grace explained. "However, Liverpool was insistent that we not stain Zapala with an outsider's blood. Here, by the shore, where the tide cleanses the beach twice a day—this is the best place for our confrontation."

Given the approaching storm and the prospect of a gunfight, I felt the only thing missing was the angel of death himself. Almost on cue, Lord Baltimore pointed toward the top of the dune above me. The sheriff and I looked up to see JV standing on the crest. Beside him were the two dogs the Ratchet had brought to track us. The angel of death had arrived, accompanied by the hounds of hell.

"Good Gawd," the sheriff mumbled. It would not register in his mind that what he saw was real. "Blue!" he barked. "Shoat Thang!"

Neither dog stirred. They looked up at JV, who stood silent and motionless. In JV's eyes, there was no emotion, no judgment.

"Blue, Shoat Thang! Come hyar!" shouted the sheriff.

"Sheriff, please," said Lord Baltimore.

"You are way outta line hyar!" bellowed the sheriff at JV and me. "Both of you are way outta line!"

"Your men are indisposed," said His Lordship. "Your dogs, as you can see, are also indisposed. I have your ammunition. And you've been without cocaine since yesterday afternoon."

The sheriff stared dumbly at Lord Baltimore, slowly beginning to realize his predicament.

His Grace pulled from his pocket a yellow, crumpled piece of paper—the very same piece I had last seen at the Cherokee Grove Motel. He held it up for Sheriff Pooler. "Do you remember this?" The sheriff squinted to read what was on the paper as it fluttered in the wind. "It says 'Megiddo Beach,' if you recall. You now stand on Megiddo Beach."

The officer seemed stunned.

But His Grace wasn't through dispensing revelations. "Your career as a lawman is ended," he informed the sheriff. "I wouldn't be at all surprised to see the state police at the dock back on the mainland, waiting to take you into custody."

The sheriff attempted a smile. "Now, you're bluffing."

"Am I?" Lord Baltimore calmly reached into his pants pocket and pulled out a small stack of photographs bundled together with a rubber band. "These might be of interest to you," he said, tossing them on the ground at the sheriff's feet. "They're snapshots of a certain drug deal that occurred in the woods the day of your political rally, not long before Captain Sandy met his unfortunate end. I think the shot of you and him together came out pretty well, considering the lighting. I didn't get the deputy's best side, but he's readily identifiable, just the same."

The sheriff picked up the packet and inspected the photographs one by one, slowly at first but with increasing rapidity as he progressed, as though viewing a nightmare he wished to end quickly.

"Both the GBI and the FBI have a set of those pictures," said His Grace. "What's more, the Georgia Bureau of Investigation has a bundle of cash with your fingerprints on it. The very same bundle you're holding in the third photograph."

This bit of news left me doubly curious as to how Lord Baltimore always seemed to possess an obscenely large bundle of money.

The sheriff's fist clamped around the photos. He let them drop onto the sand. Then he turned toward JV and me. What I saw startled me. His face was ashen. His mouth hung open, and he appeared to be in a state of shock. He looked like he had gazed upon the face of the devil himself.

"The GBI has already taken Tim's deposition at the trading post. Since Willie wasn't at Twin Oaks Apartments, the FBI travelled to his hospital bed to get his statement," continued His Grace. "And I have it on good authority that your friend the would-be state senator is already distancing himself from you." He paused a moment, then added, "The wicked are destroyed suddenly and without remedy."

Juba go down to Megiddo Beach
Juba he learn what de Goot Book teach
Say Juba, huh Juba

"This man," shouted Sheriff Pooler in a hoarse voice, pointing at His Grace, "is wanted for questioning! He is aiding and abetting a fugitive of the law. You," he continued, pointing at JV and me, "are in violation of state and federal law."

The sheriff's attempt to exert his authority was quickly squelched by His Grace. "Sir, you cannot break the law for personal gain and try to enforce it when it suits your needs. You long ago undermined your own authority."

I don't know why I felt pity for the sheriff. Much as I despised him, I could not help seeing his life as a tragedy. He was a modern-day Macbeth, misdirected by greed and ambition, an Achilles brought down not by an arrow but an opiate. I could see the final curtain on the horizon as the leading edge of a squall line came into view. The tempest had arrived.

The sheriff, collecting himself, raised his hands, conceding His Lordship's wishes. "Fine," he said. "You want a duel? Fine with me."

JV said nothing. I was too shaken to move or speak.

"Sheriff, would you care for a smoke?" His Grace asked, as

cordially as if they were old friends.

The sheriff declined.

"Then you won't mind if I do."

"Damn you!" shouted Sheriff Pooler. "Whoever you are!"

Lord Baltimore loaded the sheriff's gun and tossed it to him. "I am Lord Baltimore," he replied, extracting a fresh cigar from his vest pocket. "Duke of Zapala."

The sheriff stepped back several paces and checked his weapon to ensure it was in working order. He looked up and studied the sky over the island, then turned and pointed his pistol at Lord Baltimore. "Shoot!" he commanded.

"Not until I have my smoke."

"Damn you to hell!" cried the sheriff, firing one round after another at His Grace's feet.

The second most memorable image I will take to my grave is that of Lord Baltimore stubbornly attempting to light a cigar in the stiff breeze, totally oblivious to the imminent gale behind him and slightly irritated by the bullets ripping through the sand at his feet.

At last, he lit the thing and returned his attention to the duel. "You have one round left," he remarked. "I would use it wisely." With that, he discharged round after round from his own gun into the sand. "Now, we're all square again. Sir, what would you have me do?"

Sheriff Pooler stared at His Grace. Then he whirled and pointed his gun at me. "I'll shoot the boy!"

His Grace didn't miss a beat. "Fine," he replied. "Then I'll shoot you, and there'll be two less witnesses to worry about."

Thank you, Lord Baltimore, for your concern over my safety, I thought. The sheriff wavered, then decided that card wasn't worth playing.

"See here," His Grace said. "You know what I say is true. You'll never even see the election. And you've nowhere to run. You're not going out there," he said, pointing toward the storm. "You'll be easily hunted down on Zapala."

The sheriff must have understood the truth of His Grace's words, for his shoulders visibly slumped. "No," he said, shaking his head. "No one takes me. Not you. Not the feds. Not no one. I run this here county, and I leave office when I say." He bowed his head briefly, then straightened and stared right at me. "Boy, tell 'em I went out on my own terms."

What happened next remains the single most vivid image in my memory. It is one I would gladly remove, if it were possible. The sheriff steadied the gun at his side and turned to face Lord Baltimore. His Grace braced himself against the wind and awaited Sheriff Pooler's move. Neither man flinched for at least a minute. Then the sheriff began to lift his gun in slow motion. His Grace's eyes widened as Sheriff Pooler continued to raise the gun. When I realized what he intended, I called out a warning. Whether he heard it or not, I will never know. The sound of the gunshot hit me like a blast of compressed air. Everything stopped for one horrific moment. The wind ceased to howl. The hurricane ceased its advance. Nothing moved until Sheriff Pooler's body fell to the ground.

When time did resume, it seemed that everything was louder and moved faster. The wind, silent a moment before, blew at a deafening pitch. Lord Baltimore was at the sheriff's side before I regained the use of my legs. When I saw the wound that was once the sheriff's left temple, I fell to my knees and regurgitated. One of the dogs whined and whimpered. The other let loose an ear-splitting wail. Soon, both were baying. His Grace sighed deeply and said nothing. He shook his head.

When I was back on my feet, Lord Baltimore nodded at JV.

"Get to the dock," JV instructed me. "Kenneth's waiting on you there."

"I'm not going without him," I firmly replied, much to my own surprise.

JV looked down at me. Then he pointed toward the horizon. "See that? It'll be here real soon. Don't worry about Lord Baltimore. Now, get going."

"I have to know," I said to His Grace. "Would you really have shot him? Would you have let him shoot me?"

His Grace fired the remaining round at the storm and tossed the gun into the sea. "We'll never know," he replied.

I looked back for JV, but he and the dogs were nowhere to be seen.

"I'll tend to the body," His Grace said. "You must leave now."

This time, I conceded.

I climbed the dune and headed down the path to the woods. I broke into a dead run for the north end of Zapala. On the way, I regurgitated again, sickened by what I had seen, for abandoning His Grace, and for not intervening in some fashion.

It was in this state that I came upon the lumbering backside of Bucephalus blocking the entire path. I squeezed by the ox where the trail widened and found Liverpool moving as if on a Sunday-afternoon stroll.

"Gen'l'man," he said as though I'd been there all along. "Stoam bring big water."

I replied that I was aware of the storm and that His Lordship and Sheriff Pooler were still at Megiddo Beach.

"*Comme il faut*," he replied. "Dat mean, 'As it should be.' "

"The sheriff's dead!" I cried. "We're all in trouble. I mean *big* trouble!"

Liverpool came to a halt. He looked me up and down as if searching for evidence of a fever. "He sho dead?" he asked.

"I saw the whole thing!"

Liverpool shook his head and let out a long whistle. Then he made a clicking sound. "Gawd wa bored wif him," he said. "Nah, go on. Get on out yuh. An doan tell no one."

"Surely, you're coming with us. I mean, you're coming to the mainland with Kenneth and Jenny, aren't you?"

The ancient one spit on the ground at the side of the path. "I came in dis yah worl on a hur'cane, an I go out on a hur'cane. It de Lawd's will. His will be done. Cain't change dat. Ah been on top a Zapala, now Zapala on top a me. It de natural way. Zapala all de time be on top in de end."

These words did nothing to assuage my confused state of mind or allay my fears that His Grace, JV, and Liverpool were doomed if they did not leave the island immediately.

"But ah almos foget," he continued. "I hab a gif fuh you. Come yuh."

I stepped closer. He lifted the Saint Christopher from his neck and placed it around mine.

"Dis yuh were belong to Fadda. De ol man Couper gib it to him fuh goin to Shiloh wif de young marse. De young Couper, he kilt in de battle. Fadda go on de battlefield an fine him. Yankee shooter fire on Fadda an hit him in de ches. Fadda get back to safe place an tek off he coat. De Sain Chrisfer done stop de minie ball. See dere?"

I took the Saint Christopher in my hand and looked at it. In the center was a small, concave depression. I could feel the half bubble on the other side where the Union soldier's bullet had pushed the metal outward.

"De Sain Chrisfer alluz protek de trav'ler," he said, tapping it with a forefinger. "Yuh weah dis an never tek it off."

"This was your father's?"

He nodded. "Fadda bring young mista Couper all de way back tuh Zapala. De ol man give Fadda plenny land. De gov'ment tek it away attuh de war an split it up fo freedmans. Den de gov'ment tek dat away an give it back to Couper fambly, an Mista Couper, he gone by den. But de gov'ment don't tek de Sain Chrisfer. He protek me trav'lin tru life. He goin protek yuh on yo travel. Tek him. Tek him an go."

In vain, I attempted to return the medal, which was possibly Liverpool's only material possession. And I made another attempt to persuade him to come with me, offering to carry him if necessary. So earnest were my pleas that he uttered something that sounded like "*Contego,*" which caused Bucephalus to assume an aggressive stance and make threatening sounds. I realized that Liverpool was staying on the island come hell or high water—two very likely occurrences. I had no choice but to graciously accept the gift and leave.

I had gone about five steps when Liverpool called my name. I turned.

He winked at me. "*Pax vobiscum,*" he said.

I waved and turned to go on. It was a few seconds later that I realized those were the very words he had spoken in the dream I had. I wheeled to ask him what they meant. Just as I had dreamed, he and his ox were nowhere to be seen.

I pressed on to Folktown at a steady trot. On the outskirts of town, a solitary figure came running toward me. It was Brantley.

"Man, c'mon! Boat's a-leavin'. Let's get offa this island quick."

We dashed the final leg through town and headed straight for the dock. We were within sight of the boats when I saw in a side alley JV and two blindfolded deputies—the Ratchet and the Hyena—with their hands tied behind them. JV motioned us to remain silent and move along quickly.

We reached the dock out of breath. Only two boats remained. The *Mattie III* was loaded with passengers. I panicked at first because I recognized no one. Then I saw Jenny and the child. Another boat, the *Hannah*, was tied up nearby, its motor idling. I assumed it was the boat that JV, His Grace, and the others would take.

Kenneth hit the throttle the second we tumbled on to the *Mattie*, and we were off for the mainland.

Thus ended my stay in Camelot.

CHAPTER 19

We ride out the hurricane.

"Sheriff's boys spent last night on the bluff," Kenneth informed me when I entered the pilothouse. "They'll come over on the *Hannah* soon as I let you off on the mainland."

As he steered us into the sound, I asked how the sheriff and the Ratchet had depleted their ammunition.

He explained how he and JV got them to fire at various noises in the night. JV had then lured the deputy away from where I had last seen him.

"JV, he get de dogs to barkin, an ol deputy come a-runnin. He tink dey got loose an got someone treed. All de time, de sheriff callin, 'It a trap, it a trap! Come back, durn fool!' But de deputy doan pay no mind an run fo de dogs."

"I don't understand. Why didn't the dogs attack JV?"

"JV a man that . . . He got power over creatures. He learn from de Montagnard over there in Vietnam an de Cherokee. Make a deer eat out his hand. Make a wild dog fetch a stick. Ol hound dogs recognize they real master when he show up. He what you call a kindred spirit with dem."

The sky darkened as we made our way among the whitecaps in the wide channel.

"Where Tilly is?" he asked.

"Last I saw, she was on a sand dune dueling with the storm."

"You tink she out dere using the unknown tongue an plantin root to turn back dat hur'cane?"

"It sure looked like it to me."

"I tell you, she prayin up a storm to God Hisself, jus like any other Christian," said Kenneth. "She put on a good show with de root, but I know who she turn to when tings gets rough. She turn to God in a heartbeat, an don't you doubt it."

By the time we reached the mainland dock, a light rain had begun.

"I'll let y'all off here," Kenneth said. "You go with Jenny an Papa to Milledgeville. We got some folk up dere out in de country."

"I'm supposed to watch out for Brantley."

"Who told you that?"

"Lord Baltimore. I'm supposed to keep Brantley out of trouble."

Kenneth laughed. "You done a good job keepin him an you outta trouble on Zapala. I tink Lawd Balt'mo want to fine you an know he can trace Brantley quicker, cause all he have to do is fine trouble. Brantley just a beacon fo to fine you. He like a lighthouse. Lawd Balt'mo like a ship. He fine Brantley, he fine you."

"What if Brantley doesn't want to go to Milledgeville?"

"Guess you better do what de bossman say. Stick to de boy."

Judging by the sky, I guessed that the bossman was squarely in harm's way back on the island. As I climbed the wooden steps leading up to the bluff, I looked back at Zapala and could not help noticing how small and flat it appeared.

Brantley and I followed Jenny into the parking lot. She held the tightly wrapped child securely in her arms. I turned to wait for Kenneth, only to see him pull away from the dock and head back out the way we had come.

"Now where's he going?" Brantley demanded to know.

"He's taking the *Mattie* down the coast," Jenny said. "He lost the first one tying it up to a dock during a storm. It's safer out there."

"What happened to the second *Mattie*?" I asked.

"Caught fire out to sea. Papa spent two days in the water that time. Come on!" she beseeched. "Ain't much time."

As she said these words, a shiny red sports car flew into our path and stopped inches away. At the wheel was the man who had sold me the ghost sunglasses. It was Kenneth's father, Kent.

"Great," Brantley said. "The four of us and a red-headed baby in a red sports car. Do you think we'll get pulled over?"

Jenny looked him up and down. "Honey, you want to wait around for a better ride?"

"Get yo'selves in yuh!" Kent hollered through the open window.

Brantley and I piled into the backseat. Jenny took the front passenger seat. As we exited the parking lot, a state patrol car pulled in, just as Lord Baltimore had predicted. I assumed the men inside it were looking for the sheriff and his deputies.

The next hour was sheer terror, as Kent had not yet mastered the concept of power steering and power brakes. It was as though a novice rider had been given the reigns of a thoroughbred after years of riding a mule. However, we soon outran the rain on the westbound blacktop that took us inland.

Kent turned on the car radio but could only tune in weather reports. "We know de wedda!" he shouted at the dashboard. "It rainin."

At length, he found a station actually playing music—or at least a facsimile. It blasted forth from the speakers.

Coppa on muh ta-yell (boom, boom)
I'm a go tah ja-yell (boom, boom)
Coppa in muh mir-ruh (boom, boom)
Coppa gettin near-ruh (boom, boom)

The verse was repeated numerous times before Jenny complained it was disturbing the boy. She reached over and switched off the radio. The lyrics must have disturbed Brantley, too, for he turned frequently thereafter to see if there was indeed a coppa on our ta-yell.

Kent had the annoying habit of pulling to the side of the road every so often to "check de vitals," as he put it. Apparently, his last vehicle had required constant monitoring of engine fluids in order to reach its destination. At each stop, he announced to us from beneath the raised hood, "Oil okay! Tran'mission okay! Coolan okay!" Then he slammed the hood, jumped in, and burned rubber. Brantley attempted to convince him that the constant checks were unnecessary, going so far as to explain the advances engineers had brought to the modern automobile. But it was no use. Kent had spent a lifetime coaxing third- and fourth-hand vehicles to move and raiding them for parts when they refused. His experience had left an indelible imprint on him.

After a while, his occasional meanderings off the shoulder of the road became routine enough that I settled down. Most of the coast had already been evacuated, so the back highway we traveled was open.

We had been moving along at a good clip for a half-hour or so when we crossed a long bridge and came upon an overturned truck in the middle of the road. Its contents had spilled out, and numerous flattened items remained on the asphalt. The trailer was completely empty of cargo, and not a soul was in sight.

"She stripped," Kent remarked as he slowly made his way around the hulk. "Don't wreck round yuh. Dem folks tek everthin. Cain't trus no one."

I found that comment rather interesting, since he was the man who had taken my last dollar in exchange for a pair of ordinary sunglasses.

Since he had slowed down for the wreck, Kent took the opportunity to stop the car to check its health. And that was when an odd thing occurred.

Brantley, who was sitting behind Jenny and the boy, got out of the car. I thought he was going to offer Kent some friendly auto advice. Instead, he grabbed the child from Jenny's arms and ran away before she could react. By the time she had her seatbelt off and was standing in the road, Brantley had made good his escape into the underbrush.

"Let him go!" shouted Kent. "Dat white-folk bidness. Don't angry up the blood over sech foolishness."

Though she was nonplused at Brantley's actions, Jenny was not as upset over the loss as I might have supposed. I apologized profusely for Brantley and told Kent that I was under Lord Baltimore's instructions to stay with the kidnapper.

"Oil okay!" he hollered.

Jenny gave me quick instructions on how to care for the baby and how to contact them in Baldwin County.

"Tran'mission okay!" Kent yelled.

I told her I would do my best to retrieve the boy.

"Coolan okay!" shouted Kent. He slammed the hood and called out to me, "Ef Lawd Balt'mo say foller dat boy, yuh foller!" He got back into the car. "An don't buy no mo fake sun shades," he said, laughing. Then he laid rubber at my feet.

After they passed out of sight, the realization descended upon me that I was once again alone on a deserted highway, only this time with a hurricane close on my heels. My first order of business was to track down Brantley. I plunged into the woods at the spot where he had disappeared and began calling his name.

"I'm right here," he said angrily from the bushes behind me.

"You're gonna attract someone."

The boy seemed none the worse for the sudden snatch and mad dash for the bushes. He appeared interested in the tree limbs, which were blowing ever more violently in the stiffening breeze.

"They left us here, you know," I said.

"Suits me fine."

"That was pretty rude of you."

"I got as much right to him as she does."

I failed to see the logic in that statement, since it was not he who found the child and took him in. And it was not Jenny who robbed a store, got caught, was sentenced, escaped, and became a fugitive. Nor was it Jenny who had the lack of sense to be standing unsheltered in the middle of unknown woods with the wind howling and the smell of rain in the air. All in all, I would have preferred to be in the sports car rather than with Brantley. But as time was of the essence and finger pointing would serve little good, I determined to seek cover.

"Well, what's your plan now? You're still wanted by the law, and now you've got a baby to care for."

"We'll set up camp here," Brantley said.

"You sure?"

"Positive."

I thought the plan lacking in merit. "We passed a bridge back there," I said. "I saw some houseboats. If we're lucky—"

"Let's go, dude! Storm's a-comin'!"

In fact, the first wave of rain enveloped us before we made it back to the highway. We endured endless windblown sheets of water before stumbling upon the bridge. I knew we had reached it because I walked, head down, smack into a road sign. The horizontal, driving rain stung my eyes when I looked up and read the name: Altamaha River. Brantley had the sense to walk backwards, thus protecting the boy from the rain. Even so, I knew the worst of the storm was by no means upon us. A brief encounter with hail prodded us beneath the bridge span, where we found some protection. The sound of the deluge on the road above us made conversation almost impossible.

"We can stay here!" Brantley yelled.

I glanced where the bridge's foundation met the road. Some homeless travelers already occupying that space eyed us in a way that was unsettling. Brantley saw them, too, and quickly changed his mind.

"Where'd you see -ouse-oats?" he asked.

"*What?*"

"*Where'd you see the houseboats?*" he shouted into my ear.

I pointed to the north side of the river. Though I knew they were not far off, I could see nothing but a wall of water.

He nodded in that direction. "Come on!"

We negotiated a treacherously wet and narrow trail that paralleled the river. The rain momentarily slackened enough for us to spy a dock where three houseboats were moored. They were nestled in a small harbor sheltered by a tree-covered finger of land jutting into the river. Narrow plank walkways led out to them.

The first was an A-frame structure with a flimsy porch framed with four-inch columns. Two-by-four rails and plywood decking encircled the porch. Its occupant greeted us with a shotgun before we had completely crossed the walkway. He advised us to go back to the highway and never return.

We met a similar fate at the next one, a flat, rectangular houseboat with a cheap railing encircling the roof. I supposed that the roof served as a sunning or fishing deck. This time, we actually made it to the end of the walkway before a woman with a snarling dog turned us away.

"Ain't no use," lamented Brantley. Then, raising his voice for the benefit of those inside the houseboats, he called, "Ain't no Christians living here! Turn away a baby in a hurricane!"

His words did not have the hoped-for effect on the occupants we had encountered. But they must have fallen on someone's ears, for the door of the third houseboat opened to reveal a middle-aged woman of medium build beckoning us to come inside.

To be invited into someone's abode under such circumstances stirs deep emotions. Elation, relief, and faith in one's fellow man are certainly in the mix. I'm confident that the feeling of being accepted into a prestigious club or a Wall Street firm cannot equal it. In the split second when one is pulled from a maelstrom into a warm, dry home, all is right with the world.

Of course, to say that her home was dry would be misleading. It was evident that the roof needed repairs, for numerous pots and pans were laid out in order to collect the water drips. The interior consisted of one great room with mostly beige furniture sitting on a brown shag rug. A kitchenette nestled in one corner, while a loft was built against the opposite wall. Two smaller rooms were positioned side by side near the front door. One was the bathroom, the other a bedroom.

Her name was Connie.

An elderly, tall man came out of the bathroom holding a wrench in one hand. "Ever tried to fix a sink with a busted wrench?" he demanded of me.

I replied that I had not.

"There's two kinds of people," he said, holding up two fingers. "Thems who got the right tools, and thems who ain't."

He was introduced to us as Ange, or something like that. Because the ferocity of the rain had increased again, I didn't catch his name. After that, Connie referred to him as "Sweety," "Cutie," or the "Old Goat." They were a giving and caring couple who provided us too-large but dry clothes and food. The only thing they seemed to want in return was for us to tend the pots and pans as they filled up. Rather than repair the roof, it was their practice to simply pour collected water into a sink that discharged into the river.

Connie immediately took to Junior—which was how we introduced the boy to them—and tended to his every need. Brantley helped out as much as possible. That pretty much left me and Ange to pass small talk as we rode out the storm. I referred to him by name as little as possible. When pressed, I called him Ange, trailing the last part so it could have been Andrew, Andy, Angie, or Angel. The only visible sign of his name I saw was an old envelope he used as a bookmark for a fishing magazine. The label on the envelope had only the initial of his first name printed on it.

Our host favored asking me questions that were intended to promote the hardships he had endured while revealing the relative easy life enjoyed by those of my generation.

"You ever been stuck in a storm with no one to help you and not a dollar in your pocket?" he asked.

I said I could not remember such a time, wondering if he recalled that he had just denied me that privilege by allowing us into his abode.

"Didn't think so," he said. "This generation has gone soft! I remember . . ."

It must have been an hour until that anecdote ended, a banker being the antagonist and a rail car Ange's refuge. The moral, according to Ange, was that "there are two types of people. Thems that help others, and thems that help themselves."

This was followed by another question: "Ever had to get a crop in on time or the bank would foreclose on you? Ever had that happen to you?"

I replied that I could not recall such an incident, but that I had been late with my homework on occasion.

Of course, that wasn't good enough. "It's the young today. They're lazy."

Thus began another hour, the antagonist remaining the ever-deceitful and heartless banker. "There are two types of people," he told me as we moved into the moral phase of the tale. "Him what's got money, and him that ain't. Today's youth don't understand about hardship."

Before he launched into yet another yarn, I took the opportunity to empty several water-filled vessels. Ange astutely observed that it was raining harder than before. Drawing a parallel between Noah and our predicament would not have seemed far-fetched at that moment, for a new squall line of black clouds descended upon us, issuing forth bolts of lightning and deafening thunder. It was as if the devil had arrived, sowing hail and harvesting trees.

I had until that point believed that Ange and Connie were keeping the conversation light and behaving nonchalantly in order not to betray their fear of the coming destruction. But Ange's comment about it being a real "gully washer" caused me to rethink things. Looking around, I noticed that there was no television, no radio, no newspaper, and no telephone.

"How do you stay in touch with current events?" I asked.

"Pssh. We don't care none 'bout townies' doin's. We keep to ourselves and don't bother no one."

Brantley picked up on my line of inquiry, setting down his beer. "You mean y'all don't know about the hurricane?"

"What hurricane?" Connie wanted to know.

Ange's face turned a whiter shade of pale.

Brantley nodded in the direction of the storm. "That hurricane," he casually replied, tilting the beer can up for a sip.

At that moment, small limbs and leafy debris began to pelt the side of the boat. The first real wave of the storm was showering us with vegetation from across the river a quarter-mile away.

Ange and Connie's stunned silence was followed by an explosion of quick, decisive movements on both their parts. Ange dove outside into the tempest to secure things outside. Connie began to pull from a closet and a cedar chest life preservers, an inflatable raft, a small hand pump, and flares.

I could see Ange having a tough time unraveling rope in the pelting rain, so I hustled out to help him.

"Take down them storm shutters!" he yelled above the mayhem.

At first, I didn't comprehend his command. Then I noticed that plywood coverings latched to an overhanging section of roof were attached to hinges just above each window. Each storm shutter was suspended by a thin rope tied to a post. With help from Ange, I was able to lower the shutters and secure them. However, it took all my strength to move around to the side of the boat facing the river. The wind was so fierce that I found myself pinned against the window I was trying to cover. I could see whitecaps moving toward me as a downdraft pushed the surface water sideways across the river.

Ange made his way to where I was. He jumped over the railing and into a small boat tied to the side of his domicile. Then he loosened one of the ropes that kept the craft attached to the houseboat and rocked it over on one side. Water quickly flooded it, and the small craft had almost completely disappeared by the time Ange climbed back over the railing. He then tossed an anchor overboard. It banged hard against the side of the boat before disappearing below the surface. Seeing me pinned against the window, he raced to help me unlatch and let down the shutter. The wind slammed it hard against the frame. We latched it down and headed back around the side of the houseboat, which was no small feat, for the wind did its best to blow us over the rail.

When we returned to the safety of the living space, I could see that Connie had prepared for any emergency. With the windows boarded up, very little light remained. Candles had been set on the coffee table in the middle of the room. Ange and I changed into his last available sets of clean, dry clothes, and we all settled in amid the howling wind and rain. Though my hands trembled, Ange and Connie were the picture of contentment, holding hands and softly singing hymns.

When we first arrived, the river had been very low, with several feet of bank visible. But before nightfall descended upon us, only a foot of bank remained. And though the worst of the storm swept through by evening, enough rain was dumped inland that the spit of land protecting Connie and Ange's residence was soon overrun by upstream flooding. The last thing I recall from that night was being awakened by a passing train. I heard a sharp crackling sound. Then I drifted off to sleep again.

CHAPTER 20

After the deluge . . .

I woke the next morning to the restful tones of a light but steady drizzle on the roof. Ange was standing on the porch assessing the damage. I stumbled outside and stepped over numerous tree limbs to stand beside him. The landscape was one that I did not recognize.

For two or three minutes, I didn't say a thing, and he didn't move an inch. All he seemed capable of doing was shaking his head in disbelief, and for good reason. For starters, the houseboat next to his was demolished. All that remained were chunks of styrofoam and plywood. The houseboat next to it had altogether disappeared. The river was filled with debris—trees, limbs, pleasure boats, houses, decks—all flowing swiftly downstream, ultimately past Zapala and into the Atlantic.

I wondered how His Grace had fared. I wondered what had become of Liverpool and Bucephalus. And Tilly and Kenneth. And I wondered if Zapala had been a dream. Who would believe I had spent several days on a remote island with a root doctor, a Latin speaker, and this person called Lord Baltimore? I scarcely believed it myself.

Nor could I believe what I saw on the shore. A four-by-four post protruded from a pine trunk. The trunk had snapped in two, as though ripped away by a giant hand. A swath of destruction ran up the slope. The limbs of the trees that stood on either side of this path were bent inward toward the swath. Ange was looking there, too. The telltale signs of a tornado. The freight train I had heard in the night.

"What was the name of that one?" Ange said.

"The hurricane?"

"Yeah."

"I don't know what it was called."

"Well, they oughta call it By-God William Tecumseh Sherman!"

I doubted the general's best efforts could compare to the damage we now surveyed. I suggested we inspect the boat next to us for survivors, but Ange informed me he had already done so.

"Old Lady Preston's under it somewhere. Jake, the boy two down, musta cut his lines and rode downstream. You boys are plain lucky they turned you out. Coulda been the end of you."

Later that morning, after helping Ange and me salvage materials from Mrs. Preston's place, Brantley informed me that the ropes holding Jake's houseboat had snapped and were not cut.

There was only minor damage to Ange's boat, mostly to the roof. Connie told us we were sent to them by the Lord, that she and her husband would have perished had we not brought Junior to their door. She further stated that Junior was obviously being preserved by the Lord to achieve great things in life. However, I believed that the Saint Christopher given me by Liverpool had something to do with our being spared. Naturally, Brantley attributed our luck to the power of the root he now possessed.

That afternoon, Ange, Brantley, and I raised the john boat, set its small Johnson outboard motor aside to dry out, and paddled to the bridge. From there, we walked several miles up the highway to a cross-roads at which stood a gas station and a small food mart. Our purpose was to catch up on the news and to purchase supplies. We learned that the hurricane had come ashore between Zapala and Savannah and continued inland, flooding rivers and streams and knocking down trees. St. Simons and Brunswick had been spared, so I was confident that my family was safe.

Obtaining food was another matter altogether. The store was overrun with people from all walks of life. There was no bread on the shelves and no canned goods. What little stock remained consisted mostly of bagged chips, cookies, and candy. No bottled water was available, and absolutely no batteries of any kind were to be found. We did manage to buy several six-packs of ginger ale, a case of beer, two large bags of chips, a pack of hot dogs, and a number of gooey pastries of questionable shelf life.

An icebox sat outside the store near the double glass doors. It was guarded by the store owner, who held a shotgun in one hand and issued one bag of ice per customer with the other. The going price was two dollars a bag. By the time we arrived, only a few bags remained, and the line of people was long. A man and a woman actually began to bid for a bag, but the store owner would have no part in it.

"You shoulda got here early," he said.

"Just you wait," Ange told us, pointing at the highway. "Tomorrow, they'll be a truck across the road sellin' ice for twenty dollars a bag."

He scowled at us, but I believe his anger was directed more at himself for not keeping informed about the weather and stocking his home with supplies. Fortunately, Ange and Connie had built a cistern on the roof to store rainwater for drinking. Their bathing was accomplished in the river, so we were not in as dire a need of water as others appeared to be.

"There's two kinds of people," Ange went on to inform us. "People that take advantage of others, and others that get took advantage of. You see if that truck don't pull up over there tomorrow like I said. I betcha anything."

Ange used a pay telephone to report his missing neighbors to the police. I thought doing so would upset Brantley, as it might draw suspicion upon him. But either he did an admirable job of masking his feelings or he was genuinely unconcerned due to the protection of the root.

We discovered two things in the Atlanta paper.

The first was that the hurricane was named Henry—or Hank, as it was now affectionately known.

This sat none too well with Ange. "Hank!" he complained. "What kinda name is that for a hurricane, 'specially this un? Shoulda been called By-God William Tecumseh Sherman, from what I seen."

Brantley, on the other hand, was so taken by the hurricane's name that he resolved to apply it to the boy. His reasoning was that Hank had a "born with money" sound to it, and that one's name was a determining factor in how one turned out in life. "Take Brantley," he said to me privately. "A name like that gets you in jail, follerin' a crazy dude around some island, and ridin' a hurricane out on a houseboat."

I declined to point out that the name Ensworth had put me on the same island and in the same houseboat, and that one's actions played a larger role in determining the course of one's life. I further declined to point out that Hank was a name easily associated with being penniless, heartbroken, and melancholy, a state that only an equally despairing and forlorn country tune could pacify.

The second thing we discovered in the paper was a small side story that included a photograph of Sheriff Pooler and Brantley beneath the headline, "Authorities Search for Sheriff and Escaped Felon." The story quoted Deputy Adrian, the Ratchet. In his eyes, the sheriff was a bona fide hero who personally hunted down desperate criminals at the risk of losing his job by neglecting his campaign for elected office. The photo of Brantley did not do him justice, the person in the snapshot appearing much younger and more filled out and having much shorter hair. The Brantley standing next to me was gaunt, weathered, and shaggy. Perhaps that was due to his not having slept well in recent days. Add to that the young child under his care and the profile of a desperate criminal was almost obliterated.

In the course of walking to and from the crossroads, we were passed by numerous ambulances rushing to various emergencies. When we got back to the bridge, we came upon the orange trucks of a Georgia Department of Transportation crew inspecting the site for damage.

"What's all the sirens about?" Ange asked one of the crewmen.

"Listen," the man replied.

We did. I heard buzzing sounds in the distance.

"Hear that? People are cutting themselves up left and right with chain saws, trying to clear fallen trees. Never fails after a hurricane."

We had no such problem, as Ange possessed only hand tools. "Never need to waste no gasoline on 'em," he informed us on the way back to the boat. "Save it for the 'Rudes," he said, referring to the twin outboard Evinrude motors that powered the houseboat up and down the river.

We spent the next few days making repairs to the houseboat and searching for any sign of Mrs. Preston. We also cleared the path that led to the highway—a slow process, since it was partially submerged for two days and since a great number of water moccasins had been driven to higher ground by the flooding. But Brantley, Ange, and I managed not to get bitten or hurt while cutting and moving the heavy debris.

On Thursday, Brantley and I hitch-hiked ten miles to the delightful burg of Doctorville to seek employment. A large, burly truckdriver immediately picked us up. He was hauling an empty ice truck back to

Macon. On the way to Doctorville, just as Ange had predicted, we passed a truck on the side of the road selling small bags of ice for twenty dollars each.

"Criminal," our host fumed as we passed the price-gouging ice purveyors. "Twenty a bag. Some people . . ."

"How much you sellin ice for?" asked Brantley.

"Fifteen!" barked our hairy host. "And not a dime mo'."

We correctly assumed we would be able to find work with clean-up crews. We spent the next several days being hauled with a gang of other men from this or that destroyed dwelling to remove and repair things as best we could. The pay was seven dollars an hour. Most of the gang consisted of poor locals and migrant workers from Mexico who had finished harvesting the onion crop. Though communicating with one another was not easy, I managed to convey to one of them that I was heading to Savannah and that he might seek employment there. He was Esteban, a small fellow about my age. Even the hint of going to Savannah unnerved him. I learned from him that migrant workers often disappeared around the docks of that city and ended up as unwilling crew members on cargo ships in need of deck hands. As the migrants usually had nowhere to turn for help, they soon learned to stay away from port cities altogether.

There was one incident involving Esteban and several of his countrymen that greatly altered my opinion of Brantley. It occurred the second day of our employment, a hot, humid morning. Our crew had been dropped off to clear the remains of a barn devastated by the hurricane. The incident made me realize how those who occupy a low rank in society often find solace in abusing those whose status is even lower than theirs. This was the case regarding several ill-educated and slovenly young men on our crew who began to badger Esteban and his friends. They were led by a brutish fellow in his mid-twenties named Wayne. For most of the morning, their derogatory remarks about the Mexicans went unheard, though their quick glances toward the migrant workers left no doubt as to whom they were ridiculing. As long as our crew chief was present, nothing untoward occurred. However, the moment he drove off in a pickup truck to replenish our water supply, Wayne leapt into action. He walked past me and deliberately bumped Esteban, who was dismantling a section of fallen roof. Esteban said something under his breath, which Wayne used as an excuse to push him to the ground. I looked around for Brantley but could not locate him. The only workers nearby were a few of Wayne's friends and three other migrant workers, Fernando, Gil, and Hernani.

Esteban, now disconcerted, forgot how to communicate in English. Wayne kicked him and let forth a torrent of slurs and insults. It was then that three of Wayne's cohorts took the opportunity to assault Esteban's amigos, who had rushed to his aid.

I stepped in and attempted to mediate. Wayne accused me of being a "wetback lover." I replied that he was no more than a bully, upon which he took a violent swing at me. Thanks to His Grace's training, I evaded it. However, before I could respond in kind, one of his cronies knocked me to the ground. My eye began to swell immediately. I rose and leapt onto Wayne's back, but he flicked me off as a bear might dismiss a pesky bee. I again attempted to enter the melee and managed to bring one of Wayne's boys to the ground. As Hernani and I struggled with the assailant, I noticed that Gil and Fernando were admirably holding their own despite their lack of size. Esteban was quick enough that Wayne had a hard time getting a grip on him. Hernani, thinking I could handle myself, abandoned me to assist Esteban.

It was then that I heard a great thumping sound and looked down to see Wayne on the ground clutching one knee, howling profusely and writhing in agony. Brantley, wielding a two-by-four, stepped over him and hammered hard on the back of my opponent. He then descended on Wayne's compatriots still in the clutches of Gil, Hernani, and Fernando. One of them escaped unmolested, but the other felt a jolting blow of the board.

When it was over, Brantley instructed the transgressors to remove Wayne from his sight, to hit the road, and to not return. They retreated from the field of battle defeated and deflated.

"That's how you deal with their kind," said Brantley, breathing heavily. "Them kind don't understand talk. They understand this," he said, holding up the board as if it were King Arthur's sword.

Wayne and the others did not return that day or the rest of the week. And though I didn't tell him, my estimation of Brantley grew considerably.

The farmer who owned the barn made us lunch. He also gave us each a pack of cigars he had hand-rolled from his tobacco crop. Brantley set about smoking one of his. I resolved to save mine for His Grace.

At the end of the day, we received our wages. My work with the crew brought me the first honest money I had earned and seemed a far greater treasure than all that I had accumulated through my father. Therefore, I was extra careful in how I spent it. Brantley and I offered Connie and Ange something in the form of rent. However, they stubbornly refused our money.

We spent that Saturday redigging burial plots at a local cemetery, since a good number of recently buried caskets had been forced to the surface by the water saturating the ground. Returning home that evening covered in dried mud, we immediately jumped into the river to bathe. We had no sooner undressed than a boat belonging to the Georgia Department of Natural Resources pulled alongside the houseboat. Connie and Ange walked on to the deck to greet the ranger, who reached over the rail and handed Ange a document.

"Well," said the ranger, surveying the boat, "I'm afraid it's official."

"What's official?" Connie asked.

Ange handed Connie the document and eyed the ranger.

"You folks have thirty days to vacate the river."

This bit of news stopped Brantley in mid-lather.

"I ain't vacatin' nothin'," Ange replied.

The ranger explained that the "powers that be" in Atlanta had determined that houseboats such as Ange's were not built to code and posed a hazard to the public. Ange pointed out that he had constructed his home himself and that it had withstood the hurricane, whereas many manufactured houseboats were so much flotsam floating downriver.

"Sir, I'm just doing my job," the ranger answered.

"It's them developers behind it," Connie said.

This made me wince, for the bulk of my family's wealth was derived from the building of homes, hospitals, and office space. In fact, I was an heir to one of the leading catalysts of development in the area. But I was quite sure that realtors and builders were not behind the eviction.

"It's gettin' so's a man cain't live in his own home," said Ange. "Them developers won't be satisfied 'til every man, woman, and child lives in one of their houses. No, sir. I ain't movin'."

"Okay, now. You can petition—"

"And I ain't petitionin' nothin' either! Some politician wants to drive me from my own home, he can come down here and tell me hisself. I got a barrel of buckshot he can take back with him."

"Okay, okay," said the ranger, scratching his head. "I'm just informing you what the new law is. You have some options you can follow in that document I handed you. But if I was you, I'd start making other living arrangements."

Ange stared coldly at the man.

"Oh, yeah, one other thing," continued the ranger. "We found Mrs. Preston's body." Ange and Connie said nothing. "She got caught up in some low-hanging tree limbs about ten miles downstream. Thought you'd want to know."

He backed his boat out and was on his way. The four of us followed the craft with our eyes until it rounded the bend. I looked back at the couple. Ange's lower lip momentarily quivered. Whether that was due to rage or sadness, I could not discern.

"Don't worry 'bout it," said Brantley. "They're puttin' up some shelters over in—"

"We ain't goin' to no shelter," Ange said abruptly. He took Connie's hand and turned to go inside.

Brantley and I took our time washing, so our hosts could discuss the matter in privacy.

We never did discover what became of the other neighbor, Jake. However, while hunting for game in the woods one afternoon, Ange found the remnants of a pole, the kind used for maneuvering a houseboat in shallow water. Ange was certain it was the same pole Jake used. It had bite marks presumably left by Jake's dog. Even more curious was the array of rotted trout he discovered in the woods, more evidence of a tornado's passing across the river.

Connie had another visitor that day as well, for upon our return home, she presented us a playbill on which was printed the headline, "Hurricane Hank Tent Revival!" This perked up Connie and Ange's spirits considerably. They wanted us to be their guests at the gathering. We would be in the presence of none other than the Reverend Ezekiel Eleazer Loop—"Preacher Loop," as he was commonly known. The fun was to begin at noon with an "Old-Fashioned Bar-B-Q"—as opposed, I guessed, to a high-tech barbecue of fried motherboards and computer chips.

My first thought—and perhaps Brantley's as well—was to devise some reason to remain on the boat the next day, instead of going to the revival. I could complain of exhaustion-induced muscle cramps from overwork the previous week. Brantley might invoke his wish to stay with Hank, since he hadn't seen much of the boy lately, due to our work. I half expected him just to state, "I ain't goin'," and be done with it.

But Connie made a compelling case for us to attend. After all, we had been spared by the storm, whereas our neighbors had not. And it was not asking too much for us to spend one day in celebration of our blessings. And though she didn't mention it, I felt that since we had a roof over our heads, decent meals, and someone who gladly coddled Hank day and night—all free of charge—we could not refuse.

It rained again that night and continued until late in the evening. The river rose quickly, as it had not yet returned to normal after the recent flooding. This gave me some hope that the revival might be postponed.

That night, I dreamed of my father. I saw him standing under a tall pine tree. He looked on me with a broad smile that assured me he was proud of me or of something I had done. He spoke, but I could not hear him. I came closer but still could not hear. He smiled again and waved. Then he faded from view altogether.

CHAPTER 21

*Brantley and I witness
the Miracle of the Evinrudes
and attend a revival.*

When I awakened the following morning, I decided to employ my exhausted-from-manual-labor strategy, which meant that I needed to remain bedridden until noon. Brantley's snores told me that his somnolent state was no ruse.

I knew my strategy was doomed to failure the moment I heard water lapping against the hull and realized we were moving. I sprang from my blanket nest and looked through a window to see Ange poling the houseboat into the river. By the time I got outside, he had fired up the two Evinrude motors and we were moving upstream.

"'Bout time you sleepyheads was up," he said as he steered us around the land jutting into the river. He guided the boat past midstream toward the opposite bank.

Connie came outside with Hank and laid him on the pine picnic table to change his diaper. We had chugged our way upstream for about five minutes when I popped the question.

"What about the big revival?" I asked, feigning disappointment.

"That's where we're heading," Ange replied. "It's about ten mile upstream." He began to hum "Amazing Grace."

I realized the error of my ways, the chief one being that my plan called for me to remain on the boat, when I should have been off the boat when it left.

"See there," said Ange. "The good Lord wanted you two at this meetin'. Gave y'all plenty of sleep so's you could be rested up for it."

One of the Evinrudes sputtered, then ceased to function altogether. We were in midriver when the second engine gasped and died as well. Ange didn't panic. We were too deep for the pole to reach the bottom, so he plugged away at getting first one motor, then the other to start.

Connie offered friendly advice at first. "Did you try the choke?" she asked. "Maybe it's flooded."

"Naw, hit ain't flooded," replied Ange, scratching his head. "Propeller ain't snagged on nothin'. Danged if I know what it is."

I saw no reason to worry until it dawned on me that we were drifting downstream on the swift current—on a collision course with the bridge's concrete pilings. When I realized our predicament, I immediately made plans to abandon ship.

"Go wake the boy," Ange said calmly.

I went inside, shook Brantley out of his slumber, and half dragged him on to the deck. He quickly sized up the situation and got down to the business of repairing the left motor.

"All right, all right," he said, coming alive. "You work on that engine. I'll work on this un."

With that, he and Ange began earnestly to pinch, pound, and pull on all the engine parts available to them.

By then, I had formulated a backup plan in my head. I would dash aboard the john boat and use it to pull the attached houseboat out of harm's way. The plan was flawless, except that the smaller boat had been left behind at the dock.

At that moment, a curious thing occurred. Connie began to sing "Rock of Ages." She was perhaps two bars into the hymn when Ange ceased to fiddle with his engine and joined in with a passable baritone.

Okay, they've both given up hope, I thought.

Brantley threw his hands up in disgust and announced that he could find nothing wrong with his Evinrude. If he began to sing along, I would take it as a sign that all was lost.

"Look, y'all," said my astute colleague in a matter-of-fact tone, pointing ahead of us. "We're fixin' to hit that bridge."

I'm sure the fact was not lost on Ange and Connie, but they sang bravely on in spite of the danger. Indeed, we were closing in rapidly on the structure much like the *Titanic* once sped toward its iceberg.

"Oh, ye of little faith," said Connie, not fretting in the least.

"Amen," Ange chimed. "You don't abandon the Lord, and He won't never abandon you."

The moment he said those words, a cool, refreshing wind blew across the water.

"I ain't abandonin' nothin' but this here boat," Brantley retorted. "I'm takin' Hank an' my faith with me, an' I wish y'all would come along."

At that point, we were perhaps fifty yards from a piling. Ange shook his head at us and grinned. Then he yanked hard on the starter cord of the left Evinrude. It cranked up immediately. He yanked on the other cord, and that engine, too, sprang to life. He turned the motors far to the left and swung the houseboat away from the bridge.

We said nothing to them for the duration of the trip, though

Brantley did whisper to me that he thought Ange had rigged the outboards to perform on cue for our benefit.

We eventually came to a landing on the east bank where a dozen or more houseboats were tied up. Ange docked. Brantley carried Hank as we scaled a narrow path to the top of a bluff. From there, we followed a trail wide enough for two people. It wound its way through the woods for a half-mile or more before opening on to a rectangular pasture maybe a hundred yards wide and twice as long, surrounded by pine trees. Pickup trucks and rusted cars covered much of the field in no particular parking arrangement. In the center of the pasture was a large, green canvas tent that was open on all four sides. There were enough chairs and benches beneath it to accommodate at least three hundred people. Nearby was a tent filled with tables holding a variety of dishes, including fried chicken, beef and pork barbecue, corn on the cob, sweet potatoes, creamed corn, biscuits, hot dogs, hamburgers, potato chips, coleslaw, pecan pies, chess pies, and sundry other foods.

Within five minutes, I lost track of the others and found myself wandering aimlessly and taking in the sights. I spent most of the afternoon eating more than necessary and listening to small clusters of singers harmonize on "Swing Low, Sweet Chariot" and "Shall We Gather at the River." Musicians accompanied them on guitars, banjos, and harmonicas.

In general, those in attendance clustered into groups according to age. The older folks like Ange and Connie hovered around the food tent. The rest of the adults gravitated toward the singers and musicians, while the children flew freely about in a radius of fifty yards, much like electrons whirling around the family nucleus. Those my age occupied the hinter regions of the field. Like comets, they swooped down upon the food tables every so often, then swooped back to the outer limits. They were well behaved for the most part, but a number of them appeared to be more intimate in their parked vehicles than I would have expected on such an occasion.

I decided to rest when the heat of the day was at its worst, for I anticipated a long night ahead of us. I came upon a rattletrap of an old school bus and crawled beneath it for shade. I was just about to doze off when a dust-covered truck pulling a camper drew up near the bus and parked. Two men and a woman got out of the truck and stretched as though they had just completed a long ride. Indeed, the Oklahoma tag indicated they had crossed several state lines to get there. The man and the woman who had exited the vehicle on my side scanned the immediate area, as if to determine they were not being watched. Both looked to be about fifty years of age. The driver, fortyish, then appeared in my view. The three entered the camper and closed the door behind them.

I must have fallen asleep for some time, but the sound of arguing voices awakened me. There, standing beside the trailer, were the two men and the woman, along with a bearded fellow wearing red suspenders that strained against a paunch that had obviously seen its fair share of food tents—and enjoyed every one of them.

"Look, Joey, we want it up front this time," said the driver in a loud voice. "Not like in Carolina."

"You know he's good for it," retorted the large man, attempting to keep the volume down.

"Don't listen to it, Jimma," the woman advised. "We heard this sermon last year."

"I don't wanna hear two words outta you, Gertie. You've done your share of hustlin' evangelists in your day. You and Frankie," said Joey, pointing at her companion.

"Pay up now or we're outta here," said Frankie, taking Gertie's hand.

"All right, all right," said Joey. "I'll be back in thirty minutes with half the money. But you cut out on us and you know what to expect. Loop's got a lotta friends on the circuit. He's got a mean temper and a meaner left hook."

Jimma, the driver, thought for a moment. "Okay. Half now, half later."

"Fair enough," said Joey, adjusting his suspenders. "You get ready. I'll be back in a half-hour."

He departed, leaving the three to discuss the merits of their negotiations.

"I'd love to sic ol what's-his-name on Loop," said Frankie.

"Who?" Jimma asked.

"You know. That sheriff down there 'round Medway."

"Pooler?" Gertie asked.

"Yeah, Pooler."

"Now, that would be a fight," said Jimma.

"Make more money sellin' tickets for that than doin' this ol thing," said Frankie.

Sensing it would be unwise to loiter further, I quietly exited from underneath the other side of the bus without being noticed. I returned to the tent area, where I came upon Brantley, who was playing with Hank. I was touched by the genuine interest he took in the boy. Up until then, I had thought it a passing fancy that would wear off. It was only a matter of time before the law caught up to him, and I didn't want to reveal my thoughts about the child, knowing that Brantley might be separated from him at any moment. Fortunately for us, Ange and Connie didn't follow the local news and never once inquired about our backgrounds.

As I turned this thought over in my mind, I became acutely aware of a presence nearby. I turned to find a gorgeous young lady staring at me. I must admit I did not expect to encounter such a creature under the circumstances. Her eyes were the azure of a tropical lagoon, and her dark brown hair cascaded down her bare shoulders like a waterfall. As for the rest of her features, little imagination was needed, for the eye had only to behold what was revealed by a dearth of clothing. My first thought I cannot reveal. My second thought was this: *How did she manage to get out of her home dressed like that?*

"Who're you?" she wanted to know.

I searched my mental index of names but could not locate the one I knew to be mine. "Ensworth!" I blurted the moment it came to me.

"My name's Holly. Papa wanted to call me Molly, and Mama wanted to call me . . ."

I absorbed none of her conversation. She spoke for five hours—or perhaps it was only five minutes—before I realized that she had asked me a question.

"Um . . . What'd you ask?"

"Where you from?"

"Oh. I'm with . . . I mean, I'm from just downstream. You know, Ange and Connie."

"You mean old man Aleph and Connie?" she asked, pointing to the man I had known as Ange up until that moment.

"You're quite sure his name is Aleph?"

"That's him. I see 'em here every year," she said as she snuggled up to me and put her arm around my waist.

"Are you from here?" I inquired, attempting nonchalance while coming very close to passing out. Her perfume was a strange blend of orange marmalade and onion that offended my nostrils. But her physical allure and the warmth of her touch were overpowering.

"I just told you all that, silly. Papa's Reverend Loop. We travel the South doin' revivals," she said, running her slim fingers through my hair. "That's our bus over there."

I turned to look. Sure enough, a long touring bus was parked near the revival tent, its diesel motor idling and twin air-conditioning units humming. Painted in large white letters on the bus was "Mission Of Mercy Crusades." A large, red cross was painted on either side. A small pair of boxing gloves dangled from one of the crosses.

In smaller letters were the words, "Reverend Eleazer Loop—Missionary Evangelist, Servant of God."

As I read this sign, the bus door flew open and an imposing fellow appeared on the top step. *Tall, stern,* and *vigorous* were the words that leapt to mind. Long, white hair flowed behind him as he marched in our direction. His pointed beard gave him a rugged, Western look— the Buffalo Bill of the revival circuit. Indeed, he looked like he had seen a few battles in his day. He was a man capable of intimidating others. A man not given to light conversation. In short, a man best left alone. A man much like my father.

"Holly!" he bellowed, his voice bouncing off cars and echoing across the field. His eyes fixed laser-like on me as he addressed his daughter in a lowered voice. "Getcho tail back in heah and get some clothes on, ragamuffin," he growled through gritted teeth.

Holly rolled her eyes. "Yes, Papa."

They passed each other as she made for the bus and he headed for me. I tried to run, but my feet seemed rooted in the soil. I recall none of the specifics of what he told me, but the upshot of it was that my chances of continuing in good health were in direct proportion to the amount of distance I kept between myself and his daughter.

After that, he strolled off to partake of friendly fellowship with some of the gathered. I leaned against the hood of a truck to regain my composure. That's when I saw Gertie's beau, Frankie. Only this time, he was walking on crutches. I thought it odd that he could be so quickly injured and so lucky in finding a pair of crutches. He appeared to have a game leg.

But the parade of oddities had only just begun.

Several minutes later, I spied the woman, Gertie, creeping along, bent over as if in pain. At first, I thought she had lost something and was scanning the ground for it. But soon, two young men approached her and offered to help her to the food tent. She refused their assistance and pitifully shuffled along on her dreary course.

It wasn't long before a third invalid, Jimma, made his entrance. This was accomplished despite a severe limp and a left hand that had assumed a cramped and grotesquely bent position.

An hour later, the sun, having witnessed enough nonsense for one day, began its descent. Fireflies lit up the darkening field. Not long after that, three distinct horn blasts from the reverend's bus summoned the believers to worship. Without a word, the crowd shuffled en masse toward the revival tent. Since I was one of the last to enter, I was ushered up front, where a number of seats had been left vacant. There was no opportunity to stand in detachment outside the tent at this gathering; it quickly became apparent that everything was under tight control. A group of organizers, about ten of them, sat on a small platform in front of me. Chief among them was the well-rounded Joey with his red suspenders. Holly, now dressed in a rather plain, drab brown dress, entered the tent and took her place among them.

After several minutes, Joey rose from his seat and stood humbly, solemnly in front of the crowd. The tent was very quiet while he bowed in silent prayer. Then, with a jerk, he lifted his head and launched full force into "I Saw the Light." I was startled by the abruptness of the song's start and equally surprised by how quickly the congregation joined in. I mouthed along, faking it as best I could. Looking up, I noticed Holly staring right at me.

We were hitting the second chorus when the headlights of Reverend Loop's tour bus began to blink on and off. A single spotlight shone on the door as it opened. Like Moses descending from Mount Sinai, Reverend Loop emerged from the bus. Instead of two stone tablets, he carried a large, white Bible. He seemed transfigured since I'd seen him not an hour previous. He wore a pure white, shimmering suit that complemented his white hair. He strode purposefully across the small space separating the bus from the tent and walked down the aisle greeting people. By the time the song ended, he had made his way to center stage. He called out in a thunderous voice,

"Hallelujah, brothers and sisters!"

"Hallelujah, brother!" the crowd replied in unison.

The evangelist began with a brief prayer of thanksgiving on behalf of all present for surviving the storm and gathering in that field to hear the Word. Thanks were also given for the congregation's monetary contributions to the reverend's ministry, so that he might continue helping lost souls elsewhere. We then waded through a half-dozen hymns and the passing of offering plates. Several prayers assured those in attendance that the return on their manifest munificence would be tenfold.

My initial mistake was putting too much money in the plate the first time it circulated. When it came back around, I noticed my neighbors putting more money in, having had the good sense to keep their donation small the first time. I struggled to keep up with the songs, mouthing the words as best I could. Two children near me observed that I was hymnally challenged and sang all the louder to prove their superiority. A final passing of the plate found me, under much peer pressure, contributing the final installment of almost fifty dollars. I hesitated a moment before feeling the burning stare of the reverend upon me. As the plate disappeared up the aisle, I saw an entire day's wages go with it.

"Friends!" boomed Preacher Loop. "Rejoice in the presence of our Father Almighty, who hath deemed it right and just to guide us safely through the recent destruction."

This was not a bad prelude. I had feared that the reverend might be of the fire-and-brimstone persuasion. Until that moment, I had fully expected Old Testament burnt offerings of "an he-goat and a bullock" to be placed on an altar.

I relaxed as he led us in a rousing rendition of "When the Roll Is Called up Yonder, I'll Be There." He further put me at ease by making a few light comments and alluding to his former days as a boxer. Judging from his cauliflower ear and bent nose, I highly commended his switch from pugilist to evangelist.

"I was laid out on the canvas of a boxing ring up there in Louisville, brothers and sisters, when the Lord's Word came to me," he said. "A young fighter named Cassius Clay had put me on my back in the third round. The light was shining down on me from above, and I saw a vision. I saw the light of God in all His glory above me. I heard Him giving me the final count. And I promised the Lord that if He gave me one more chance, I would repent and spread the gospel. When I came to, I vowed to change my life one hundred and eighty degrees. The first thing I did was to take that canvas I fought upon and put it over my head. That's why I'm here today under this canvas tent spreading the light of the Lord to all who will listen, the believers and the nonbelievers." This he said looking dead at me. "I made a vow to minister to those who have heard the Word of God and to the stiff-necked sinners who refuse to bow to God's will."

A hundred voices around me said, "Amen, brother!"

It was then that the sermon took a turn for the worse—at least for me. I must admit, however, that he made a compelling case for justifying why the hurricane had descended upon us.

"With deadly accuracy, God Almighty exposes the sinners of the world using natural disasters guided by His unwavering hand!"

"Amen, brother!" replied a chorus of worshipers.

"Floods and pestilence are His road signs. They point the way to a stiff-necked people. Drought and fire are His spotlights. They shine upon the sinners hiding in their dens of iniquity. The tornado and the avalanche are as cross hairs on the scope of His rifle. They target the wayward, who are condemned to perdition!"

"Amen, Brother Loop!"

"The blizzard and the hurricane are His brushes. They paint a wide swath upon the homes of heathens."

"Amen, brother!"

"And who do you think He has chosen to follow the floods, follow the fires, and follow the hurricanes to weed out the sinners and spread the gospel?"

Of course, the correct answer was that Reverend Eleazer Loop had been chosen to chase natural disasters with revival meetings, at which those in attendance learned that it was because of their sins that they had been the recipients of God's wrath. I suspected there was little difference between the reverend and those who sold ice at inflated prices to hurricane victims.

I wondered what Tilly would say about the reverend's theory of sinners bringing disaster upon themselves. It would be an interesting debate. Were witch doctors in Africa responsible for the hurricane, or did sinners attract it? Perhaps it was both. Or perhaps it had something to do with seasonal changes in the atmosphere and water that occurred every year regardless of whether or not man existed. Another thought occurred to me. Tilly, like the reverend, used natural disasters to gain control over others. Only it seemed to me that her intention was to protect, whereas the reverend had a dollar motive.

"The hurricane that swept through here is no more than a whisper of wind where those of you condemned to eternal damnation are going!" howled Reverend Loop. His eyes fairly blazed, and his hair seemed to take on a reddish hue.

Poor Brantley shook in his metal folding chair. Hank was all smiles, as the constant shaking of Brantley's legs must have seemed like a carnival ride.

Another chorus of "Amen, brother!" swirled about my head, but the reverend would have none of it.

"Don't you dare 'Amen, brother' me, ye children of Satan!"

"Tell it, Preacher Loop!" someone shouted.

"The devil himself hides behind the cross. Never are ye more vulnerable to Satan than when ye think ye are safe in the confines of a holy sanctuary. You drop your guard for one moment, and the Lord of Darkness will floor you with an uppercut," he said, swiping a fist through the air.

"Ame—" someone started to say but stopped short, having been caught in the cross hairs of Preacher Loop's formidable stare.

The reverend continued on a rampage for several minutes before quieting down. But it was only the lull before the storm, for it was then that he jumped to the Book of Mark.

Quoting from the Bible, he boomed, " 'And these signs shall follow them that believe, in My name shall they cast out devils; they shall speak with new tongues; they shall take up serpents; and if they drink any deadly thing, it shall not hurt them; they shall lay hands on the sick, and they shall recover.' This sayeth our Lord."

Joey stepped forward carrying a box. Reverend Loop then proceeded to prove that he met all of Saint Mark's requirements. You could hear the crickets in their night song as the crowd grew silent. Like the seasoned performer he was, the reverend closed his eyes, raised his left arm skyward, and seemed to go into a trance. He then began to speak in a babbling tongue I could not understand. A woman sitting near me, apparently also in a trance, began to loudly proclaim this or that prophecy, as though interpreting the reverend's babble. I can't recall much of what she said, but the upshot was that seven seals were to be broken, four horsemen were to ride into town, and then things would pretty much take a downward turn.

Reverend Loop stopped babbling as quickly as he had begun. The woman finished her proclamation, and all was quiet for a moment. That is, until the reverend jammed his hand down inside the box that Joey held. I should be forgiven for falling out of my chair—and I was not the only one who did so—for the reverend pulled from the box a rattlesnake that looked to be three inches in diameter.

" 'They shall take up serpents'!" he shouted. "Ye sinners! Ye who shy away from the serpent! Reveal yourselves to the Lord God Almighty!"

He spent a good five minutes flipping the snake around his neck, holding it out for others to touch, and generally terrifying much of the crowd.

" 'And if they drink any deadly thing, it shall not hurt them'!" boomed the reverend.

With this statement, he took the snake's head and pressed its fangs against the side of a glass, spewing venom inside. He placed the rattler back in the box and, without hesitating, swallowed the contents of the glass. He then paced up and down the center aisle with arms spread wide to show that nothing could harm him.

" 'They shall lay hands on the sick, and they shall recover'!"

No one moved. An awkward hush fell over the throng. No one, it seemed, dared approach the reverend. But I suspected several would be coming forward to be freed of their newfound afflictions. And I did not have to wait long before Jimma made his dramatic and pathetic walk up the center aisle to the front of the tent. Like a wayward son, a lost lamb, a babe in the woods, he approached with arms outstretched, stumbling, crying, beckoning for forgiveness and for freedom from his pain.

"Brother!" the reverend said loudly after Jimma finished his long and arduous journey. "You have a game leg and a paralyzed hand, do you not?"

"I do, reverend," Jimma replied with bowed head.

"You've been cursed with these afflictions for many years?"

"Twenny-fo."

"Twenty-four years, brothers and sisters!" the reverend repeated. "Do you believe in the healing power of God?" he asked Jimma.

Uncontrollable sobbing overcame Jimma, whose shoulders heaved up and down like a pneumatic hammer. "I believe," he wailed at length. "I believe!"

No sooner had Jimma repeated those words than Reverend Loop threw out the palm of his right hand and struck him hard on the forehead.

"*Heal!*" the reverend cried. "In the name of God!"

The blow sent Jimma hurtling back into the waiting arms of several men who had positioned themselves to catch him. The healing "touch" was forceful enough to send sweat from Jimma's brow spraying in all directions.

This, I quickly concluded, was what the crowd had come to see. Forget the snake and the venom; we were now entering the really entertaining portion of the event.

The crowd watched intently as Jimma regained his senses. He sat up quietly and shook his head as though coming out of a deep slumber. Then he held his left hand and inspected it in astonishment. Disbelief spread across his face as his hand rose higher and higher and the paralytic grip loosened. He opened and closed his hand and stared at it gape-mouthed. One would have thought he had just unearthed a rare treasure.

"Praise the Lord," he said, barely managing to squeak out the words. Then he rose and placed his weight on his right leg, gingerly at first, then with more assurance. "Praise the Lord," he said, a little more loudly. The next thing I knew, he was walking in quick, little circles and dancing a jig. "*Praise the Lord!*" he bellowed.

Jimma's "*Praise the Lord!*" was met by three hundred of the same. Hallelujahs and amens resounded through the tent.

" 'They shall lay hands on the sick, and they shall recover'!" thundered the reverend once more. "Who else among you is ready to accept the healing power of God?"

My guess was that Gertie might find it an opportune moment to be freed of her ailment. I was right, for the poor wretch was at that very moment making her way up the aisle.

"Sister, you have many a grievous sickness within you."

"That I do, rev'ren," Gertie responded in the feeblest of voices.

"And you have carried these illnesses for many a year."

"Sixteen year, rev'ren," she quivered. "Help me. I'm so scared I don't know what to do."

Whap! went the reverend's hand on her forehead. Only this time, he held her by the shoulder with his left hand so she could not immediately fall away.

"Out, ye demons! Come out, Satan's servants! In the name of God the Holy Father, I command you to leave this woman forever!"

Then *whap!* went his hand against Gertie's forehead again.

"Heal, in the name of God!"

This time, he let her go, and she plunged backward into the waiting arms of the handlers. I believe that Gertie's slow recovery was authentic, since she had likely been knocked semiconscious by the evangelist. Like Jimma before her, Gertie ultimately regained her feet and jumped around like a spring colt.

It was when Frankie began to painfully shuffle forward that I determined to put a stop to the charade. He was within ten feet of the reverend's outstretched arms when, to my own surprise, I found myself standing and announcing for all to hear, "These people are frauds!"

The effect of my words was like lightning—or, in the reverend's words, like "spotlights" that "shine upon the sinners." Everything came to a halt. The poor, afflicted fellow stared at me with open jaw. The laser beams in the reverend's eyes temporarily flickered off. The congregation held its collective breath, and I knew it was time to deliver the goods.

"I saw these three drive up in perfect health, reverend. They met with that man right there in the red suspenders and demanded money. Then I saw them—"

"Child of Satan!" boomed a voice that blanketed the field. An earthquake erupted from deep within the reverend. "The mark of the beast is upon you, thou demon-possessed truth-slayer."

"This boy's a-lyin'," Joey wailed. "I ain't never seen these people in mah life."

"He's a liar," Frankie joined in. "I ain't never seen Joey either!"

The fact that Frankie knew Joey's name seemed not to matter to those in attendance. I was met with hostile rebukes from all sides. It was at that moment I realized I had failed to learn the lesson Lord Baltimore taught me at the Cherokee Grove, when I proclaimed that I, an outsider who didn't know the lay of the land, would make the county aware of Sheriff Pooler's dealings.

"He's wicked!" Holly cried. "He tried to attack me."

"I seen with it my own eyes," the reverend said. "Thou black-hearted sinner!"

But all was not lost, for I knew that if Connie or Aleph didn't come to my rescue, Brantley certainly would. I didn't have to wait long, for I saw my good friend rise and pass Hank into Connie's arms.

"He's got the evil eye!" shouted Brantley, to my total consternation. "I seen that ol witch doctor on Zapala put the evil eye on him, an he didn't even flinch."

"He's a good boy," Connie protested in my defense.

"I knowed the boy was trouble," I heard Aleph say.

"He's got the evil eye!" Brantley declared again, this time lunging at me. He grabbed me in a headlock and pulled me to the ground. I thought he was making a move to bite my ear when he whispered loudly, "Go down hard an' come up saved if you wanna get outta here in one piece."

Then he leapt to his feet and held high for all to see the very root that Dr. Owl had made for him. "An' this here's the root he carries around!" He flung it to the ground as though terrified.

Preacher Loop wasted no time in capitalizing on the evidence piling up against me. "Don't hurt that sinner!" he yelled. "He's possessed by demons!"

A dozen hands pulled me to my feet, and then a dozen feet stomped the root beyond recognition. It occurred to me that I might have faced a similar fate if not for Brantley. I also realized that my friend had sacrificed his prized possession to save me.

"Brothers and sisters! Ye of little faith! Doubt no more! Behold the power of God!" the reverend called, preparing to perform a feat that even I was anxious to witness. " 'In My name shall they cast out devils'!" he shouted. " 'They shall lay hands on the sick, and they shall recover'! *Heal!*" he howled. And with that, he simultaneously slammed the palm of his left hand hard on my forehead and that of his right on the forehead of Frankie, the cripple.

When I regained consciousness, Frankie was already dancing and whooping it up. Three hundred "Praise the Lord"s ceased in mid-utterance when I sat up. Three hundred sets of lungs held their breath while I struggled to remember where I was and what I was doing.

Fortunately, I caught Brantley's eye and recalled my predicament. Thinking quickly, I assumed a sitting posture and slowly raised my eyes toward the ceiling. This I managed to do in ever so slight degrees that it took half a minute to fix on an overhanging light bulb. I knew I had to achieve "Praise the Lord" status in order to exit with my body parts intact. So I emulated Jimma, only doubling the effect by slowly lifting both arms toward heaven and assuming as sanctified and awe-inspired a facial expression as possible without the benefit of the practice he had enjoyed.

A collective "Ah!" escaped the lips of the onlookers, and I knew that success was just a matter of navigating the homestretch without falling out of the saddle. I accomplished this with a slow-motion rise from my sitting position. I kept my eyes on the light bulb and assumed a fully extended position, hands raised skyward, before unleashing a show-stopper that surprised even me. I issued forth a steady stream of incoherent babbling that mimicked Tilly's unknown tongue and Reverend Loop's gibberish. I also tossed in several computer acronyms for good measure—in particular, Alt-Delete, Abend, GIGO, NetBios, and TCP/IP seemed to go over well with the audience.

" 'They shall speak with new tongues,' " moaned the reverend, apparently moved by the experience. "Praise the Lord, our God Almighty."

His words were echoed by all present.

I babbled a few more moments, waiting for the woman who had earlier interpreted the reverend to translate my message. But as she never came forward, and as the crowd became more riotous, and as I had run out of tricks, I did the only sensible thing. I fainted.

I was carried out of the tent and set down upon one of the food tables. I feigned unconsciousness for some time and even dozed off while Preacher Loop called for people to witness for the Lord and come forward to be saved. I was awakened by the sound of flies buzzing around a bean dish near my head. Preacher Loop was leading the congregation through one more hymn. I sensed someone standing over me. It was Brantley.

"Man, I thought they was gonna tar an feather you," he snickered. "That was somethin' else."

I opened one eye to ascertain if anyone else was nearby.

"Seein' the light, speakin' in tongues, then collapsin' an' all. That was somethin'," he repeated, shaking his head in disbelief.

"What's going on now?" I asked.

"They's finishin' up. Your actin's got 'em fired up. Ol Ange got to—"

"Aleph."

"Huh?"

"His name is Aleph. I just found out."

"Who told you that?"

"Holly."

"That preacher's daughter?"

"The very one."

"Man, she hit on me big time."

"You, too?"

"Had to fight her off. I don't want no trouble from that preacher dude."

"What about Ange?" I asked, using the name out of habit.

"You mean Aleph?"

"Yes, yes. What were you saying about him?"

"Man, he an' Connie started testifying about the Miracle of the Evinrudes."

"The what?"

"Those rusty ol outboard motors. Said we was about to smash up against the bridge pillars when the 'spirit of God moved across the face of the waters' and came upon them. And them Evinrudes started up just in time to save us."

"Why didn't they mention the tornado that hit the two house-boats next to us? Now, that's a miracle in my book."

"I don't know. But it played pretty good. Bunch a folks wanna see them 'Rudes now. We're the hit of the revival."

Sure enough, as I peered back toward the tent, I could see a small group of men huddled around Aleph as he reenacted the pulling of the starter cords. His heroic pantomime was interrupted when I spied a man walking toward us.

"All right, who you boys workin' for?" he asked. With the tent lights at his back, I could just make out that it was Jimma.

"What?" asked Brantley.

"Come on. How much they payin' you?"

Brantley started to respond, but I caught his arm. If I had learned nothing else from my experience with Bertie McGrady, it was that a con man could be conned. I sat up and locked my eyes on Jimma's.

"We're taking home five each," I said.

"F-f-f-," Jimma sputtered like the outboard motors I had heard earlier in the day. "Five hundred apiece?"

"You saw what happened in there," I said. "You folks didn't do anything new."

"I oughta—"

"You oughta what?" Brantley snapped, though I'm not sure he understood what our conversation was about.

"Look," I said, "we didn't know about y'all until tonight. What you get paid is between you and Joey and you-know-who. We just do what we're hired to do."

Perhaps Reverend Loop was right about my being possessed.

"Aw, I've had enough of this preacher. Y'all can have him," Jimma muttered. He turned and walked off into the night.

I know not what became of Jimma, Gertie, and Frankie, but I suspect they have been cured of many an ailment since that evening. Neither do I know—or care—what became of Reverend Loop.

Brantley and I soon made our way back to the river with Aleph, Connie, and Hank. We were accompanied by several dozen flashlight-carrying believers who were keen to see and touch Aleph's Evinrudes.

"There they are!" he proudly announced when we reached the houseboat. "This un's 'bout twenty year old," he said, pointing at the left motor. "That un ain't much newer."

The flock came aboard and took turns caressing the motors. They were indeed miracles—the miracle being that they still operated at all.

"Yes, sir," Aleph sighed, "they seen many a storm, many a winter, an' many a blisterin' hot day."

"I just hope they get us outta here," Brantley said quietly. "'Bout had enough of this stuff."

The motors started right up. As we pulled away from shore, a dozen flashlight beams shone on them. Whether it was fatigue or the lingering effects of the preacher's blow to my head, I believed at that moment that there could be something to Aleph's assertion about the miracle.

It didn't stop that evening. The next morning, we were awakened by the sounds of numerous motorboats. I made my way outside to see what the commotion was. Word had spread up and down the river, and the inhabitants were streaming in to see, touch, and photograph each other with the blessed outboards. Someone placed a bucket on the deck, and the visitors contributed modest donations toward a new home for Aleph and Connie. No doubt, the Evinrudes would hang above the mantel of their next domicile.

I tried to explain to several of the shrine's visitors that a tornado had destroyed the neighboring houseboats while leaving Aleph and Connie's virtually unscathed. I even showed them the twisted trees that marked the tornado's path. But each one quickly lost interest and returned to bask in the glow of the divine Evinrudes.

When Brantley stepped into the sunshine and found himself being photographed with two others near the 'Rudes, I knew our time with Aleph and Connie was nearing its end.

"I'm outta here," he told me several minutes later as he stuffed his belongings into a plastic trash bag. "You comin' or stayin'?"

"Why do you want to leave?"

"I can't have every fool 'round here snapping my picture. Look at this," he said, shoving Saturday's paper in front of me.

His photograph was on an inside page above the caption, "Escapee Still at Large. Suspected of Killing Sheriff Pooler." The article related how the sheriff's body had been found on Zapala by "the vagrant known as Lord Biltmore" and that Brantley was the chief suspect. Of course, I knew the truth but had been instructed to tell no one.

"But you didn't do it. I'll attest to that."

"It don't matter. His boys'd string me up before I get to trial."

"What about Hank?"

Brantley stopped packing long enough to think that one over. "He stays here. I'll come back and get him when I get settled somewheres."

That sounded reasonable to me. I was sure Connie and Aleph would see to the boy's needs. I was very close to wishing Brantley luck and shaking his hand good-bye when I recalled my promise to His Grace. I also recalled what Brantley had done for me the previous night. By giving up his root, his protective shield, Brantley had relinquished his peace of mind. And although my father had advised me to owe no person and to have no one owe me, the bruise on my forehead was a reminder of my indebtedness to Brantley, which I could not ignore.

"I'm going with you. But we can't stray too far."

"Ha! I'm plannin' to hitch to Arizona or somewhere out there. Get as far from here as I can."

That was a side trip I had no intention of taking, for I had plans to be in Savannah. An idea hatched in my head.

"You know, Susan is working somewhere around here," I heard myself say.

The trash bag slipped from Brantley's grasp and fell to the floor. "My Susan?"

"I think so," I said, hoping I was right.

"And," he said very deliberately, "just how do you know about her?"

His question demanded a delicate answer—one that would sound plausible yet be tactful enough so as not to offend his memory of her.

"I met her in a brothel, I think."

Of course, that was neither the answer I meant to give nor the one he expected to hear. The ensuing scuffle resulted in a broken coffee table, two bent chair legs, a broken picture frame, and a shattered window. My nose bled, as did Brantley's lower lip. In addition, we suffered numerous scrapes and would have accumulated more had Aleph and two other men not intervened.

"You got the evil eye again?" Aleph demanded of me. "Huh?"

I said nothing.

"Naw. It weren't him that started it," Brantley said at last. "Anyhow, we're gonna be leavin' y'all this mornin'. You mind keepin' Hank?"

While Aleph was agreeable to keeping the child, he was less enthused about our decision. "There are two types of people," he informed us. "Thems that's responsible nuff to keep a child, and thems that leave it to other folk."

Brantley flushed crimson. "I'll send money!" he said. He then emptied his pockets, laying thirty dollars on what was left of the coffee table. "And I'll pay for the damages. This here's a down payment."

I, too, contributed a few dollars to the cause.

Once calm was restored, Aleph and his cronies exited to resume their stations outside by the Evinrudes.

"What were you doin' at a brothel?" Brantley asked after several awkward moments.

"It was a roadside hotel. I had no idea—"

"What was *she* doin' there?"

"They were all working for the sheriff and his friends."

"Did you—"

"Of course not!"

"That's all I wanted to know," said Brantley.

"It's where I met Lord Baltimore. Well, sort of."

"That ol buzzard! Did he—"

"No, no. He had a room to himself, like me. It was he who got Susan to leave there. That's why I want us to stay in the area. She might still be around here."

"Well, thanks for tellin' me, I s'pose," he said. "Sorry for bustin' your nose."

"It's quite all right. Sorry for busting your lip."

Brantley tied the top of his bag and walked out. I gathered my possessions and followed. Stepping into the sunlight, I had to shield my eyes from the intense rays coming from above and reflecting off the water. I heard Connie softly sobbing. Brantley had just broken the news.

Connie didn't have to be asked to care for Hank. She volunteered to do so. "He so reminds me of Virgil, my firstborn," she said. "God rest his soul."

"That won't be necessary, madam," said a voice from the far side of the deck. The distinct aroma of a Sancho Panza once again greeted my nostrils. Lord Baltimore stood alone, leaning against a handrail. "The lads and the infant are coming with me. Sir," Lord Baltimore said, addressing Aleph, "I understand that you're being evicted from these premises and are in need of funds for a new home."

"Friend," Aleph replied, "you got that right."

"In that case," His Grace said, pulling an immense bundle of cash from a pants pocket, "please accept this donation on behalf of myself, Brantley, and Ensworth." He approached the outboards and plopped the bills into the bucket.

"Mister," said Aleph upon recovering from the shock, "I done witnessed two miracles in two days. Praise God Almighty!"

"There will be a third miracle today," His Lordship said. "But it requires the presence of these three and transportation to get them there. Is it possible for you to take us upstream?"

"Brother, I'll carry you on my back if necessary."

Connie, on the other hand, didn't seem so happy. His Grace seemed to comprehend this. He huddled with the old couple for a moment and whispered something I couldn't hear.

"Right. We're off then," His Lordship said to Brantley and me. "You two come with me. Bring the little one as well."

"Where we goin'?" Brantley asked.

"Do you believe in miracles?" His Grace replied.

"Maybe. But not for me," Brantley said.

"I sure do," said Connie. She and Aleph were beaming from ear to ear.

"Well, then," His Lordship said to Brantley. "You have nothing to lose and everything to gain by coming with me, whether you believe in miracles or not."

Connie hugged us good-bye and kissed Hank a dozen times. Aleph, His Grace, Brantley carrying Hank, and I climbed into Aleph's fishing boat. Aleph pulled the starter cord and pulled away from the houseboat. In another minute, we were heading upriver. A flotilla of boats followed in our wake, the occupants wishing to see the third miracle, I assumed.

Brantley and I waved at Connie, not realizing that we were seeing her for the last time. Hank was too mesmerized by the water to care what was taking place.

CHAPTER 22

In which I witness a reunion . . .

We made our way around two or three bends before anyone spoke. I can't say if Brantley felt it, but it occurred to me that something of significance was about to take place.

"Where we going?" he asked.

"You shall soon see," His Grace answered above the motor's drone.

"Did you really kill the sheriff?" Brantley wanted to know.

"Of course not."

"You that Biltmore fella?" asked Aleph.

"I am," replied His Grace. "The papers never get the name right."

"Well, you're among friends, brother. River folk don't care much for the gov'ment, includin' the law. They're the one's cain't leave us be and runnin' us off our property."

"Then who did?" Brantley demanded, switching the subject back to Sheriff Pooler.

Lord Baltimore held a finger to his lips. "No more questions. All will be revealed soon enough."

It was perhaps half an hour before we came upon a railroad bridge spanning the river. By then, the boats following us had lost interest and returned one by one to the known miracle, rather than chasing an unknown one that may or may not occur. His Grace pointed to the shore near the base of the trestle. Aleph directed the boat there. We disembarked and scrambled up a steep embankment to the train tracks.

"Remember," Aleph called as he backed the boat into the river, "there's two kinds of people. Thems that know everything and let you know it, and thems that don't know nothin' and act like they do." He nodded knowingly and raised an eyebrow to lend importance to his observation.

I supposed that this was his prized pearl of wisdom saved for special occasions, such as guest departures. "How do you know the difference between the two?" I asked.

Aleph was momentarily caught off guard but quickly recovered. "That comes with experience," he replied with a smile. "Til you know the difference, you're a sittin' duck." He howled with delight, hit the throttle, and was out of sight before we reached the summit.

"Our destination is two miles in that direction," said His Lordship, pointing east.

We proceeded along the train tracks, Brantley carried Hank. I wore my backpack and toted Brantley's sack.

"What do you make of Aleph and his wife?" His Grace asked.

"They're good people," I said. "Aleph isn't too keen on the younger generation, though. He tends to inquire whether or not I've endured this or that hardship."

"That's quite natural. Each generation laments the passing of the old ways it helped to destroy and blames the changes on the current generation. You'll do the same in due time."

"How did you find us?" I wanted to know.

"Ha! That was simple." He asked me to put the pieces together.

"One hundred dollars is yours if you will but use some logic," he said. "Think for yourself, boy."

"Where are you getting all this cash?" I inquired. "And this time, don't say, 'Money begets money.' "

"Fair enough. As our friend Aleph might say, there are two kinds of people. Those who find money and can't hold it, and those who find money and make more. It's a God-given gift to make money. I happen to have that gift. Now, this bill is for either of you," he said, waving it in one hand.

I thought it over. Were I in his shoes, I replied, I would surely have known where Jenny and Kent were and would have contacted them. They would have told me where Brantley and Ensworth were last observed. I would have poked around that neighborhood until I found someone who had seen them.

"Praise be, young man," he said, handing the bill to me. "You have just earned a day's wage simply by using your head. It's a habit worth adopting. I knew from Kent the precise spot on the highway where you abandoned him. From there, it was a simple matter of finding the commotion, for you two have an absolute genius for getting into trouble. When I heard about this business with the Evinrude engines, I knew you would be nearby."

I disclosed how the houseboat had been sure to wreck against the bridge piling and how the Evinrudes had mysteriously started at the last, fateful moment. I jokingly noted that the event was now being called the Miracle of the Evinrudes, expecting His Lordship to laugh along with me.

"Typical of man," he said. "Ever demanding proof of God's existence, yet reasoning it away when it is revealed."

When I described the debacle at Reverend Loop's revival, he said, "Seems to me you would have learned on Zapala the futility of rebuking a people's faith."

Indeed, there was little difference between island superstition and fire-and-brimstone preaching. No outsider stood a chance in attacking those beliefs or the spiritual leaders the believers turn to for guidance.

"But your intentions were admirable," he continued. "Reverend Loop is one God-botherer not to be toyed with."

Brantley was strangely quiet the entire time we conversed. He walked behind us, brooding. I half expected him to run off along one of the many paths leading into the woods on either side of the tracks. His Grace must have sensed this as well, for he often encouraged Brantley to keep up with us. Then, to ensure his allegiance, His Grace offered to carry the child. To my surprise, Brantley didn't protest. Hank immediately took a liking to His Lordship. We took turns carrying the boy, who behaved admirably, considering it was his mealtime.

His Grace said nothing further until we came upon a highway that intersected the railroad. It was the Coastal Highway. There, he brought us to a halt.

"Master Brantley, do you know the story of Jonah and the whale?" he asked.

"Sure. Jonah got swallered up by a whale and spit out on the shore. Some old fish tale, if you ask me."

"Well, the tale demonstrates by way of analogy that we sometimes get a second chance at life. In this instance, you are Jonah and the hurricane is the whale. You have been snatched out of prison, blown off course, and deposited here. You, my lad, have an opportunity to start anew. It is a rare blessing, one I hope you can appreciate."

Brantley looked to me for an interpretation, but I had none to offer.

"Do you believe me when I tell you your life is about to begin anew?" he asked.

Brantley did not respond.

"Do you believe, Master Ensworth?"

I shrugged my shoulders.

"Come, then, and see for yourselves."

Lord Baltimore turned and proceeded northward on the highway. We had not gone two hundred paces before a small truck stop appeared on our right. It was not the large, modern sort of truckers' restaurant and service center, but an old, two-story, square building surrounded by a parking lot. It had three gas pumps in front that didn't appear to be in use. A sign nailed to the second story advertised the place as Edna & Earle's Eats. Lace curtains and a window air conditioner on the second story suggested that Edna and Earle resided above the restaurant.

We were about to enter the establishment when Brantley stopped. I sensed that he feared a trap was being laid for him.

"I ain't goin' in," he declared.

His Lordship grabbed Brantley by both shoulders. They locked eyes.

"My dear boy, there are no police inside. And far be it from me to offer advice, but were I in your shoes, I would deem this an excellent time to turn myself in."

"Well, you ain't in my shoes," said Brantley, trying to pull away.

"Hear me out. Sheriff Pooler's office and the entire county government in Medway are under investigation by state and federal agencies. Prisoners and local citizens are coming forward to testify against the corruption under the sheriff's rule. The county commission is under investigation. The judges are under investigation. City officials are under investigation."

This information interested Brantley. He well knew that he faced a life of looking over his shoulder and that, sooner or later, the long arm of the law would catch him.

"Here is the name of an excellent lawyer in Brunswick," said His Grace, stuffing a business card inside Brantley's shirt pocket. "He will take your case. He owes me. He will get you a fair hearing. Turning yourself over to the authorities will be to your advantage."

Brantley remained unconvinced. "I ran from Pooler 'cause I feared for my life. Ain't no way I'm turnin' myself in."

"That's precisely your case! You were subjected to cruel and unusual punishment. You even feared death at the sheriff's hands. Now, Jenny and Kenneth have agreed to testify on your behalf. You were with them when the sheriff was with me on the beach. That clears you of the murder charge. JV will also testify to that, provided they locate him. And I have already made a statement concerning the sheriff's demise."

His Grace let Brantley go and started to enter the restaurant.

"One thing I gotta know," said Brantley. "How'd he die?"

His Grace responded as though he had been asked what time it was. "Oh. It was a suicide."

We followed His Lordship into Edna & Earle's and took a booth near the front door. Brantley sat opposite His Grace and me. Hank sat in Brantley's lap, reaching in vain for the condiments on the table. I had just begun to scan the breakfast menu when His Grace spoke up.

"The service here is atrocious!" he growled.

He got up to find a waitress. A minute or so later, he came back and motioned for me to follow him.

"Be right back," I said, grabbing several packs of crackers from a basket on the table.

Brantley shook his head and grinned. "No tellin' what'll happen next round that dude."

I got up and started for the entrance, where His Grace stood.

"Hey, Ensworth," Brantley said. He looked at me for a just a moment, then smiled. He held out his hand. "Thanks, man. It's been a trip."

For some reason, no words came to me. I simply shook his hand.

"What is it?" I asked His Grace when I got to the cashier's counter.

"You are now no longer under any obligation to Brantley," he whispered.

"Good. Why is that?"

"Watch."

No sooner had he spoken than I heard a soul-piercing shriek, followed by the sound of glass crashing on the black-and-white-checked linoleum floor. It was the sort of spill that requires all restaurant patrons to stop eating, talking, and listening and to turn and inspect the damage. I saw a pretty, young waitress with close-cropped hair standing over a tray of broken water glasses. Her apron and dress were wet. Yet she remained frozen, eyes fixed on Brantley and Hank. She seemed familiar, though at first I could not place her. Then I saw the gap in her teeth.

Her chest began to heave uncontrollably. A dead quiet hung over the entire restaurant. I—and I'm sure the other patrons—had no idea what would happen next. What transpired was something few people ever have the privilege to witness.

"My baby," she said, her voice breaking.

Hank began to cry.

Next came a voice that seemed not of human origin: "*My baby!*"

Brantley, who had been as transfixed by the spill as everyone else, snapped out of his trance. "Your baby?" he wailed across the room.

Hank, still in Brantley's arms, reached out with both hands and kicked with his legs, trying desperately to get to Susan. Brantley slid out of the booth and moved slowly toward her.

"Brantley," Susan moaned.

Tears coursed down her face. She suddenly found the strength to move her feet and ran into the outstretched arms of her son and his father. The three melted into a quivering mass of sobbing flesh and sank to the floor.

"Dear me," sighed His Grace with more than a hint of annoyance. "They do carry on."

However, as I scanned the room, I noted an entirely different reaction among the onlookers. A waitress who no doubt knew Susan's plight openly wept. A number of weathered truckers' eyes welled up. And I heard more than one sniffle among their ranks. These men had probably seen it all on the road. Births. Deaths. Triumphs and tragedies.

The silence was too much to bear, and the sniffling had to be drowned out. Someone started clapping in one corner of the room. Someone else clapped. A moment later, the entire restaurant erupted in a spontaneous cheer for the new family.

His Grace threw his hands up and disappeared outside. I looked back once. Brantley and Susan were still embracing on the floor, rocking back and forth. Scattered applause continued.

His Grace was halfway across the parking lot when I caught up to him.

"What now?" I asked.

"You have an appointment in Savannah, do you not?" he replied, chewing the end of a Sancho Panza.

"No. I mean, what happens next with Brantley?"

"That's entirely up to him."

"Shouldn't we—"

"You should get on with your life and let Master Brantley get on with his. There is nothing better to settle a man down than a wife and child. If they aren't enough incentive for him to mend his ways, I doubt anything will be."

A train whistle blew in the woods ahead of us.

"We'll miss that if we're not quick about it," His Lordship said.

He broke into a trot. We were within a hundred yards of the tracks when I saw the train engine cross the highway. Twenty or so boxcars had passed by the time we reached the tracks. His Grace grabbed the handrail of the next passing rail car and scrambled up. I misjudged the one after that, and the next one as well. The next two were flatcars, which I let pass. The end of the train was quickly approaching. I looked to my left and saw His Grace disappear around a bend in the forest. The train was picking up speed, and I had to leap to grab a rung of ladder. I managed to gain a hold, but my legs were still dangling, and it was not without a struggle that I finally managed to gain a foothold as well.

I climbed to the roof of the boxcar and sat down. Looking back, I could see that only one car remained. Though still somewhat panicked, I was nonetheless exhilarated by the feeling of riding the rails through the Georgia pines. The tops of the trees zipping by on either side were a mesmerizing reddish gold in the morning light.

I saw His Grace hopping from car to car toward me.

"Thought I'd left you behind," he said as he climbed up from a flatcar and plopped down next to me on top of the boxcar. He propped himself on his side using one elbow while he lit a Sancho Panza.

"Speaking of which," I said, "I'm having second thoughts about leaving Brantley back there. What about Susan and Hank?"

His Lordship waved off my concerns with a sweep of his hand. "They'll be taken care of. A trust has been established for their well-being."

"Why didn't you just give them the money back there?"

He seemed perturbed at my question. "I rather suspect that the young man would have been tempted to take the money and run. As long as he doesn't know about it, he might just follow my advice and obtain the pro bono services of my friend in Brunswick. Susan is eligible to draw annuity payments immediately."

"Well, I guess that might work out for the best," I said, unable to find much fault with his reasoning.

I fashioned my backpack into a headrest and lay down my head. I was soon transfixed by the treetops, which, to my mind, resembled church steeples speeding by one after another. I thought about Reverend Loop and Holly. I forgot all about her accusation and recalled only her beauty. I had earlier omitted that part of the story but now recounted it for Lord Baltimore. It wasn't easy for me to admit to him that I might have fallen in love with her.

"Until you can discern true love from infatuation, I suggest you avoid attaching your heart too ardently to any young lady," he advised. "Youth confuses passion for love, never having loved before."

"The heart doesn't lie," I protested.

His Grace said nothing for a while but slowly puffed his cigar. "The heart is easily fooled. It receives competing signals from the brain and other areas of the body. So it sends out equally confused signals, which reason wrongly interprets as love. Do you follow me?"

I told him I did, in order not to appear foolish. I regretted bringing up the subject and wished to change it immediately.

"Tell me about the hurricane. What happened?"

His Lordship was lost in thought. "What happened where?"

"Megiddo Beach. What happened after I left?"

"Oh, well, yes. I suppose some explanation is due."

He changed his position until he lay staring at the sky. The cigar shifted in his mouth several times, and I assumed he was collecting his thoughts so as to leave out no details.

"See that sky? If I were to describe the colors in it to you, without you seeing it for yourself, you might call me a liar, and I wouldn't blame you."

"Yes, go on." I was certain he was drawing an analogy between the sky and Sheriff Pooler.

"It's God's palette. He really outdid Himself with this morning's sunrise."

"The hurricane, the hurricane!" I said, realizing he was nowhere near the topic that interested me.

"Yes, yes. I'm getting there. If I were to describe to you what happened on the beach after you left, you might be equally disbelieving."

I patiently endured the silence while he puffed away.

"You may not know this, Ensworth," he said at last, "but my ego is prone to getting the better of me at times."

I choked on one of the crackers I'd taken from Edna & Earle's.

"Just as the sheriff underestimated me, I failed to appreciate his powers at that moment. For somewhere in him, there remained vestiges of the man from years gone by. In his day, he won the respect of his comrades in wartime, and later that of the people of his hometown—enough so that they voted him into his father's former office. But that was years ago, before the temptations became too great. I must tell you that I didn't expect him to take his own life."

"You didn't see that coming?" For some reason, it gave me satisfaction to know that His Lordship was not always in control of things.

"I did not."

His Grace closed his eyes. Just when I thought he was drifting off to sleep, he again spoke: "I fully expected that he would fire at me."

"And would you have shot him?" It was the question I had wanted an answer to ever since leaving the island.

He looked at me. "If you must know, had he fired upon me, I would have indeed defended myself. However, I have seen the location and the hour of my death. That wasn't it."

"Why did he take his life?"

"Loss of position in his community. Loss of status. The threat of prison. For too many men, their jobs are their lives. Take that away and they have nothing to live for. There was nothing for the sheriff back on the mainland. That and the fact that he was undergoing withdrawal from cocaine. One can never predict the actions of a man addicted to drink or drug."

Lord Baltimore slammed a fist down hard on top of the boxcar. He snatched the cigar from his mouth. "It happened too fast." He stared ahead, his gray hair flowing like a silk scarf in the wind. "I should have seen it. I did not wish for that man to die. That was a lost soul, that one was. A shipwrecked saint."

I waited for what I judged a respectful amount of time before returning to what I was impatient to know.

"Then what?"

He rubbed his head. "What happened next? A little wind gust called Hurricane Henry blew in. I spent the next ten hours tethered to the upper limb of an oak tree. I secured his body as best I could to the roots, but the storm surge got it. They found his remains floating not far from where we discovered Captain Sandy. The islanders believe their souls will duel in eternity. No one will lay crab traps near there now."

"What about Liverpool and Tilly and JV?"

"Tilly and JV made it through fine. They rode out the storm in the old lighthouse on the north beach. Liverpool, well, I'm not sure what happened to that rascal. By the time I left, no one had found Bucephalus. That's a good sign. An ox carcass is easy to find. And where they find Bucephalus, they'll find Liverpool."

I clutched the Saint Christopher that dangled around my neck. Liverpool had said that Zapala was always on top in the end. I wondered if those words had come true for him. Zapala had certainly come out on top where the sheriff was concerned.

"Why didn't you tell the local police about the sheriff? They think Brantley did it."

"Ha! Now, that's a good laugh. I told the authorities everything I told you."

"And they didn't believe you?"

"The Crazy Limey? The Fruit Loop? They didn't believe a word of it, even though the autopsy clearly showed the wound to be self-inflicted. No one wanted to believe it. They scoffed at my assertion that I challenged Sheriff Pooler to a duel and concocted a story about a fugitive attacking him from behind."

"Surely, his deputies know better."

"Those two? Bah. They weren't about to admit they'd been so

easily led around the island and then captured. They claimed that the storm separated them from the sheriff."

"But you sent the GBI evidence. Don't they believe you?"

"They received evidence. They don't know who sent it."

"So Brantley doesn't stand a chance!"

"Oh, I think he'll do all right. What with the other investigations and the autopsy, which revealed cocaine in the sheriff's system, the trial will likely move to Brunswick. Brantley's solicitor has the film from my camera, along with Kenneth's and Jenny's depositions. I'm confident the murder charge against Brantley will be dropped."

"But he'll still go to prison."

"Oh, undoubtedly."

"For how long?"

"For the length of his original sentence, I should imagine. Though with your legal system and the overcrowding of the prisons, it's likely he'll be out in a few years."

"That's a lifetime!"

"No, no. On the contrary, that's life." He meditated for a minute. "A shame, really. That boy. He could use some guidance."

"Well, what do you propose?"

He drew heavily on his cigar and exhaled a long stream of smoke. "Nothing I can do for the lad. He refuses instruction, and I have business elsewhere. And while we're on the topic of instruction, young master, it occurs to me you've learned some useful lessons on this journey."

"Useful? I don't see how they can help me."

He rubbed his beard. "No. And I don't suppose a child learning the alphabet fully appreciates its importance. But a solid foundation is necessary. Come, now, you've surely learned something."

I thought diligently. "I suppose I've learned that a little money goes a long way. I've learned that a lot of money doesn't necessarily last long. I've learned that there are those who will give you the shirt off their back, even though it's the only thing they own. And I guess I've learned that things balance out in the long run."

His Grace said nothing, but I perceived he was pleased with my answer.

"There is one other thing," I began. It had been on my mind ever since leaving Zapala. "It may be that my stay on the island will be the most exciting time of my life. And though I couldn't wait to get home, I now regret not enjoying my time there, even though much of it was spent in danger."

"Aha!" cried His Lordship, seizing my arm. "You've had a taste of Eden. You've been in the Garden, and you want to go back. Now, you've an inkling of how Adam felt after the Fall."

I replied that my principal desire was to reach Savannah.

"Do you have an address?" he asked.

I looked inside the backpack and read the street number on the envelope: "Three twenty-six and a half Bull Street."

His Grace nodded. "You'll be there before evening."

With that, he lay back and promptly fell asleep.

CHAPTER 23

We reach Savannah.
Sweet destiny . . .

We arrived on the outskirts of Savannah and hopped off our rail car as it slowly passed through a crossing. I quickly realized that we were near the dockyards. Immense warehouses lined the left side of the train tracks. Beyond them were towering gantries used to load and unload freighters. Tin-roofed shanties bordered the right side of the tracks. Most of them had small porches on which sat weather-beaten sofas and chairs, as well as dockworkers' boots left outside to dry.

I was all for proceeding quickly to the downtown address that was my final destination. However, His Grace thought a celebration was in order and suggested we duck inside one of the numerous bars. I suspected he was more interested in a shot of scotch than in cele-brating my arrival.

"Which of these establishments do you find to your liking?" he asked.

To be frank, none was particularly inviting. The least offensive was a hole in the wall called the Grotto, a run-down bar recessed in an alley between two brick warehouses that probably dated to colonial days. It seemed the light of day had not made its way down that alley since then.

A cloud of smoke billowed out when I opened the door. Red lights dimly lit the interior. I thought, *The entrance to the underworld must be something like this.*

"Let's try another place," I said.

Two doors down was another bar. A shattered sign hung over the doorway. If the Grotto was the doorway to Hades, this establishment was certainly the service entrance. It took us some moments, once inside, to discern our surroundings. What came into focus was a seedy joint decorated with worn, grease-laden posters of ships, cheap ships-in-bottles, and a motley crew of patrons to match. It was perhaps one of the last joints that had not given way to tourism. It was the type of place Jack the Ripper would have frequented had he been alive and visiting on holiday.

"Are you certain you want to stay here?" I asked.

"Quite," he replied with confidence.

We found a table near the back. I ordered a Coke from a girl not much older than I. His Grace asked for a scotch. The drinks were promptly brought to us, and I gulped mine down. As I did so, I noticed a man sitting on a stool watching the television that hung over the bar. He looked familiar, though I could not decide where I'd seen him before.

His Lordship looked queerly at his glass. "I don't know what they're using for whiskey. This tastes bitter."

Our waitress placed two more drinks on the table. "Compliments of him," she said, pointing to the man on the stool.

It was Jeremy, the man whose life we had saved on Zapala.

"Don't drink that," said His Grace.

I had just taken a sip of my new drink. "What's wrong?"

His Lordship raised the glass to his nose and sniffed. "Blast," he said. "We must leave, quickly."

Jeremy strolled up to our table just then. "I thought I recognized you two."

"Yes, well, we were just leaving, thank you," replied His Grace, trying to rise.

Jeremy held him down with one hand. I, too, attempted to rise and realized that I could not. The room seemed to grow even dimmer than it already was.

"You know," said Jeremy, "you saved my butt over there on that island. But heck, I can't have people around here know I attempted suicide. Wouldn't look good. I took your advice, sir. I'm in a business now that can support me and my wife in the manner to which we're accustomed. It's a right nice business at that. We're moving up the social ladder, and I just can't afford for anything to jeopardize that. Understand?"

"What's he talking about?" I asked His Grace.

Lord Baltimore placed a hand on his forehead and leaned heavily on the table.

"I loaded up your drink with twice the dose," Jeremy said. "It works pretty quick. But you won't be out for too long."

"Blast," His Grace replied weakly.

That's the last I recall of that afternoon.

I came to my senses several hours later with a throbbing head and a queasy stomach. I felt a cold wall at my back and realized I was propped in the corner of a small, rectangular room. It was dark and empty except for myself and three other bodies. A metal door with a round window was to my left. Another round window was next to the door, and a third was on the wall behind me. Two plastic bottles of water sat by the door—our refreshments, I supposed.

One of the other bodies stirred. It rolled over, and I looked upon

His Grace's countenance. He groaned and rubbed his eyes.

"Blast," he quietly remarked.

"You already said that."

He sighed heavily and massaged the back of his head. " 'Nothing amazes me so much as the labyrinth of follies I have wandered in all my life.' "

I had by then come to my senses enough to have apprehensions.

"Where are we?" I asked.

"Look for yourself," he replied.

I pulled myself to my feet and wobbled to the round portal on the wall behind me and looked out. Far below, the Savannah River flowed alongside our ship. The sun was low in the sky.

"We're . . . We've been . . ."

"Shanghaied?"

"Yes!"

"Now you know Jeremy's new line of business. I blame myself. I knew something was awry the moment we stepped into that establishment."

"I can't believe it. Shanghaied in Savannah."

"Believe it. Many foreign shipping companies pay slave wages to crew, who jump ship at the first port of call. The captains have to replace them by any means at their disposal, and the shipping firms don't know—nor care—as long as the goods are delivered on time."

"This is inconceivable!" I protested.

"Well, someone conceived it. And Jeremy supplied the bodies. You, me, and those poor blighters."

"Isn't that tyranny? Forced labor?"

"Most definitely."

"It hardly seems fair."

"Yes. And your point?" he said. "Now, how do you plan to get us out of here?"

I looked around the room, thinking he must be addressing

someone else. In one corner lay two unconscious men who appeared to be Mexicans. It was then that I recalled Esteban's story of immigrants being sold to captains of merchant ships.

I suppose I was too much in shock to be petrified. The only emotion I felt was anger, made worse by His Grace, who seemed not to care whether he was being shanghaied, dueling with a sheriff, or hanging on to an oak tree in the middle of a hurricane.

"Were you speaking to me?" I inquired.

"I'm tired of bailing you out of predicaments," he said. "It's your turn."

I threw my hands up in despair and resumed gazing out the window.

"My boy, do you believe me when I tell you we will be free within the hour?"

"I don't see how."

"Hasn't everything I told you turned out to be true?"

"Yes, but . . ."

He felt around in his pockets. "Well, they've taken my cigars," he said.

I felt for the Saint Christopher medal Liverpool had given me. It was missing.

His Grace then reached beneath his beard and extracted half a Sancho Panza, which had been attached to the underside of the beard with a tiny clip. A single match was pressed into its tip. "They never check under here," he commented, obviously no stranger to being kidnapped. "I got the idea from a bloke in Pakistan. The beggar walks into a shop, hides twelve combs inside his beard, walks out, and no one's the wiser." He reached beneath his beard once more and pulled out several folded hundred-dollar bills, which had also been clipped on.

"What are we going to do?" I asked.

"First, we'll want some attention. Tell me what you see outside."

I walked to the door and surveyed the ship. The deck was covered with stack upon stack of cargo containers. "I see stacks of containers."

"Good. Describe the ship itself."

I peered around the deck as much as possible through the dirty window. "It's pretty rusty. Ropes lying here and there. It's messy."

"Anyone on board?"

"I see a couple of fellows." Both were poorly dressed and slump-shouldered. They were spraying down a section of deck with a hose.

"Describe them."

"One is about my size. In his forties. The other looks Asian. Taller. In his twenties. They don't appear to be any more enthused about being here than I am."

"Excellent." He shoved back against the wall to make himself comfortable. "Let me know when you're ready to proceed with the escape," he said, lighting his cigar.

"I don't believe lighting that thing is such a good idea."

"Think boy, think!" he commanded. "Everything you need to free us is at your disposal. Recall our first two meetings."

By then, I knew better than to argue, so I set my mind to the matter at hand. I soon realized that the only thing the two meetings had in common was that I thought the bungalow and later the trailer were on fire. Then it occurred to me that His Grace's cigar might be used to create the illusion of fire. And I knew that fire on a ship was a dread danger.

"We'll draw them in here with smoke and overpower them," I blurted.

"Open that window by the door," he ordered, rising to his feet.

Enough smoke had already built up inside that it spilled out through the portal upon my opening it. His Grace walked to the open window. He leaned close to the opening and blew a steady stream of smoke through it.

"Each man must learn to be the captain of his own ship," he said. "Your destiny lies in your hands."

He puffed steadily away, issuing great, billowing clouds of smoke. It wasn't a minute later that I heard several excited voices on deck shouting, "Fire! Fire!" I then heard running footsteps approaching our room.

"Do you believe," His Grace asked, looking at me with a mischievous grin, "that the four of us will be free of this place within the hour?"

For some unaccountable reason, I felt a strange serenity that bordered on excitement. It was a most unexpected but welcome feeling. I smiled and nodded my head. "Yes," I said. For the first time since we had met, I believed.

"Stand by the door, lad," he instructed. "Recall what you've learned about self-defense. When they come through, feed them one at a time to me."

A key turned. The door flew open, and the two men I had seen outside burst in. The older one carried a fire extinguisher. The Asian carried a club. He also wore my Saint Christopher.

To be fair, their eyes had not adjusted to the relative darkness, so they were therefore at a disadvantage. As no one tried to escape, they must have assumed we were still unconscious. The first man was fiddling with the fire extinguisher to make it work when he bumped into me. I shoved him in the general direction of His Grace. The Asian, on the other hand, took a calculated swing at my head. I held my ground, blocked the blow, and used his momentum to sling him toward His Lordship.

The first man was already lying face down on the floor. His Grace had moved so quickly that I missed seeing whatever blows he imparted. He then pivoted and in one motion disarmed the second crewman and jabbed him hard in the midsection. The man bent over in pain, and as he did so, His Grace flipped the Saint Christopher over his head and into an awaiting palm. He then handed it to me. His Grace held the Asian against the wall with one hand and brandished the club menacingly with the other. The man's eyes were wide with fear. But instead of delivering a crushing blow, His Lordship lowered the club and pulled a hundred-dollar bill from his pocket.

"One now, one when we get off the boat with our belongings. Understand?"

The man nodded.

"Be quick about it."

I poured the bottled water on the Mexicans, rousing them. The Asian then led all of us to a room where our belongings were laid out on a table. I expected the fellow to flee and find help the first chance he got, but he stayed by our side as we regained our possessions and made our way to the gangplank. His Grace conversed with him in an incomprehensible language. The sailor spoke with great animation. I got the gist of what he was saying without a translator.

"The crew's ashore," His Lordship informed me. "They're looking for more poor blokes like us."

"He wants to come with us," I said.

"Wouldn't you? This ship's a disgrace. A rust bucket. Poor blighter got snatched aboard himself at the last port. Come on, then," he said to the man. "This way."

Lord Baltimore, the two Mexicans, one crewman, and I were back on dry land a short time later. The migrants jumped on the first freight train leaving Savannah. His Grace and I headed toward downtown with the crewman.

"What about that guy at the bar?" I asked. "Jeremy."

"What about him?" replied His Grace.

"Shouldn't we do something?"

"Yes," he replied, "I suppose we should."

CHAPTER 24

I deliver the envelope.

We proceeded past the last warehouses of the shipping district and reached the waterfront tourist area known as Factor's Walk. We soon passed two cannons set side by side and came to a large, brick building, where His Grace halted.

"Wait here," he instructed me. "Don't move."

I read the sign above the doorway through which Lord Baltimore and the crewman passed: "U.S. Customs House. Port of Savannah."

His Grace emerged alone a few minutes later and urged me to follow him.

"Right. That takes care of our friend and that Jeremy fellow. Quickly, now. They think I'm in the lavatory."

"What about the ship?" I asked as we made our way across Bay Street.

"That vessel isn't going anywhere. However, another boat is leaving this evening. And I have every intention of being on it."

We strolled down the beautiful palm- and oak-lined streets of old Savannah and through a number of exquisitely maintained parks adorned by statues and fountains. His Grace pointed out homes of historical significance.

"Now, that one there," he said, indicating a fine brick mansion, "was occupied by General Sherman after he captured Savannah and presented it to President Lincoln as a Christmas gift. And that porch over there is where Lafayette stood for a parade held in his honor in the year . . ."

This went on ad nauseam, until I felt like I was walking through a museum.

"Do you recall the two cannons we passed? Gifts from General Washington on his visit to this city. Now, Booth—you know, the one who shot your Lincoln—was a famous actor who frequently performed in that theater right there."

I asked him how he knew all this.

He asked me how I did not.

"Perhaps," I said, "because I didn't think it important."

"Well, I can assure you it is important, and I'll tell you why. If you go back a mere twenty-one generations, you'll realize that it took several millions of people in that small expanse of time to create you. These are people who lived in times we can scarcely conceive. Their lives are worthy of study. Each generation must learn for itself the great truths. However, by studying the lives of those who have preceded you, you can accumulate much wisdom and avoid some of the errors each new generation is doomed to repeat."

"Does that have something to do with that Wheel of Truth you mentioned to me and Brantley?"

"It does indeed."

"And this wheel can tell you what is going to happen?"

"For the most part, yes. There is nothing new that hasn't happened many times in the past. The patterns are all there for those who have eyes to see."

"Is that so? Well, maybe you can reveal what will happen to me next."

His Grace studied me. I felt as though his eyes looked past mine and searched the depths of my being, just as Liverpool had done.

"It is a great gift and a great curse to know the future. Do you really want to know what lies ahead for you?"

What lay ahead for me, I knew, was a sumptuous dinner, then a ride home to resume the comforts of a lifestyle I had previously enjoyed. But I wanted to hear his version.

"Yes," I answered, "I do."

"You're sure?"

"I'm quite sure."

"In that case," he said, pointing over my shoulder, "turn around."

I did so. Across the street stood an antebellum house. The address was 326½ Bull Street. I had arrived.

"We're here!" I shouted. "My journey's over."

His Grace smiled. "Your journey, Master Ensworth, is about to begin."

"We part here, I suppose. Thanks," I said. "Thanks for looking out for me."

He said nothing, continuing to puff away on his Sancho Panza.

I stared at the ground for a few awkward moments. Then, mostly out of manners, I suppose, I asked where I might reach him.

Without batting an eye, he answered, "Seek where I am not. There will I be."

"Okay . . . ," I replied, not having a clue what he meant.

I started to leave, then remembered the gift I had received. "Wait a minute," I said. I reached in my backpack and pulled out a handful of cigars. His eyes lit up. "I got these from a man whose barn I helped rebuild after the storm."

His Lordship accepted the gift and smiled broadly. With that, he was off.

I crossed the street and opened the iron gate leading to 326½, the offices of Demere, Frederick, and King.

His Grace's voice boomed across the street: "Peace be with you! Cheerio."

I nodded and waved good-bye.

The brick steps led up to a glossy black door. I pulled and released a brass door knocker shaped like a lion's head. As I waited for the door to open, I looked back and saw His Grace striding away at his usual quick pace, trailing puffs of smoke behind him just as he had done on Zapala. He disappeared around a corner as the door opened.

"Yes?" asked a venerable gentleman. He looked me up and down as if appraising a dirty mop a peddler wanted to sell him. I couldn't blame him, for I'm sure my appearance was not in keeping with the Harding name—at least not the Hardings he was acquainted with.

"I'm, uh . . ." I extracted the envelope from my backpack. "I was told to deliver this."

The gentleman eyed the letter suspiciously and closed the door. A moment later, it was whisked open.

"You . . . You're Ensworth Harding?"

"Yes."

"Frank Harding was your father?"

"Was?"

What little facial color he possessed suddenly drained from him.

"Who is it?" a voice called from inside.

"What about my father?" I asked. It was obvious he had disinherited me as he'd threatened, though I couldn't understand why, as I had been true to his instructions.

The door swung wide, and a distinguished-looking man about Lord Baltimore's age pulled me inside. He introduced himself as Bruce

Demere, who I recognized as a friend of my father's, though he had aged considerably since I'd last seen him. Before I knew it, I was sitting in a comfortable leather chair in front of a large desk. On top of the desk was a miniature folk-art sculpture of an owl painted red and green. I immediately knew it to be a Liverpool original.

"My God, boy. Where have you been?"

I didn't see that it was any of his business. In fact, I wanted an explanation about being disinherited.

Before I could respond, two other men entered the room and introduced themselves as Mr. Frederick and Mr. King. They sat down as Mr. Demere stepped out briefly. I could hear him instructing someone in another room to call my mother and inform her I was alive and well. Then he returned and leaned on his desk.

"Here," I said, holding out the envelope with the law firm's name and address on it. "My father asked me to deliver this to you. Tell him I kept my part of the bargain."

Mr. Demere accepted the envelope and opened it. He read the brief note inside, which was attached to a small cardboard container. He looked at me. "Ensworth, it is with deep and profound regret that I must inform you that your father passed away two nights ago."

He stared intently at me, possibly to confirm that I had understood what he said. The truth is I did understand the words, but the meaning escaped me, much the way someone who has been wounded might not at first realize it.

"The note instructs me to play this in your presence," he continued. "It's from your father."

He tore open the container and placed a tape into a cassette player.

"Ensworth, I have a cancer," it began. There was no mistaking my father's voice. "Doctor Oliver tells me I don't have much time. That's why I sent you on this excursion. When I saw the latest x-ray, the first thing I thought about was that I had failed in preparing you to face life on your own. Your inheritance is no guarantee against people who will prey on you until nothing is left. And money certainly won't guarantee happiness. Another reason I did this to you is because I didn't want you to see me as I enter the final stage of this disease. I asked an old friend, known to you by now as Lord Baltimore, to guide you on your journey. My hope is that by the end, you will have learned a few things, chief among them that you can fend for yourself and be self-reliant. If you make it to the address on this envelope like we discussed, it means you can do anything you want to in life. One more thing. I know I never said I love you. It's not something that comes easily. I don't think my father ever said it to me, although I knew beyond all doubt how he felt. The point is, Ensworth, I love you. And I'm very proud of you. Take care of your mother."

That was the entire message.

I looked up at Mr. Demere. It was then that his words sunk in. "He's dead," I said. "My father is dead."

"I'm very sorry."

A secretary poked her head in the door and announced that she was having trouble locating my mother.

"Excuse me, " Mr. Demere said. "I need to make a phone call. I'll be right back."

The burden of consoling me thus fell on the reluctant shoulders of Mr. Frederick and Mr. King, who cleared their throats in preparation for this unexpected but familiar duty. One of them—I didn't notice which—began a well-rehearsed consolation speech that began, "The tragic loss of our good friend Frank Harding will be felt for years to come."

Perhaps I was simply too tired or numb at that moment to find solace in their words. Another secretary came into view and asked if there was anything I needed, but I was oblivious. I knew then why I had dreamed about my father two nights before. It was the only dream about him I had ever had.

There was more talking, the content of which was fuzzy at first.

"We've set up a trust fund per your father's wishes," someone said. When a legal document was placed in front of me, I knew that I had to get fresh air and clear my head.

"Excuse me," I said weakly.

To my amazement, no one tried to restrain me as I walked to the door. It was only when I reached for the handle that I perceived movement behind me. I quickly exited, leapt the wrought-iron fence, and bolted down the sidewalk.

Why I sought Lord Baltimore at that moment, I cannot say. Perhaps I realized a kinship had grown between us, one I had refused to recognize before.

It didn't take me long to find my way back to the parks we had walked through earlier. I made a quick search of two of them before I recalled that His Grace had told me he had a boat to catch. I raced to the waterfront and made my way among the cobblestone streets toward the wharves—that is, until a police car pulled up a block away. I assumed the attorneys had called the authorities to find me.

Not knowing what else to do, I blended in as best I could with the thick crowd of tourists. I found a bench near the river as first dark descended. It was clear that I wouldn't be able to find His Grace at night among the many ships occupying berths on both sides of the Savannah River.

And I felt I had lost two fathers that day. It is during such moments that one wants to be alone. At least that's the way I felt. Naturally, a flock of tourists then descended upon me to better view a large container ship gliding up the channel on its way to the Atlantic. A few of them attempted to take photographs in the fading light.

Something urged me to inspect the freighter more closely. I turned and spied a solitary figure standing near the ship's pilothouse. He leaned on a handrail, a cigar protruding from his mouth. Long, gray hair blew freely in the breeze behind him.

I stood to get a better view.

Even though I was surrounded by people, he saw me. He removed the cigar, held it out toward me, and bowed ever so slightly in acknowledgment of the gift. Then he put it back in his mouth and unleashed several large plumes.

I watched the ship until it disappeared in the night. That's the last I saw of His Lordship, His Grace, Duke of Zapala, Lord Baltimore.

THE END